contxt

FARRUKH DHONDY

FRAGMENTS AGAINST MY RUIN

A Life

First published by Context, an imprint of Westland Publications Private Limited, in 2021

Published by Context, an imprint of Westland Books, a division of Nasadiya Technologies Private Limited, in 2024

No. 269/2B, First Floor, 'Irai Arul', Vimalraj Street, Nethaji Nagar, Alapakkam Main Road, Maduravoyal, Chennai 600095

ISBN: 9789360450892

10 9 8 7 6 5 4 3 2 1

Typeset by Jojy Philip, New Delhi

Printed at Manipal Technologies Limited, Manipal

FRAGMENTS AGAINST MY RUIN

CONTENTS

UNCLES AND CARROM BOARDS

Stepping out of the terminal at Bombay airport with my rucksack and bottles of duty-free, I was accosted by the taxi drivers competing for fares to the city.

'Unkal, unkal, unkal,' they called out.

The calumny of Time.

When we were teenagers, we would gather on the corners of the streets of Poona, greeting familiar passers-by and, on occasion, depending on our mood, would offer mild provocations to strangers. To those unfortunate passers-by with shiny bald pates, we would shout, 'Oi Carrom Board!' I look in the mirror now, and my thinning white hair promises to perhaps confer precisely that epithet, the teasing torment, on me. Calumniating Time.

My earliest memory—though my mother, Shireen Anita, always disputed its accuracy—was kicking the wall against which my swinging baby-cot was placed. My mother insisted that I only slept in that sort of cot till I was a little more than a year old and that it was never placed against a wall I could reach with my foot. Arguing the point, my masi, my mother's sister, recalled that once when the bedroom in which my mother, sister and I slept was being painted, the cot had been shifted for a few days to my grandad's room and placed against the wall, and that, yes, I had got my foot stuck between the wooden bars of the cot's sides and had set up a howl. I don't remember it as my first memory of pain but as a way of making the cot rock. Perhaps that's fanciful, and I shouldn't call it a memory at all as it doesn't bring to mind an image of my infant leg but only of the wall and the Coca Cola–shaped brown wood bars of the cot's side.

Then, no memories, not even flashes, till I was in Quetta. My father, Lieutenant Colonel Jamshed Dhondy, was an officer in the British Indian Army, and a year or more after I was born in 1944, he was transferred to the Military Staff College in Quetta in the as-yet-undivided India. We had a house in the cantonment, the army settlement of the town, and four strong memories of that time stand out.

I must have been two years old. There was a kitchen window outside which, in the garden to the side of the house, there was a chilli tree, and Aslam, my father's army 'orderly', a soldier assigned to my father's personal duty, stopped me plucking the chillies and carried me away from it.

There was a stream somewhere in the distance over barren, rocky land, and hills far away beyond it. When we were put to bed, my sister Zareen and I could hear the wolves howling. One day, as we were taken on a stroll towards the stream, a porcupine appeared at the edge of it and rolled itself into a spikey ball, which someone, perhaps Aslam or Chandri, the ayah who came with us from Poona and looked after us, pointed out.

One day, my mother asked us to assist in making gingerbread men. She shaped the dough, and Zareen and I placed currants for the biscuits' eyes. We expectantly waited for the gingerbread men to emerge from the oven, but when they did, we noticed that one of the two was cracked in the middle. Zareen immediately said she was having the whole one. I said I was. My mother, quite rightly anticipating a noisy fit of dispute, tried to reason with us. The gingerbread would crumble in our mouths anyway. We were having none of it. Then, inspired perhaps by the judgement of Solomon, my mother took a knife and cracked the whole one precisely like the other. That was it. The two of us were on the floor, crying and kicking our legs.

Our father walked in and, hanging up his army hat and stowing the baton he carried, came into the kitchen to ask what was going on. Mum, in distress now at the ingratitude of us brats, told him the story.

My father took charge. He put the two gingerbread men on a plate and invited us to follow him. We were intrigued. He walked out the back door from the kitchen and then round to the front of the house. We followed silently.

'Now, watch,' he said and, lowering the plate so we could see, crushed the two biscuits into crumbs. Then, lifting the plate, he flung the crumbs with a determined flick onto the roof of our bungalow.

'The pigeons will have a surprise picnic,' he said and walked back into the house.

At the end of the year, perhaps for Christmas, the officers of the Military Staff College planned a funfair in the campus grounds for the children of the officers and soldiers of their regiments. The junior officers dressed as clowns to entertain us. I didn't understand the intent of the costumes or the painted faces with huge red lips and white foreheads. They terrified me. I cried and clung to Chandri. My sister and other children entered into the spirit of the afternoon. I was marked as a spoilsport and taken home.

In 1947, when I was three and my sister was just five, the subcontinent won, or was granted, its independence from British colonial rule and was consequently divided into India and Pakistan. Quetta was deep in Pakistani territory. The regiments of what had been the British Indian Army were divided down religious lines, and the officers were offered the option of deciding their country. The Hindu and Sikh officers naturally opted for India. The Muslims from my father's regiment and others who came from the territories that had become Pakistan naturally chose to stay. Other Muslim officers with families, ties and history in the Indian territory would make their way to India.

These seemed inherent or even inevitable choices. My father, being a Parsi Zoroastrian and neither Hindu nor Muslim, was urged by some colleagues to stay in Pakistan and serve in its army. But our family belonged to Bombay and Poona, and besides, my father was ideologically with Mahatma Gandhi, opposed to the division of the country and thought the creation of Pakistan a tragedy.

Riots broke out in the border towns as millions of Hindus and Sikhs fled Pakistan and, equally, in the opposite direction, Muslims crossed the border from India as refugees. Martial law was declared. My father was called away from Quetta to the Northwestern towns when his regiment was enlisted to enforce it.

My mother was left with us two children and Chandri. In the following weeks, all the Indian Army families were loaded onto a crammed and military-protected train to cross the border to India. I have no memory of the journey, but my sister remembers the compartment which was meant for four but had perhaps twelve women and children in it. What should have been a two-day ride, guarded by soldiers armed with machine guns on the compartments' roofs, took four or five days.

My mother, for the rest of her life, would occasionally recall the horror, the sights and sounds of slaughter, as refugee groups from both sides crossed each other in bitterness and hatred.

I am spared the memory.

When I was five or six years old, my father was transferred to Madras. I began school in the Presentation Convent, Church Park, which was a few hundred yards away from the house in Lloyd's Road, where we occupied the spacious first-floor flat. Below us, on the ground floor, with a porch for parked cars and our terrace directly above it, lived an American family called the Huxleys.

By this age, the early memories evolve into recollections of day-to-day existence. Chandri would walk us to school each morning, and on the opposite side of the pavement sat, or perhaps lived, a man who suffered from severe leprosy. He had his mat spread out, with pots and pans and several aids to daily existence by his side. A canvas cover hung on the wall of the church behind him. He would grin at us as we passed by and move his head back and forth like a chicken, perhaps to amuse us. Zareen and I named him 'Mr Wookoo', the word we invented as a verbal description of the bird-like back-and-forth movement of his head.

Over the weeks—or was it months or even a year?—his leprosy caused his truncated fingers and toes to ooze pus, and when the police drove him away from his station at the head of Lloyd's Road, he camped a few hundred yards down our front gate. The day after, he was gone, leaving his mat and the meagre bundles and utensils of his street-abode on the pavement outside our house. I remember Mrs Huxley and my mother going out with bottles of disinfectant to pour on the spot he had occupied.

It was at that age I was made aware of sex. In the next house, beyond a floral hedge in what I thought was an expensive garden, there lived a boy called Christopher, who was a few years older than me. We used to meet by passing through a thinning part of the dividing hedge. One day, messing about in his garden, he suggested that we 'play koonjis'.

I didn't know what he meant, but he asked me to take down my shorts just as he was doing so that we could rub our penises together. I did as he said and rubbed my diminutive prick against his foreskin but didn't understand the objective of the activity. At that age, there was no possible stimulation. It appealed to me as just something vaguely forbidden, as one's private parts should remain private and not be seen by anyone except one's parents, one's sister and Chandri.

I don't know whether Christopher derived any pleasure from the 'game' he initiated or whether he had played it with anyone else.

My awareness that a prick had more uses than as an outlet for piss came when a lad called Abraham, a Tamil Christian in his late teens, was assigned to look after me. We used to play a sort of child's cricket, and he would take me for walks in the botanical gardens opposite our house.

My father drove a maroon Mercury whose registration plate, MSP 9673, remains somehow in my memory. Its garage was to the side of the house, and I often went in there, got in the driver's seat and held the steering wheel, pretending I was zooming down the roads and highways.

One day, Abraham led me into the garage where the car was parked. We got into it and pretended, as usual, to drive. Sitting in the passenger seat, he loosened his trouser belt and fingered himself erect. He seemed totally absorbed as he masturbated. I asked him what he was doing, and he said, 'Soon the milk will come out, watch.' I watched, and it did.

Abraham, dragging his trousers up, said I wasn't to tell anyone.

I was intrigued and couldn't keep it to myself. I told my father that Abraham had brought milk out of his 'soosoo'. My father calmly said he shouldn't have done that and it was naughty. I didn't see Abraham again, and when I asked where he had gone, was told that he had to return to his village. I don't think it occurred to me that my report of the incident had led to his dismissal.

Are early memories reliable? They are retained as sights, sounds and the precise emotions of elation or fright. While later memories, when the moulding fabric of language wraps itself round perception and experience, are retained partly as words and formulations, or perhaps that's just a writer's conceit.

SECRET PASSAGES

At the age of eight, I was settled in Poona in my maternal grandparents' house, where two of my aunts, Shera and Amy, lived. My parents thought it best that my sister and I lived in one place and were educated in a single school till we matriculated instead of shifting with the family as and when my father was transferred from one military station to another.

In our house on Sachapir Street on the border of Poona cantonment and Poona 'city', the rooms followed one from another. The architect, if indeed there was one, had no concept of or respect for privacy. The building had been thrown together. The room I shared with my sister was a curtained-off area, with the curtains hanging between two solid wooden wardrobes, leaving the other side of the cordoned-off section as a corridor to the dining room. My study space was an area on the back veranda, where my writing table and a small cupboard for books partitioned me off from the doors that opened to the dining room and to my sister's and grandfather's rooms.

A retired land records official, my grandfather would sit every morning on the front veranda at a felt-covered bridge table that would be set up for him, working at his vast stamp collection. Grandpapa, or Mamawa-ji as we called him, would do his stamps in the morning, have his lunch, take a nap in his large four-poster bed and go for a walk in the evenings. Then dinner and bed.

It was a lesson in getting on—the loss of ambition and any manner of conquest, even everyday ones. Life was done with, and there was now the routine and the waiting. It terrified me, and I resolved never to follow in those sterile footsteps.

The school chosen for me was supposed to be the best boys' school in town. It was undoubtedly the most expensive and had been primarily a boarding school for the sons of British soldiers and officers in the days of the Raj. Bishop's, as it was called after a nineteenth-century Anglican prelate, was run on the lines of pseudo British public schools, and by the time I went there, it had a headmaster and staff of mainly Anglo-Indian and Eurasian teachers. There were two notable exceptions: the PE (physical education) and games teacher, Mr Sewell, an ex-sergeant-major in the British Indian Army, and Mr Aitken, the tall, thin Englishman who taught geography. They had both remained behind after Indian Independence, when the captains and kings of the Raj had departed. The reason for them staying on, it was said, was they had each married an Anglo-Indian lady and would perhaps not be accepted by the British community back in Blighty.

I went to school riding a small red bicycle, accompanied by Dara Cama, a neighbour and friend. Dara was three years older but was in my class. As his father had been the chief minister of a princely state and a friend of the maharaja, Dara and his siblings, growing up in Chhota Udaipur, had spent their childhood in the palace and hadn't been sent to school. They had been indulged till the age of eight or nine, and only on coming to Poona, a few years after Indian Independence, had their father considered their need for fast-track tuitions in English and for them to be sent, when they were sufficiently proficient, to English-medium schools. Dara had a man-sized bike, and we came and went from school together as he became my friend and protector. We grew up through our teens as inseparable friends.

After August 1947, when the kingdoms of the rajas and maharajas were annexed into the Indian and Pakistani republics, Mr Cama lost his comfortable, idle status. The family moved to

Poona to our neighbourhood. Not used to doing any work as the dewan, Mr Cama had no profession as such and had brought with him from the palaces of Chhota Udaipur a bank balance, hundred Rolex and other Swiss-made watches, French-tailored suits and his wife's jewellery endowed by the maharaja. This loot served his family for a while.

But Mr Cama took to spending his days at the Parsi Gymkhana, some miles away in the military part of the cantonment, gambling at cards with other club members. He also went regularly to bet on the horse races during the season. Before the money ran out, he had taken the precaution of buying two rickety, old trucks and hired two young Parsi boys to drive them, contracting the trucks out to people who wanted goods transported between Poona and other cities.

Over these years, with only the income from the trucks, some of which was purloined by the young drivers, the bank balance vanished and the jewellery and the Rolex watches sold or pawned. The family was reduced to living frugally.

Dara's mother took to stitching her daughter's clothes at home, and from the spare cloth, she fashioned all of Dara's underwear. The entertaining aspect of this frugality, for us, his insensitive friends, was that the tight 'chuddies' with no elasticity made him uncomfortable when riding a bicycle.

As teens, we would go in a gang to see English and Hindi films at the theatres. In the intervals, at the urinals, while the rest of us would unbutton or unzip our flies, Dara would have to pull down his trousers and the tight home-made cotton underwear to his knees, exposing a hairy behind to astounded men and boys in the queue behind him.

Dara graduated from our college in Poona a year before I did. He went to work in the distillery of a mutual friend's father, and when, after graduation in 1964, I went to Cambridge, Dara followed a year later, to live and work in London. He got a job in the sports department of Harrods, a luxury department store, from where he would walk home to the bedsit he rented in South Kensington.

On his way home, he would pass a Catholic church and, one day, decided to go in. He made regular visits in the evenings, just to sit in the quiet, he said, and was approached by the priest who noticed his silent vigils. He became friendly with the priest. Soon after, he told us, his friends who met in the evenings to go down to the pub or share a meal cooked on a gas ring in one of our bedsits, that he, an atheistic Zoroastrian, was converting to the Catholic faith.

He gave up his job at Harrods and took on a job with the Kensington and Chelsea Council, cleaning the streets. He said it was in line with his faith. The people he hung round with, myself and others, were all atheistic socialists and quite committed to talking about socialism and its rejection of 'superstition'. Dara remained stoically silent, even saying Jesus would approve of our faith in social progress and equality.

He went on to study theology in Wales and then took holy orders as a Catholic priest. He was sent by the church as a missionary to Bolivia, and we continued to meet with him on his annual visits to London. He was still fond of his food and drink and was the best of company, a sort of Friar Tuck in our crowd.

When he returned, after several years in Bolivia, he was assigned to a church in Gloucester. He tragically developed cancer in his tongue, and as the disease began to spread, the doctors said nothing could be done to stop it. He accepted his fate and went to pass his days in a Catholic hospice for priests in Gloucestershire's countryside.

I went to visit him. The priest in charge of the hospice said Dara was in a solemn, depressed and probably fearful state. He couldn't speak and had to be fed through a surgical hole in his abdomen.

He scribbled on a slate he had been given to say he was happy to see me. It was a tiny room with a bed and a basin, and on the wall was a cross and a picture of Madonna and the child. A window opened onto the Gloucestershire countryside.

Dara pointed to it and wrote on his slate, 'A good place to spend this time, nature in glory.'

'Never mind nature,' I said. 'Where's the secret passage to the nunnery?'

He shook his head but couldn't resist a smile, which broke into a grin as he picked up his slate and wrote, 'You'll never change!'

As a nurse came in and with a funnel poured medicine into his unbandaged abdomen, I stepped out of the room and returned when she left.

'See that? Only way to be fed,' he wrote.

'Let's get a good bottle of rum, and I can pour half of it down your funnel.'

He laughed again. We chatted, with him scribbling and me telling him about the people we knew. The priest in charge looked in once or twice and, after a few hours, it was clear I was being asked to leave. It was prayer time. I said I would return the following week.

Dara died five days later. His funeral was attended by hundreds of his parishioners who flowed into the street. I was told fifty-eight Catholic priests, eight of them bishops, were there that day. I drove behind the hearse to the burial ground, and as they buried him, the priest asked me to say a Zoroastrian prayer.

I joined Bishop's in the fifth standard. The rest of my class had been at the school for two years already. All the boys in my class were older—I was eight, while most of them were nine and ten years old, and some, who had repeatedly failed exams and were compelled to repeat the year, even eleven or twelve.

A lanky boy called Uday Laad got hold of me in my first week of school and asked if I knew about sex. I said I didn't. Giggling, he formed his fingers into what he contrived as a model of the penis and with the fingers of his other hand a circle as a model of the vagina.

'This is what your daddy does to your mummy,' he said.

Another lad, watching this disapprovingly, brought a fist down on Uday's hands.

'He's a new boy, don't teach him all this rubbish.'

This was Alfie Gordon, one of the boys who had assumed the role of being the moral conscience of the class. Uday sneaked away. Relentless talk of sex by my adolescent companions punctuated a lot of my school life.

I was still pre-pubescent when an anxious episode overtook me.

'Buy Nixoderm from your chemist today,' was a regular ad on the commercial service of Radio Ceylon, to which we children, from the age of nine onwards, were addicted. It was the only radio station that featured two commercial 'Hit Parades', one featuring the ten most popular English and American pop songs and the other of Hindi. Listeners had to endure the advertisements in between.

The ad for Nixoderm had a beguiling offer: 'Guaranteed to end all skin troubles or money back!' It was guff we simply ignored, except one night I felt my groin aflame, a burning sensation round my crotch. With a hand mirror I bent to see what the fucking hell was tormenting me.

The skin was crimson red. There wasn't much I could do to relieve the burning itch. I tiptoed to my aunt's room in the dark, knowing that if our dogs, chained to the dining table in the night, heard any unusual movement, they would bark and wake up my aunts and my sister, and I would have to explain why I was prowling about at night. Of course, my affliction, a disgrace, would have to remain a secret.

I picked up a jar of my aunt's cold cream, hoping it would bring some relief or at least lessen the urge to itch. I knew it was a face cream and not medicinal, but hope sprang eternal. It did nothing at all to relieve my discomfort.

I spent a restless night wondering how I, never having had sex, had caught the clap or some other venereal disease the older boys joked about. I couldn't believe that this disease, which I had heard was a punishment for those lads who frequented sex workers, had affected me, aged ten. Was it bad that I had, unlike other boys in my class who did it openly, never masturbated? I eventually fell asleep but woke up the next morning with the same burning in my crotch.

Turning on the radio to the breakfast-time broadcast, I heard the Nixoderm ad. Here at last was a straw to clutch at. I would dress and go with all the pocket money I had saved to buy records (perhaps it would suffice) to get some Nixoderm, the guaranteed miracle cure.

It was the school holidays, so I got out of the house on my bike and stopped at a chemist's. I asked the price from a young assistant who looked so bored he didn't look askance at my young years. He brought the green tin from the shelf as though Nixoderm was my daily bread. I took it home, shedding grateful tears, confident that nothing could intercede as Nixoderm 'guaranteed to end all skin troubles or money back'.

But when I rubbed it into my groin, a shooting pain spread concentrically from my crotch—an agonising, unbearable, fresh burning sensation.

I felt that I would die if I couldn't wash this poison away. I rushed to the backyard and sat under the cold water from the tap, rubbing my crotch and inner thighs as hard as I could bear.

At which point our cook, Hukam Ali or 'Hukams', came out of the kitchen and asked what I was doing. Beyond caring about humiliation by that point, I told him about my burning crotch. Hukams turned the tap off and fetched cubes of ice, asking to see where it hurt.

'Hai Allah,' he said. 'You've got a bad case of dhobi's itch! Putting water on it will make it worse.' Looking at my crotch, he let out a terse expression of disdain in Urdu, that all dhobis were conceived out of wedlock and were constantly drunk.

'That crook your aunts employ always stinks worse than a skunk,' he said. 'He doesn't wash any clothes. He just dips them in filthy water and hangs them up to dry. I know these scoundrels. You have to go to the doctor today.'

Hukams insisted he tell my aunts that I caught this from my chuddies. I went to our doctor, reassured that it wasn't some sexual disease. Doctor Frenchman—yes, a Parsi with that name—checked me out and said yoghurt would ease the itching.

'But, can this be cured?' I wanted to know.

'We'll try,' he said and, smiling to confirm a suspicion, added, 'but we won't try Nixoderm!'

For days the touch of underwear hurt, though the burning lessened. I was on the road to a recovered crotch.

So now, wanting to work the guarantee and see if Nixoderm's adverts really meant what they said, I got hold of the green tin and went to the chemist's. But my intention was cut short when a new attendant with a friendly grin asked how she could help. What was I to say to a teenaged girl? I turned away.

Bishop's was, through tradition, very sports-oriented. As it began as a school for British soldiers' sons who would all one day return to Britain, there would have been no compulsion for them to acquire academic qualifications. It was in the 1950s, when I was a pupil there, that the school was induced to produce the professional classes for the future of independent India. The school was pressured by parents and by the general zeitgeist of the country to alter its priorities. Our parents wanted us to graduate with the grades and qualifications that would enable us to join institutions of further education, which would in turn qualify us as engineers, doctors, lawyers, scientists, academics and administrators of this vast and diverse country.

And yet, there remained in the school a distinct bias of honour and rank towards those boys who excelled at sports and only a cursory attention or kudos afforded to those who were good at studies—the 'swats'. But the world and the future belonged to these swats, and there was a creeping, if reluctant, realisation that the 'all-rounder' who could master goal-scoring on the hockey field and the physics of the electromagnetic field was to be most valued.

The day-scholars, sons of professionals and business families in the main, would excel at studies, perhaps because they were pushed into homework and extra reading at home. From the fifth standard onward, for me, there was no question—I would be in the competition for the highest marks in any and every subject we were taught. If I fell below the rank of third in the class, my guardians and I counted myself a failure. Still, the pride of place in the school was reserved for sportsmen.

I was clumsy at sports and so always among the last to be picked by the captains of the various teams. Perhaps the humiliation of not being a passable player at any of these sports (except once when I won the 200 metres athletics prize) pushed me towards attempting to show-off in different ways—telling stories or reading books that none of my contemporaries would attempt.

There was in the cantonment a decrepit building on East Street, the Albert Edward Institute. In the days of the Raj it used to be a popular lending library. The three rooms of the building were still filled with dust-laden books, but these were rarely borrowed by the mostly ageing patrons who came by to read the daily papers. The old Goan gentleman with a well-lined face who sat at the librarian's desk had been there, he said, for forty years.

Together with Dara and Rashid, friends of mine who also had intellectual conceits, I joined the institute, and we worked our way through the shelves, reading indiscriminately, with no idea of the literary worth or ranking of a book. I read through perhaps ten of the novels of Thomas Hardy and four of those by someone called Marie Corelli without any guidance as to the difference in their literary status. They were all books, stories to read and talk about with the other two lads.

One of the books we discussed was *Vendetta* by Marie Corelli. Its opening sentences, as I remember them, were:

'I, one Fabio Romani, am dead. Dead and yet alive.'

Could there be a more intriguing beginning to a story?

In my ninth standard, Mr Rais caught our imagination in his first class of general studies by saying it was about time we had some lessons in sex. He drew some crude diagrams on the board and was pleased with the attentive response from the class.

In the next session, he launched into a diatribe about the dangers of masturbation. He said that the sperm spilt at the climax of masturbation came from a liquidisation of a nerve behind the eyes and that if one continued to wear away the nerve through persistent 'self-abuse', one would certainly and steadily go blind. It was an alarming assertion, warning or thesis, and those in the class who were known for 'pulling their wire', as the expression of the time went, began in panic to question Mr Rais.

Hadn't he said in the last lesson that the sperm emitted from the male went into the female to make babies? So, surely that too would wear away the nerve behind the eyes? No, said Mr Rais, the liquid that the female organ emitted sealed that particular nerve and so there was no danger. Regular sexual intercourse was safe.

I was not yet pubescent, and though I had witnessed other boys doing it, had never had the inclination to masturbate. Still, it was worrying. I didn't want my friends or anyone else to go blind. Yet, it seemed absurd. Why weren't there blind boys all over the world, regretting their lustful self-abuse?

That evening, Dara, Rashid and I, with our other friend Khushroo Captain, raided the bookshelves at Rashid's house because he said there were many books on sex. We chose the ones that looked the least technical and leafed through them. One of them, an American text, had several paragraphs on masturbation and pronounced it an absolutely natural, normal and, even in one's adolescence, a physically and socially necessary activity. It explained how and where sperm was manufactured, and there was no mention of any optic nerve. The book, the cover assured the reader, was by a qualified medical practitioner and specialist in sexual matters.

We took this information back to the class the next day. What Mr Rais had told us was bullshit, I announced, addressing the whole class, all of whom had gathered round to see the book I had borrowed. I relayed the reassuring opinion of the American sexologist. I am sure it altered to some extent the respect for us swats who had brought back comforting facts from our reading.

The male adolescent obsession with sex and the unused testosterone running rife was manifest in my final years at Bishop's.

Some of the boarders would sneak out at night and go into town to visit the red-light district. The boys who lived in the dormitory, called 'military barracks' because that's what they used to be, would also wait at the three-foot-high wall that separated the back doors of the barracks from the cantonment road for the young women who collected old bottles, paper and cardboard from round there for recycling. They were poor girls dressed in sarees.

The lads would throw coins at them and shout, 'Kholo,' demanding that the girls raise their garments and display their thighs, crotches and vulvas.

My father had, over my teenage years, been transferred to different army posts. He spent years in Kashmir in an army settlement out in the wild where his regiment camped in tents. He got fed up of living in one, and being a civil engineer by education and trade and calling on the help of one of his soldiers, his orderly, he built himself a two-room house with an outhouse kitchen and lavatory, fashioning bricks out of mud and straw. The walls were made of these amateur bricks and the roof was of corrugated iron over tent-canvas fabric fixed to large wooden beams, which they made from the trees they felled.

Udhampur in Kashmir was what the army called a 'non-family station', but officers were allowed to live with their wives if the women could face life in the camp. Several officers lived with their spouses in large tents, like the ones in *Arabian Nights* films, except these weren't multicoloured but khaki and olive green.

After he had built his house and Mum had joined him there, Zareen and I visited them for a holiday. I was nine years old and my sister was approaching eleven. We were put on our first flight ever to Amritsar, from where Dad picked us up and drove us to Udhampur and to the tent he had pitched for two outside his house. We found it exciting to be under canvas and to put out the hurricane light at night, except for one night when we woke up in the middle of a sandstorm which threatened to blow the tent away. After my parents took us into their beds in the house, the tent came off its moorings and the canvas went careering uphill. A sandstorm in those parts of Kashmir meant one had difficulty breathing and had to use filters of porous cloth over the nose and mouth. We had the use, for this purpose, of my father's Parsi religious vests made of fine muslin in a religiously ordained pattern—but a shield of any pattern against dust was welcome.

My mother repeatedly asked my father if we should all weather the storm outside in case the walls caved in or the roof fell and smothered us. Dad was quite sanguine. He sat through the night and the storm and assured her that he had built the house to withstand such a disaster. It passed the test and didn't collapse.

Other officers' families were not so lucky. The next day, when the storm subsided at dawn, hundreds of soldiers were chasing tents all over the hills. Ten of the officer's wives crowded into our tiny house, one of the few standing shelters, and were given coffee and sustenance, while their husbands and the regiment's soldiers rebuilt the officers' homes.

We were then taken to Srinagar, the idyllic capital of Kashmir, in a valley with a lake. We lived in an army guest house in whose grounds there was a cherry orchard. My sister and I had never seen cherries before, and we were constantly climbing the trees and eating them.

One day, I decided to make cherry wine. We gathered a big bunch, squeezed what juice we could from them and strained the dregs away. I then added some brandy from my father's portable store and, as I had gathered, let it ferment for a few days. I found what I called a secret passage, a hole that perhaps some rodent had dug under the foundations of the building, and hid the bottle in there. Later, I drank a good draft of it. I was sick the next day, throwing up, and had to confess to what I thought, at the age of ten, was a serious crime. Dad said that being sick and consequently going without two meals was my punishment.

We returned to Poona after this holiday, and I was confident that none of my classmates had had equivalent adventures. It was a confidence that was heading for a fall. At the religious assembly of the first day, where the whole school gathered, after prayers and hymns, the headmaster summoned a group of seniors to assemble on the stage. We wondered why.

Mr Lunn announced at the lectern that this brave crew had, led by him, during the holidays been to the highest mountains of the Himalayas and had scaled, as only adventurers and mountaineers do, the Pindari Glacier, one of the challenges of the northern range. The mountaineers were each awarded acclaim, certificates and whatever else the school regaled them with, to resounding applause. Sandstorms in Udhampur and rotten cherry liquor could hardly compete. I thought it best to keep these unique adventures to myself.

The school assemblies followed a pattern of prayers and hymns from a small hymn book, the card covers in the colours of the 'house' to which each of us was assigned. Very many of the meanings of these hymns eluded me. Particularly puzzling was:

'As pants the hart for cooling streams
When heated in the chase ...'

Pants were what you wore and heart was obviously misspelt. And at the ages of eight to ten, I had no idea what this particular 'chase' was.

And where in the atlas was Sion City? And what were we, ex-colonial Indian lads, to make of 'fading is the worldling's pleasure'?

I think we understood the mood of most pop songs on the radio or the lyrics of the records we bought, though my father professed himself puzzled by 'Good golly, Miss Molly, sure like to ball' or 'Be-pop-a-lula, she's my baby'. In one of Eliza Doolittle's solos from *My Fair Lady*, I couldn't understand the line 'lots of coal making lots of heat', because in her put-on Cockney accent, 'coal-making' became 'cow-miken'.

The seniors were all herded by Mr Lunn into a choir and made to sing, among other orchestrated songs, *Shenandoah*, *The Skye Boat Song* and the Scottish ditty *Road to the Isles*, whose totally recondite words went:

> A far croonin' is pullin' me away
> as take I with my cromack to the road.
> The far coolins are puttin' love on me
> as step I with the sunlight for my load.

And then lines which I haven't interpreted ever:

> It's the cool cresses I am thinkin' oh for pluck
> and bracken for a wink on mother knee …

As well as not knowing who Bonny Prince Charlie was, the Scots' language and the geography of the Shetlands escaped us. But we nevertheless sang all of these with great gusto and to resounding applause from the Indian parents on prize-giving day.

The cane was regularly used in Bishop's to keep discipline and dispense punishments. Some boys were beaten on their bottoms in front of the class for the sin of 'not paying attention'. I was, I thought at the time, unfairly subjected to several caning in my years there. One flogging I can never forget was the result of a quirk of fashion.

There was a Baghdadi Jewish community in Poona, refugees, it was said, from persecution in Iraq. Two of these families owned the Poona Hosiery and the Imperial Hosiery, shops selling ready-made clothes for the rich of the town. My family and those of most of my friends found it much cheaper to have clothes made by the local tailors. Ready-made clothes seemed to us a luxury only Westerners and the rich could afford.

George Iny, one of my good friends from school, one day confided to the crowd of friends who met on Main Street most evenings that some fantastic gear had arrived in the Poona Hosiery. Nylon and Terylene were new fabrics of the 1950s, and we went to see what he was being effusive about. Hanging on the display hooks were multicoloured shorts made of these silky materials. Next to them, displayed on a rack were broad nylon ties—red, blue, green and yellow—with pictures of naked ladies in alluring poses.

As thirteen-year-olds, these things we must have. In the next few days, eight of us collected the price of a pair of nylon shorts and a tie each, and we determined to wear them and parade down Main Street, officially Mahatma Gandhi Road, and impress the passers-by, preferably the young female ones.

Our parade was cut short as we strolled down the pavement. A rickety maroon car drove past, slowed down and parked on the side. We knew whose car it was. Mr Lunn emerged from the driver's seat.

'Dhondy, Iny, Cama, you are all Bishop's boys!'

'Yes sir,' we said instantly, standing in the 'at-ease' military posture.

'This is a disgrace. Go home immediately, and wear these clowns' costumes to school tomorrow. Bring your uniforms in your bags and don't go to your classes but line up outside my office.' When he was annoyed, his clenched lips dipped down at each end. He got in his car and drove away.

The next morning, after we waited outside his office, he marched us onto the stage at assembly. The students stared at us curiously as they sang the numbered hymns and said the daily prayers. Then the headmaster, at the prayer lectern, pointed to us and said that the eight miscreants on stage had brought the school into disrepute by walking through Main Street dressed as the school could see.

Each of us was given three strokes of the cane as the rest of the school watched, and then we were told to change into our uniforms and go to our respective classes.

My inclination towards reading and writing was not the only defence I threw up against my incompetences at athletics. The school had a debating society where the smart alecks were invited to make speeches on chosen topics. There were interschool competitions, and Bishop's, reluctant out of class snobbery to play the local schools at football or hockey or boxing, arranged competitions with other 'public' schools, including St Joseph's in Panchgani, a hundred miles away, and the Cathedral School from Bombay. During my final year, there was to be a preliminary in school to choose contestants for these interschool competitions, and I was keen to make the cut.

I ended up being chosen to represent Bishop's to debate on 'What Would Make Our Country Great?' for the interschool competition. I had recently read *The Communist Manifesto*, having been introduced to communist and socialist ideas by a neighbour, and had worked out what I would say in the debate. India had to drag itself out of poverty because a nation with millions living below the poverty line could not achieve greatness. I had even worked out some programmes for the forcible redistribution of wealth and was practising my speech in front of my aunt's wardrobe, which had two full-length mirrors on its doors, when Zareen interrupted.

'You've got dandruff all over your back, and those pimples on your face look disgraceful. You're not going to spout your nonsense looking like that.'

I told her to get lost.

'I can get the dandruff out with some shikakai shampoo, and I can prick your pimples and smoothen your skin if you like.'

I didn't immediately agree, but remembering there would be girls from other schools in the audience and on the platform, I acceded to her beauty treatment.

Zareen was by this time in Nowrosjee Wadia College, studying for a degree in history. She was acknowledged as the belle of the ball and lived up to the accolade by following the popular fashions of dress at the time. My father wouldn't let her cut her hair though, insisting that she plait her long and lovely locks, which she carefully nurtured.

Early next morning on the day of the debate, I fetched a bucket of hot water from the wood-burning boiler in our backyard, and Zareen got to work in the bathroom on our back veranda. It was the first time my hair was being washed with shampoo; I normally used Lifebouy soap, which I rubbed on my body too. Only girls indulged in shampoo. Zareen said the proof that my hair was clean was if it squeaked when it was rinsed.

I did, however, stop her from pricking the two pimples on my face when she threatened to attack them with a needle sterilised in the flame of a candle.

Shampooed and squeaky clean, I went to the debate and was declared joint winner with another girl who argued for establishing a school in every village or some such thing.

BAD WORDS AND BROKEN RECORDS

From Udhampur, after a brief year in Assam, my father was transferred to Kanpur, the city in the northern state of Uttar Pradesh and known in British times as Cawnpore. It was there that my sister and I went each holiday during our final years at school and then in my first year at college, which I went to at age fourteen. I was among the youngest in college through the fluke of my father being transferred from the south of the country to the north. As the school year in the north and south started in different months, I spent only six months rather than double of it in the last year of school, and so was one or two years younger than my classmates. Kanpur, where I went for each holiday from the age of eleven till when I was fourteen or fifteen, was a formative period of my early adolescence.

The town was known as a manufacturing hub of textile and woollen mills. Conjoined to the army cantonment was, some miles away at a place called Chakeri, an air force station. There were a few hundred Parsis in the town, and it was the tradition of the Parsi communities, away from their concentrations of Bombay, Poona and some cities of Gujarat, to come together socially. They would all know each other and organise to meet and create pastimes, such as badminton tournaments in winter and celebrations of the Parsi new year.

Two of the Parsi families owned hotels, and a third, the Jhaveris, were the acknowledged leading Parsi family of the city, having lived there for centuries and built an empire of property on the main street, 'The Mall' as it was known. The Parsi community would go to the Jhaveris' mansion to pay their respects to old Ma Jhaveri and her bachelor son, who taught me a word which, despite my Poona-neighbourhood-endowed street-wiseness, I had never heard or used.

My father never spoke a vulgar word apart from 'balls!', which from him didn't mean a testicle or two, but just 'nonsense!'. Nothing obscene would escape his lips, no one ever heard him swear, though he always said what he meant.

The word 'sala' in Gujarati means brother-in-law, but long before my teens I knew its use was far from innocent. It indicated that the speaker had slept with the sister of the person addressed, with a vague connotation of incest, though it was normally used as a glad-handed greeting between intimate males without the literal implication.

It was the rule in our house that we were not to repeat any of the swear words which were in common use. If one slipped out in an indiscreet moment in my father's hearing, there were certainly reprimands and a threat of a rap on the knuckles, but he never raised a hand on his children.

'What would people think of your mum and dad? They'd think we are vulgar parents who have taught you these swear words and haven't infused any sense of moral or social grace. And while I am talking to you, Farrukh, wipe that smile off your face!' was the usual rebuke.

One day, Dad drove Zareen and me into town, and the three of us sauntered down the road of The Mall, which the natives of the city called 'Maal Road'. It was the high street, with mostly Raj architecture buildings. We encountered the Parsi patriarch of the town, universally known as Papa Jhaveri, the small community's godfather. With his walking stick and Western jacket, he was taking his evening walk.

Dad paused to say his 'saheb-jis', to which Pa Jhaveri replied, 'Please, Colonel Saheb, I was about to entreat you army fellows to give me a hand to get these beytichods off my land.'

He repeated this plea, pointing down the road with his walking stick. 'These beytichods deserve something severe, a tight kick perhaps. Jimmy, can't you order your army men to throw these fucking bastard beytichods out of my properties, which they've occupied? See that cinema,' he said, pointing with his stick. 'That cinema was my uncle's, who is dead. My poor blessed bejan-ji had loads of money but tiny bit of sense. He didn't notice these beytichods were by various tricks getting his signature on all sorts of official documents, including his last will and testament. The fellows cheated him with clear criminal intent.'

It was the first time I had heard that particular word. The F-word and the word for a child born out of wedlock were more than familiar to me, but this word had to mean something startlingly forbidden. I looked at Zareen, but she wasn't paying attention, and the repeated term didn't seem to have registered with her.

Pa Jhaveri continued, 'These beytichods have even, if you please, renamed our picture house, which they have illegally occupied. They are screening Hindi movies three times a day!'

I was dying to repeat the word that stood out from this harangue. It was a chance gift to my vocabulary, endorsed by no less than Pa Jhaveri through a public diatribe in the street. So when we got home, I told my mother that we had encountered Pa Jhaveri on his evening stroll and he had told us that some beytichods had moved into the Regal Cinema on Maal Road.

My mother's mouth resembled an open goal. Dad's brows came together in a knot.

'How dare you in our presence talk such rot?' Dad thundered.

I had my defence ready, though I knew it was a feeble protest. 'Uncle Jhaveri used that word "beytichod" ten times!'

Mum shook her head. She realised I was disingenuously using old, foul-mouthed Papa Jhaveri as my license to linguistically stray into taboo verbal territory.

'Pa Jhaveri is an old man, and he is entitled to speak as he likes, but you mustn't ever say that word,' she said.

She could see that Dad's patience was on a tight but short rein and so she intervened.

'Jimmy, perhaps he doesn't know what the word means,' she said and looked at me.

Dad shook his head and looked away as though he had persuaded himself to leave Mum to deal with me.

'I'm not that stupid,' I said. 'It means someone who tries some naughty things with his daughter, like kissing her and sleeping in her bed.'

Mum, though grim, was smiling with her eyes. 'Jimmy, I think it's time you explain what all these nasty words really mean,' she told Dad. 'After all, he's heard a lot of obscene stuff from people who should refrain from using such language, at least in front of kids. It's not his fault if respected elders use words like these.'

'He should have some respect for Pa Jhaveri's age,' Dad said.

'Respect for advanced years is no excuse,' Mum said. 'Common decency forbids the old from corrupting these children. What the ear hears it passes to the tongue!'

On these holidays in Kanpur, we made memorable friends. The Rawson children, Dolly, Esme, Pammy and Richie, whose father was an air force officer, formed a firm relationship with us 'army brats'. Then there were the Khory kids, Parsis like us, Dinaz, Parveen and Rustom, whose father was the chief executive of the Lalimli Textile Mills. All of us took turns sleeping at each other's houses, on mattresses laid out in verandas or drawing rooms.

We considered ourselves as close as siblings, except I had a crush on Parveen, the younger of the Khory girls. Through a chain of confessions and whispers in the gang, I was assured that she had the same feelings too. This was a great boost to my almost pubescent ego. I had always been regarded as what was then called a clumsy swat and a bespectacled 'four-eyes' in the argot of childish cruelty. Apart from these whispered assurances, nothing more resulted from the crush, except perhaps a stolen moment of the holding of hands in the dark of a cinema.

The friendship with Dolly persists to this day. We went our ways through our university years but met again when she came to London to work at the BBC and visited me in my digs in Cambridge.

For the Kanpur gang, Zareen and I were the Western Indian sophisticates with a teenage expertise in how to jive to rock-and-roll numbers, how to cha-cha-cha and how to shuffle in authentic Spanish style to the samba. We imparted this expertise to the Kanpur crowd. Music from America and Britain was the craze and fashion of the day. It set our generation proudly and conceitedly apart from that of our parents.

Zareen bought the record of a song called *Tom Dooley* by the Kingston Trio. It had for weeks been top of the charts on the Binaca Hit Parade. As we did with very many of the hits of those days, we memorised the words and tunes and sang along.

It was a morbid tune and had a melancholy chorus which went:

Hang down your head, Tom Dooley
Hang down your head and cry
Hang down your head, Tom Dooley
Poor boy, you're bound to die.

Tom Dooley had stabbed his lover with a knife, catching her in flagrante with the villain Grayson. And now he knew he would have to pay with his life for the murder. The words were without redemption or hope, ending with Tom at the end of a rope looped across the branch of an old oak tree.

The record was forty-five RPM, brittle vinyl and seven inches in diameter. My sister had a vast collection of them, a precious hoard bought with her pocket money. Among them were *Love Letters in the Sand* by Pat Boone, *Your Cheatin' Heart* by Patsy Cline and *A Little Bit of Soap* by some band whose name I have forgotten. Ballads dominated the charts in these years, the 1950s, as rock and roll was still new.

My sister took her selection of hits on holidays to wherever our father was posted.

In his study in the beautiful bungalow on Kanpur's Havelock Road in the old Raj cantonment, Dad had a Grundig tape recorder which no one else was allowed to touch. He never stopped telling us how much he had bought it for from the Indian brigadier who had returned from a tour in Bonn as military attaché, carrying back with him every electronic thing he could sell to his colleagues. He was on a diplomatic passport which allowed him to bring in a load of contraband goods, banned in those days under strict customs rules.

Our father was disproportionately proud of owning this cumbersome tape machine on which he played Indian vocal classical stuff. That was convenient for Zareen and me as we took sole charge of the hi-fi set with stereophonic sound in our front room.

Zareen relentlessly played *Tom Dooley*, the ballad of doom, love, betrayal, murder and regret. We would sing along with it.

One day at lunch when Zareen left the table to replay the record on the turntable, my father raised his hand to indicate that we should be quiet. This was the crunch; he perked up his ears, wanting to follow the song's lyrics.

'What are these silly fools singing about?' he said, frowning.

Leaving the table, he went into the front room, and we heard the clicks of the player being switched off, then the crack of vinyl snapping, before Dad came back and calmly sat in his place at the head of the now stunned and silent audience. We knew what he had done but didn't know how he would justify himself, and so a heavy silence descended as we ate our lunch.

Dad said nothing. Only towards the end of the meal did he deign, wiping his mouth, to reveal why he had reacted to a simple song in this violent way. He said it was a 'dullinder' song, a bad omen in the household, expressing sympathy for a murderer.

'You should be listening to happy songs, not this rubbish,' he said, and then, as he rose from the table, added, 'This sort of music makes America the criminal country it is today.'

LAZARUS

One incident from those Kanpur days has always given me pause and made me wonder about the mysteries of the claim that one can 'start anew'. The clichés of healing time, of haunting memories and the regret of roads not taken are perhaps true but futile. And yet, this incident poses questions. Can one countenance a complete change of life, a transformation which compels one to put the past behind and start anew, start somewhere never imagined to be possible?

The memory is so clear that I can quote conversations from it word for word.

It was one of those first summer holidays in Kanpur. I was playing by myself in the garden, digging a ditch and trying to make bricks out of mud and straw. I was going to bake them and build a dog kennel. It was a large garden with a circular lawn on which there were several cane chairs and a cane table at which my father and his friends would have a beer on Sundays.

It must have been late afternoon when I heard a gentle call from the gates, shut against the possibility of intruding cows and goats which were known to invade and eat the flowers. I looked up and saw two figures clad neck to toe in saffron robes and with near-bald or shaved heads.

'Young boy,' the older one said.

I left my pit and, shaking the mud off my hands, went to the gate. One of the monks was perhaps in his forties, though telling the age of adults was not something I could do, and the other much younger. They had cloth bags hung across their chests, and they each carried a wooden bowl.

I approached them. They were obviously not begging.

'Is your father home?' the older one asked.

'He's at the office,' I said.

I could now see that his face bore a scar from his forehead right down to his neck and perhaps further into his saffron garment. I also noticed that he clutched his wooden bowl with one finger and his thumb and that the other fingers of his right hand were missing. There was also something about his left eye which was not right. I stared at it. It must have been the first time I had seen a glass eye, but I immediately knew that it was one.

'Is you mother home?' he asked in English.

'She's inside,' I said.

'Can I speak to her? Will you call her please?'

I didn't know whether to invite them past the gate, so I decided to let someone else take that call and turned and ran to the house to fetch my mother. I told her that there were two monks asking for her.

'Monks? For me? What do they want?'

She came out of the house and walked across the lawn to the gate. The old monk smiled, even though his brows furrowed at the same time.

My mother stopped several yards from the gate. She held her hand to her mouth. No words came for perhaps half a minute.

'Hello, Shireen,' the older monk said.

My mother shook her head.

'No!' she said. 'No, please!'

'Can we come in? Is Jimmy back soon?'

'No, tell me … I mean he is, he should be, but how …'

She unlatched the gate, which they could easily have done, and stared wide-eyed at the monk.

He stared back.

'No, I am not dead,' he said. 'You are over the shock, I hope.'

'It can't be,' she said. 'Oh my god! Come in, come in. How … where … Khasi, you … Jimmy should be back any minute …'

She was indicating that they should enter the house with her.

'We can't come in. We shall sit here if that's permitted,' the man she called Khasi said.

'Yes, yes, sit here,' she said. 'What can I get you to drink? Where have you come from? Why …'

There were too many questions in her mind, probably crowding each other out. I listened, wondering what this was about and who these people were and how my mother knew them. It was probably the strangest encounter I had witnessed.

'We'll have some water,' Khasi said.

Mum looked at me, and I ran in and fetched two glasses of water.

They had settled into the cane chairs on the lawn by the time I returned with them. I didn't hear what he said to Mum, but when I came back with the water, the pallor and shock had receded from her face.

'This is a beautiful garden,' Khasi was saying. The younger one hadn't uttered a word.

Then my father's car came to the gate. His horn blew, and one of the gardeners appeared from nowhere to open it. Dad swung round the drive, parked in the porch and, tapping his thigh with his military swagger stick, strolled across to greet whoever was on the lawn with Mum. The two monks got to their feet to greet him, and Mum took a few steps forward, saying nothing.

I was sitting at a little distance on the grass and didn't stand up. I was unaware of the nature of the mystery that was unfolding before me, but I was intrigued as never before.

Dad stared at the older monk and frowned. Then the frown faded, as though he had dismissed the idea that he recognised him. 'Hello, good evening,' he said and joined his hands in what he must have taken for a pious greeting. Then he stared at the old monk again.

'Hello, Jimmy,' Khasi said.

Dad looked at Mum as though to ask what sort of trick this was.

'It's Khasi,' she said. 'He wasn't killed in Burma.'

'Oh my god!' Dad said in a whisper.

'It's good to see you settled and happy, and I've met your son,' Khasi said.

'Where ...' Dad couldn't get the words out.

'Let's sit down and I'll tell you. When I enquired round Kanpur and heard your name, I thought I'd make contact. You are the first people from the past I've been in touch with since my return.'

'You mean Ratan doesn't know?' Mum asked.

'She's happily married again,' Khasi said. 'How can I disturb that? I can only bless her. I am a monk.'

'Take these,' Dad said to me, holding out his officer's hat and swagger stick. 'And tell Gaffur to bring us tea.'

I was reluctant to leave but had to do what Dad said. Returning, I sat unnoticed on the grass behind Dad so he wouldn't send me away. I knew that some fascinating story was about to unfold.

Khasi said he was captured late in the war in 1943 at a place called Jessami in Burma. Dad told me later, answering a hundred questions, that he and Khasi had been in the same engineering college in Poona, and a year or two after graduation, they had each independently decided to join the British Indian Army. Khasi, whose real name was Khurshed Mama, a friend of both my parents, had joined an artillery regiment, and my father had joined one of the corps of engineers, the Bombay Sappers and Miners. They were both sent with their respective troops to different fronts in Burma during the course of the Second World War.

Khasi continued his story. His artillery company, commanded by a British officer, surrendered to the Japanese. The Indian officers, including him, were willing to fight to the end rather than surrender, but the odds were heavy—their supply lines had been cut, and they had lost communication for days with the rest of their regiment and the battalion. They surrendered to the Japanese, who shot the British officers and took the Indian troops captive.

Three senior Indian officers, who had, Khasi assumed, been previously captured by the Japanese, now wearing Indian National Army colours and bearing their former officers' ranks, were sent in to their prisoner-of-war camp to speak to the recent officer-prisoners.

Dad turned to me and said I should leave them. An eleven-year-old wasn't welcome to listen in any longer. I reluctantly went inside.

Later that night, Dad, actually anxious to explain the whole story to me in perspective, told me that an ex-Congress leader called Subhas Chandra Bose had started a self-proclaimed revolutionary army of volunteers called the Indian National Army (INA), whose only aim was independence from British rule. When the war broke out, my father continued, Bose went to Japan, visited Hitler in Germany and offered to side with these Axis powers against the British. He instructed all Indian soldiers captured by the Japanese or Germans during the war to switch allegiance to these Axis powers and fight alongside them against the British. Khasi did just that.

I was curious as to why a soldier would change sides, and Dad explained. It was a lesson in contemporary history, of which I knew nothing.

'Why did he join the Japanese? Weren't they cruel people?' I asked.

Dad agreed that they were reputed to treat their prisoners badly, but then he told me about the propaganda that even he and fellow officers in the Indian Army had been subjected to: about how the INA sent them pamphlets saying the Bengal famine of the 1940s had been imposed by the British as a punishment on the Indian population for nationalism; about the British using Indian troops and civilians as cannon fodder; about the Americans' supposed plan to use Indians as slave labour with the connivance of the Raj; about how the Japanese emperor Hirohito had pledged himself to freedom of all Asian nations from European domination; and about how they would, as the INA, march triumphantly into Delhi to great acclaim from the population.

My father said it was all nonsense. He was a nationalist and very respectful of Mahatma Gandhi and Jawaharlal Nehru and their stances.

I wanted to know what this thing about Khasi having been dead was. Dad continued the story.

Khasi had fought on the Japanese side, and at the end, in the last losing battle, the Japanese regiment he was with had been surrounded by British and Indian troops. He couldn't recall how or when, but he was hit by a shell. Half his face tore off and several pieces of metal pierced his body. He had umpteen scars all over and went blind in one eye. He may have been left for dead had not an INA jawan, one of those who had switched allegiance, dragged his still-breathing body back to where the Japanese had retreated.

This jawan later told Khasi that the Japanese commander hadn't wanted to leave a wounded INA soldier to die in front of other INA men and officers, and so Khasi was given the best medical and nursing attention that the retreating army could spare and found himself, when he regained consciousness, on a hospital ship which had left Rangoon in the final retreat to Japan.

Khasi was mostly unconscious, but he calculated that he must have spent more than a year in hospital and lost count of the number of times he was taken to the operating theatre to have the metal from his body removed, his smashed eye operated on, part of his brain lobotomised, his smashed fingers amputated and the bones of his jaw stapled with metal wire. Through all that, with several blood transfusions, he was kept alive. What plastic surgery was available at the time was later performed on his face and neck.

When he left the hospital after years, the Japanese gave him a pension to live on.

'He, of course, thought of returning to India when he was patched up, especially as Japan was overrun with American troops. But he was warned that India was putting what it called traitors and defectors on trial, and they could, even a year and more after the war had ended, put him on trial, imprison or execute him,' Dad said.

This was more gripping than any adventure fiction I had read. Khasi then moved in as the partner and lover of the Japanese nurse who had looked after him. He was living in a world he didn't know, and he felt he had become someone else. She was a devout Buddhist and taught him the ways and philosophy of the religion. He then went to a zen monastery, and they convinced him to return to India and preach Buddhism.

'And who is the Ratan that Mum asked him about?'

'His wife, whom we knew in college together. He found that she had married again and now had two children, his boy and another by her second marriage. We actually went to his funeral when the British government sent her a note saying he had been declared a traitor and was dead.'

In the next few days, my mother noticed that the story had had some effect on me. It absorbed me in wonder and made me very quiet. Could one really come back from the dead? Of course, I reasoned to myself, he hadn't actually died on that battlefield, only presumed dead in the chaos of retreat. But there was something ghostly about his return.

I said I didn't want to go with Zareen to the swimming pool. Perhaps they shouldn't have told me Khasi's story, my mother said.

Dad merely said, 'He has to learn how life goes.'

PARSI CUSTARD

On my first day of college, I dressed as I would for school—in shorts and tucked-in shirt with shoes and no socks—and I bicycled over the railway bridge a few hundred yards from Poona railway station to the gates of Nowrosjee Wadia College. I was absolutely oblivious to the fact that none of the boys in college, all at least two years older than me, would turn up to campus in shorts. I didn't think twice about it. Those were the clothes I possessed, and the excitement of being in a new set-up kept me from paying the least attention to what I should wear. They were what, at the age of fourteen, I wore every day. 'Long' trousers and socks inside one's shoes were reserved for festive occasions and visits to the fire temple.

I passed the day of registration interpreting the timetable, making the acquaintance of classmates I didn't know, cruising round the grounds and the canteen with boys from my neighbourhood or from my year in Bishop's who had enlisted in the same college, and together finding which lecture was in which hall.

When I got home that evening, my sister and aunts confronted me. Zareen was in a bit of a rage.

'How could you come to college dressed like that?'

I didn't understand. I had expected to be asked how my first day at college had been rather than being tackled with what seemed like outrage.

'I didn't see you at all,' I told Zareen.

'Of course, you didn't. I stayed as far as I could from you because everyone was laughing at you and at me, asking me if that was my brother dressed like a dancing monkey in shorts,' she said, raising her voice.

'Laughing?'

'Yes, you idiot, because you were wearing that!' she said, pointing at my shorts. 'Nobody wears shorts to college, you idiot.' Then turning to my aunts, she said, 'I'm not going tomorrow unless he goes properly dressed.'

My aunts seemed to sympathise with her.

'But I've got eight pairs of shorts and only one pair of long trousers, which are now too short and tight. Do you want me to wear those? And throw away my shorts?' I said.

My older aunt, Shera masi, intervened, 'Come with me, let's see what Chotelal can do.'

Had I seen anyone else in shorts? Had I noticed anyone sniggering because I was wearing them? My mind was blank.

I went with Shera masi to the tailor Chotelal's shop in Taboot Street, a quarter of a mile away. He was understanding. He promised to work into late evening, and I could pick up a pair of trousers from him that night. The next day, he would make me two more pairs. He had reams of cloth on the shelves from which Shera masi chose white, grey and khaki cottons.

The following day when I returned from college wearing my brand new long khaki trousers, I found that all the shorts from my shelf in the wardrobe I shared with Zareen had gone missing. I never saw them again.

That year, there was a permanent addition to our Poona household. No, not a new pet, but a grand-aunt, my late grandmother's elder sister, known by the name my aunts were obliged to call her: Aala masi. She was perhaps a good twenty years older than my grandmother would have been, as she was the first of seventeen children my great-grandmother had brought into the world. The statistics are notable—the first of her children was a girl, my grand-aunt, followed by fifteen boys and then the last child, a girl, my grandmother.

By the time my mother was born, fourteen of the boys, my grandmother's brothers, were dead. Some had died at birth, others in infancy and some in their teens and twenties. Only one brother had survived, and according to Aala masi, he had cheated the family and was no longer considered part of it. Only this black-sheep brother and the two girls—the eldest and the youngest of the children—had survived.

Aala masi had lived on her own in a two-room flat in a Parsi colony in Bombay—a compound of flats endowed by some philanthropically minded rich Parsi for the families of the poor—after the death of her husband, a schoolteacher. She had fallen very ill and hadn't bothered to get her gangrenous leg properly treated. She had been laid up in her flat when neighbours alerted my aunts to her condition. They had gone to Bombay and fetched her, deciding that she would live with us in Poona. Her flat in Bombay was to be vacated and her meagre possessions to be sorted and brought to Poona or dumped.

She became very much a part of the household as she couldn't venture out. A third bed in the second room of our train-like house, my aunts' bedroom, was set aside for her. She was fitted out with several fresh night-dresses, day-time gowns and a stick with whose aid she could walk to the dining room.

My aunts were strict with her, forcing her into routines, which she didn't particularly object to. They also tamed the colloquial vulgarity of what they called her 'Bombay Parsi colony vocabulary'. Early in her residency, Aala masi would say in Gujarati at breakfast, '*Oohn tho chai ni koothri*!'—I am a real bitch for tea! My aunts didn't let that pass.

'You are not to use that kind of language in our house,' they would say, scolding her.

She wouldn't understand. 'What did I do wrong?' she would ask.

My grandfather, her brother-in-law and younger than her, treated her as a necessary evil, mostly ignoring her presence. I felt that he knew the strictness or cruelty she had imposed on my grandmother, Tehmina, when the two of them were growing up, with the twenty-years-older Aala masi assuming a controlling motherly role. Now she, the eldest of the seventeen, was the sole survivor of the brood.

Aala masi would sit on her bed for half the day and on the bench on our front veranda in the mornings and evenings, observing the comings and goings of the neighbourhood. One morning, Zareen was stepping out of the house dressed elaborately in a saree, not something she would normally wear to college.

'So, whose wedding is it?' Aala masi asked her.

'It's not a wedding. I have to address the college assembly at the ceremony today. I've been specially chosen,' Zareen said.

'What's this ceremony? What for? Some pagan religion?'

'It's Independence Day, Aala masi, 15 August.'

'What's Independence Day?' Aala masi asked, her wrinkly brows and her arthritic outstretched palm questioning.

'You know, when the British left India and we were free to have our own ...'

'What? The British have left? Nobody told me.'

This was 1962, well over a decade since Independence. Living in her Parsi colony in Bombay, had she been completely unaware of the great historical events in the country—the agitation for independence, the departure of the British and the partition of the country? Had the British regime really been so remote from the people? Or had the insulation of the communal Parsi life been so complete?

Once, when Aala masi was sitting on the veranda bench for her morning outing, I was reading a newspaper article about Iran and asked my grandfather about recent Iranian history.

'The British put him on the throne,' Mamawa-ji said. 'And when Reza Shah died, this fellow, his son, was crowned Shah.'

Aala masi, who never ventured into any conversation in which Mamawa-ji was involved, broke her silence and with a tone of extreme alarm asked, 'What? Reza Shah is dead?'

'Take no notice of her,' Mamawa-ji said.

Aala masi didn't repeat the question. That evening when I returned from college and parked my bike on the side veranda, she was sitting on the bench for her evening fresh-air session. I greeted her, but she sat looking into the distance with a disturbed expression, gesticulating and muttering to herself.

'Terrible news. Reza Shah … dead!'

'He died long ago, Aala masi. What's Reza Shah to you? Why are you bothered?'

'He used to make such fantastic custard cakes,' she said.

I had no inkling of what she meant. She went on, now looking at me.

'We used to go to his bakery under the bridge in Grant Road every weekend and buy them,' she said, with an exaggerated gesture of wonder.

Obviously, some Bombay Irani had named his establishment Reza Shah Bakery, and she, and whoever went with her to buy his custard cakes, had thought this baker was called Reza Shah.

TOWERS OF SILENCE

At the end of two years in college, I sat for and performed very well in what were then known as the first-year science exams. My family had determined that I would join a respectable profession with 'scope'. They chose for me a career in engineering, with a well-planned specialisation. India was going to soon manufacture its own chemicals, and this was seen as an industry with a future. Besides, the Bombay University's Chemical Technology department was the only one of its kind in the country and admitted perhaps forty pupils each year. To be selected as one of them was a much sought-after privilege.

I was persuaded to apply, was selected and left for Bombay to live with my paternal grand-uncle, Rustom Dhondy, known in the family as Russi kaka. It was a pleasant enough flat in the old part of the fast-developing city, and I had my own room with a balcony that overlooked the street to the right and the local railway line to the left.

Russi kaka was a strict vegetarian and a dedicated patriot and Gandhian. He only wore Indian-style clothes made of handloom cloth woven by peasant co-operatives. He refused to wear leather shoes and only wore plastic slippers and shoes made of canvas. He practised yoga regularly and did some exercises such as swallowing balls of cloth, forcing it lengthwise down his gullet and then wrenching it out so as to clean his oesophagus down to his stomach. It was disgusting and, I thought, dangerous.

Though I never witnessed it, he said he had practised controlling the muscles in his lower body and had trained himself through intense yogic practice to suck oil up his penis. He boasted that his guru went further and could suck mercury up his and then spit it out. Being argumentative at the age of sixteen, I asked him what the point of it was but never got a satisfactory answer.

I travelled to college each morning by the local train which took me to the northern Bombay district of Matunga. I made a few friends on campus, but Bombay was a different proposition from the Poona I was used to. The acquaintances I made lived far apart in this rambling metropolis and there was no prospect of spending evenings or times outside college together. After the intimacy of friends and family in Poona, Bombay seemed too big, isolating and lonely. I did have friends, such as Adil Jussawalla, now a poet, and my childhood friend Fershid Bharucha, today a writer and also from Poona, but I could see them only on weekends. Everyone seemed absorbed in their own world—a contrast to the chumminess of my Poona gangs. I gradually grew bored and resistant to the lectures in chemical theory with their focus on formulae and equations. The one subject I found interesting was thermodynamics—but that was perhaps more physics and even seemed to pose philosophical paradoxes.

I was soon dodging the lectures I found boring, instead playing several hours of chess with different opponents in the college canteen. It was also the first time that I consciously sought refuge and relief in reading. I stopped travelling to and from college by the relatively fast local trains and instead took the roundabout journey by the electric tram, which ran down the spine of Bombay, and then walked a long way to college from the tram stop.

Sitting on the wooden benches of the city's trams, I would read Lawrence Durrell's *Alexandria Quartet* and his travels in the Mediterranean. On lonely evenings after university and at weekends when I didn't have any friends to visit, I would walk up

Malabar Hill, sit on the parapet and continue reading from where I had left off and wait till the twilight turned to darkness and the lights of Bombay came on below me. Behind me, the vultures would seek their nests as they hovered over the Towers of Silence, the stone structures on which we Parsis would place our dead for 'sky burial', an offering of a corpse to carrion birds.

After six months of chemical technology, I resolved this was not a career I could spend my life in. Would it entail working out quantities of chemicals which would go into some apparatus to make some drug? Could I spend my life doing that? And get married to some Parsi girl my parents introduce me to and own a Fiat car, a flat in an industrial town and have the average two-and-a-quarter children and live happily ever after? Not for me, I thought.

After telling Russi kaka I was quitting this programme, I ran away to my parents. With just a rucksack on my back, I bought a third-class ticket and took the train to Delhi, where my father was stationed and my mother and younger sister Meher lived in a flat in New Delhi's Defence Colony.

Though I wrote regularly to my parents and received responses from my mother, I hadn't told them I was coming to Delhi. I knew that my father was in the military hospital for an operation to remove kidney stones and wouldn't be home for a fortnight.

I had never been to Delhi, but alighting from the train, with hardly any money on me, I asked for directions and made my way to my parents' house.

My mother was astounded to see me turn up, unshaved and looking rough at the door.

'What are you going to say to Daddy?' she asked.

'I'll tell him the truth,' I said.

We went to visit him that evening and, of course, he was shocked and angry. He said I was ruining my life and would end up amounting to not much. The next day, when we went again to the hospital, he apologised for saying those things and suggested we collectively decide on my future. I had the distinct feeling that he wasn't trying to pacify me but my mother.

I stayed in Delhi with my mother, Meher and Chandri, the young Maratha girl whom my grandmother had employed a generation ago and who had now dedicated herself, almost as an honorary granny rather than a domestic worker in the house, to looking after my mother's children.

I spent my days doing very little apart from exploring Delhi and reading everything I could get my hands on.

One morning, my mother woke me up, shouting from downstairs, 'Farrukh! Something seems wrong with Chandri. I can't wake her up.' I rushed to where Chandri slept, already knowing that my mother had understated what she knew and couldn't face.

Chandri lay on the thin single mattress she used as a bed, covered with a patterned sheet. I looked at her. The muscles of her face seemed loose as her cheeks hung down under the weight of their flesh. I felt her pulse. There was none. I touched her breast to feel her heart. Nothing.

'She's gone,' I said.

'No, no,' Mum said, bursting into tears. 'Shall I call a doctor?'

I nodded. She should call a doctor. We would need a death certificate and certainly some advice about what to do with her body.

As expected, the doctor pronounced her dead. He said he could send a nurse to clean the body as the corpse would have messed itself. My mother refused his offer and said however nasty the task, she would do it herself for this woman who had come into her household as a teenager and stayed on to look after her sisters and brother and then her own children.

The doctor phoned the Delhi Municipal Corporation's service, which provided a hearse to carry dead bodies to the cremation grounds, the burning ghats on the banks of the Yamuna. As

Chandri's eldest and only surrogate son, I circled her funeral pyre on the riverbank and set it alight as instructed by the priest, who said the prayers and bargained for more money. I was to come back in perhaps twenty-four or thirty-six hours to collect the ashes. I told my mother that I would stay there through the night and that they should go home and come back the next afternoon or evening.

I watched the fires of several pyres being lit that evening and burning through the night with the sound of Sanskrit prayers, smoke and ash ascending into the mist.

A young 'philosopher' came and sat uninvited next to me and started preaching about the vanity of human wishes. I said I didn't need him to tell me, I knew about these. He asked for money. I gave him the change I had and said I had no more. He appeared disappointed and walked away, I supposed, to the next mourner in need of his discourse.

The death of Chandri and that night of self-communion marked the end of a phase, a curtain on a bit of family history. It was my first close encounter with death. My paternal grandmother had died when I was two, and I hadn't known her. I remember my paternal grandfather as the one who had take Zareen, my cousins Dady and Jal Mody, and me, aged four, to the Bombay zoo called Victoria Gardens. My maternal grandmother, whom I remember very well, died when I was eight. I followed her funeral procession, insisting on walking with the menfolk the few miles to the Towers of Silence beyond Golibar Maidan, the firing-range common in Poona, but I was not allowed anywhere near the corpse. Neither did her passing leave a breach in my existence. I was very fond of her and spent time with her, but at that age, I adapted without thought or sentiment to her not being there.

Chandri was different. I have told her story in verse elsewhere and it bears repetition here:

CHANDRI

I

In 1920 they began to pave
The road outside our urban neighbourhood
In Poona, where my family's home stood.
Our municipal corporation gave

The contract to British road engineers
Who in turn hired a labouring crew
To drive steam rollers and make women strew
The stones over the dust of thousand years.

The work was welcomed when it was begun,
A sign our town had joined the modern age.
Among those workers on a daily wage
Was a young girl called Chandri. She was one

Of the gang who from their relentless task
Would come to my great-grandmother to ask

II

If they could drink some water from the tap
In our front yard. She thought she'd better say
That being low caste she'd been turned away
Thirsty, but now she said no such mishap

Could break her spirit because she had seen
The worst of what her karma had decreed
Her unfortunate birth had sown the seed.
None should regret the life that might have been.

My great grandmother said, 'We have no caste
We are Parsis, and you are welcome to
The water from the tap.' The young girls crew
Would use the tap in work breaks. Then at last

The road was done, the machines, workers, all
Left, leaving one girl sitting by our wall.

III

My grandmother, a vahu* of the clan,
With four daughters of her own, came upon
This girl and asked her why she hadn't gone
With the others? So Chandri said the man

In charge of recruitment made overtures—
They had to fuck him if they wanted work.
He forced himself on her—she went berserk
And kicked him away—all of sixteen years!

My grandma asked if she'd now return
To wherever she came from. She spoke
A rural Marathi. Where were her folk?
She said she had no folk and had to earn

Her living. Her karma was bad. She said,
'Sleep with that bhadwa?** I'd rather be dead!'

IV

My grandma said that she could spend the night
On our veranda, and she would provide
Her with food and bedding. 'You can decide
Tomorrow what you'll do. You were quite right

* daughter-in-law

** pimp

To resist such advances from that swine.
Didn't the white sahibs who were in charge
Of the whole project suspect, by and large,
What was going on?' 'And do what? Undermine

The recruitment of women carriers
Of stone?' It was the accepted basis.
The mukkadams* could hire and dismiss
Girls at their whim, there were no barriers.

'The sahib bhenchods** wouldn't interfere—
So their cowardice has landed me here.'

V

My mother was at the time ten years old—
Her three younger sisters aged one to six
And four cousins the same age in the mix
Made for a fairly riotous household.

My grandmother and her sister-in-law
Proposed to Chandri that she remain there
And be their ayah, helping with the care
Of my mother's younger sisters and four

Cousins. She gratefully said she would stay
And soon became part of the family,
Telling the elders why she had to flee
And what she had to risk to get away.
She was orphaned before she was quite ten
And taken in by an uncle who then

* foremen
** sisterfuckers

VI

Sold her in a 'marriage' to an old man
Who accepted her as his virtual slave
Herding the family cattle. He gave
Her leftovers to eat and soon began

To use her body in ways she described
As torture which ended when he fell ill.
He caught smallpox and died, and in his will
Entrusted to his mother, he prescribed

The ceremonials she should undergo
To purify her to commit suttee
On his funeral pyre so that he
Could avail of her in heaven and so

That she wouldn't be a burden on those
He left behind. They thought that all widows

VII

Should face the fate of holy death by fire.
His mother cursed her saying she had brought
The smallpox to their house and that she ought
To cleanse her sins by embracing the pyre

On which her husband's body would be laid
With all his worldly goods. They knew that she
Would not die willingly
So they tied her down to a cart and made

A nephew of the clan stand guard till dawn
When they would load the body on the cart
And drive the corpse and Chandri to the ghat.
Chandri said she had struggled, screamed and sworn

At the men who slapped her and banged her head
As though to them she was already dead.

VIII

Then they gagged her and left her with this boy
By the mud track under a crescent moon.
The boy watched over her and very soon
She knew what crossed his mind. Should she employ

His lusts to make a deal and get away?
From under her gag she set up a sigh
And indicated that he should untie
The gag, and when he did, she said she'd lay

Absolutely still for him and he could
Do as he wished with her, but when he'd done
He'd pretend that dacoits had overrun
The cart and captured the girl though he stood

In their way. Chandri said, 'I am alive
By renting out my body to survive.'

IX

And now that she had told them what she was
She asked my grandma if she'd changed her mind
And if she still wanted to hire the kind
Of girl who'd done what she had, because

She didn't want this family who'd been
So kind to her to suffer any taint
From her being there. Yes, she was no saint—
Bhagwan would forgive her, he must have seen

That she had strayed only to stay alive.
My grandma was in tears and she embraced
Chandri and said, 'Ahura Mazda* has placed
You with us to make sure that you survive

The superstitious hazards of those hills
And find this home as the Lord of Light wills!'

* Zoroastrian name for god

A TOWN TOO SMALL

Dad came home after his operation, and we decided I would return to Poona and finish my science degree. I said I would dedicatedly study physics. He agreed, as after my degree, I could consider sitting for the government exams, which would, if I made the grade, enable me to join the Indian Foreign or Administrative Service.

In hindsight, the stint in Bombay and the months in Delhi was a period that influenced my future in a significant way. It was when I read everything I could lay my hands on—from myths and English literary novels to the obscure works of Lenin, which I bought in the cheap Soviet editions sold on Delhi pavements.

Five months later, I resumed my studies at the Nowrosjee Wadia College for a bachelor's degree in physics, a subject in which I had excelled in the Intermediate Science Exams that had got me into the Bombay college. Besides, physics had always interested me in a philosophical rather than mechanical sense.

Our college in Poona was not best known for its academic achievements even though its lecturers were probably amongst the best in the city or even in all of Maharashtra. It was thought of as a cosmopolitan institution with a reputation for socially advanced ways—in other words, boys and girls dated.

One of the more shameful, though possibly harmless, traditions of the college, perhaps only in the few years before, after and while

I was there, was baiting the lecturers. The 'bad boys' using the camouflage that the numbers—120 pupils in one class—gave them, would shout rude names at the teachers, calling poor Mr Agarwal, who attempted to lecture the class in calculus, 'Batata Vada', potato dumpling, when the rotund professor's back was to the class. (When I started teaching for a few brief months at a college of further education in Leicester and faced the indiscipline of students who had come to study the trades of plumbing and electricity and weren't interested in my liberal humanities, I recalled my Poona days with shame and even amused regret.)

Some of our mischief was innocent. The film about Moses, *The Ten Commandments*, came to town, and the majority of the students at the college must have seen it at least once. In the film, Yul Brynner, playing the pharaoh, issues imperial instructions to a fawning attendant, who accepts the diktat with: 'So it shall be written, so it shall be done!'

Its rhetorical subservience caught our attention, and when Mr Ketkar, our chemistry lecturer, instructed the class to take down a formula and calculate what the result of some chemical procedure would be, the class, in chorus at an agreed signal, replied, 'So it shall be written, so it shall be done!'

He hadn't a clue as to what was being said and couldn't quite characterise, even to himself, the collectively pronounced sentences as mass indiscipline or react to them as such. He decided, we thought, to pretend it hadn't happened and carried on with chemical instructions to a now attentive class. Till, of course, he asked us to write something down again.

I reoccupied my room on the back veranda of my aunts' house. Some of my friends from previous years in college were still there but were a year ahead of me. In those first days at college, old friends introduced me to new ones, and a core of about ten or so formed and discovered common interests, including literary and, of course, the snobberies that we imagined, rather conceitedly, to put us apart from other crowds on campus.

At that stage, there were no couples in our gang. There must have been attractions, but the unwritten rule seemed to be that 'love' ought to be kept in check. Separating from the rest as a couple was a betrayal. Some undoubtedly had secret liaisons, but we were all confident that these wouldn't result in the break-up of what at the time seemed to be a fervent loyalty of friendship.

One among the crowd I fell in with was a girl called Mala Sen. Her first day at college had been pretty conspicuous. She was driven through the gates, where no cars were allowed, by a uniformed Gurkha soldier-chauffeur in an official vehicle marked with the insignia of an army big shot, that of her father Lieutenant General L.P. Sen. No other student arrived like this—we bicycled or came by bus. She seemed quite grand stepping out of the car in her salwar-khameez and being picked up at the end of the day by this military-flagged car which had special dispensation to drive into the grounds of the college.

In the following days, Mala, who was in the arts faculty, was brought along to our gang by those who had befriended her during the history lectures, and she fell in very enthusiastically with our routines.

Her father, popularly known as 'Bogey' Sen, was the chief of the Southern Command, one-third of the army of India, with its headquarters in Poona. Mala lived in Command House, a grand cantonment building a mile or so from our college. It was a one-storey black-stone colonial building set in spacious grounds with a flagpole and a military checkpost at the gate, guarded by Gurkha soldiers day and night.

When the Indo-China War broke out in 1962, Mala's father was sent to Ladakh to command that war front. Their mother, separated from their father, lived in the smart part of Bombay with her husband, an ex-army brigadier called 'Tutu' Bhagat. Mala and her sister Kum Kum were left in Command House with the family's attendants.

Our gang didn't visit but rather invaded Mala's house. On these forays, we would have to wait at the gate with the Gurkha soldier holding us there till Mala had, through the staff of the house, called the duty havildar, the sergeant, who would come to the gate and instruct the guard to let us through. We drank the general's whisky and played our pop records on his hi-fi equipment on the first-floor terrace.

Mala was by any standards a beauty, and passing through the stages of attraction, infatuation and obsession as she and I got to know each other and began to dodge the gang to spend stolen moments together, I fell in love with her. At the time, I would describe the feeling I got when I saw her or even thought about her as a ticklish emptiness in my abdomen. It was a new sensation and defined an attraction I had never felt before.

Of course, I set out to impress her in any way I could, and through some twist of fate, it worked. I had nothing material to offer her, but as I was a couple of years older than her, she must have felt that our relationship would give her ways of growth, intellectual and emotional, which she wanted desperately to pursue. When Alice asks Humpty Dumpty how you can make one word mean so many different things, she isn't referring, but may as well be, to 'love'.

Mala came from an exclusive school in Dehradun and had friends and schoolmates who were from the elite families of India—daughters of the military top brass, industrialists and politicians. None of them lived in Poona, but I met some of them when she went to live with her mother in Bombay during the holidays. I would follow her, camping with Khurshed mamu, my mother's younger brother, and his wonderful wife, my aunt Freni.

Mala didn't live in the social worlds of her father or her mother, because those worlds were, through distance and the remoteness of their acquaintances and concerns, closed to her. She had no inclination to go to the clubs to which her mother belonged or to learn how to play bridge. The one thing we did do together, entering her father's world for an evening, was to go to dances at the Rajindra Sinhji Institute, the army officers' club, on occasions when wives and families were invited. We danced to the ballroom music played by a military band—not the kind that led marches with blaring brass, but quartets with a repertoire of 1950s British numbers.

In the months before the degree exams, I gave hours of the night to studying physics, chemistry and mathematics. I would start after dinner at half past nine, sitting at my table on the back veranda while the household put itself to sleep. I would work till midnight when there would be a whistle from the street outside, to which I responded by taking a break and joining the friends waiting for me with their bikes at the junction. We would ride to the railway station where the cafes stayed open all night and have a cup of tea before returning to our respective dens to study till three or four in the morning.

I did well at the degree-level exams, as I had determined and sweated to do. The obsession of wanting to get away from the small and provincial world of Poona had overtaken me. As a student in school or college, I was very happy living there. It was a town and environment for making and keeping lifelong friends, which at the time felt unique, but what prospects would I have once I left college and settled into postgraduate studies, for which my parents would have to pay, or find a job?

The world outside, which my imagination had explored through books, had made me want to experience a wider life, a wider universe. Very many of my friends would go into professions following their fathers and uncles. Some were on their way to qualify as doctors and engineers—yes, even chemical. They would find jobs in Bombay or some industrial town. What would I do? Others would join the family business, running petrol pumps, paper mills or whatever. I had no such inheritance or prospect and now thought with some desperation that the only avenue open to me was to get a scholarship to study abroad.

I was variously advised to apply for a second undergraduate course in physics—in which I now had a Poona University BSc—in England, the USA or even Russia where many Indian students went, mostly to study science or medicine. The Russian course would require one or even two years of learning the language before starting on the course of chosen study. England and the USA had no such requirement.

But I applied to universities in all three countries—Moscow, Princeton and Cambridge, England. At the same time, I applied to the Tata Endowment for the Higher Education of Indians. To continue with this application, I had to have an acceptance from one or other of the overseas universities I had applied to. Luckily, I received letters from all three, saying that I had been accepted to join the next term. I decided to attend Pembroke College, Cambridge.

During my first interview at the Tata Trusts office, I was informed that they were happy to fund my three-year undergraduate course. The chairperson of the scholarship committee, Mrs Vesugarh, invited me for a further post-grant interview.

Before the round of interviews for the scholarship, I had, in those last years in Poona, adopted the sartorial style of the American Beatniks—of Allen Ginsberg and other Beat poets who grew their hair and beards and wore loose Indian clothes. My father didn't approve and was constantly at me to have a haircut, shave my beard and wear what he called decent clothes. I wasn't persuaded by his pleas until the crunch before the Tata interviews, when he wrote me a seriously admonishing letter. I would never get a scholarship if the ladies and gentlemen of the scholarship board saw me as I was. He implored me to go by his judgement for once. I did and gratefully realised that had I not shaved my straggly beard, cut my hair short and worn a crisply ironed white shirt and dark cotton trousers, I would have probably been judged unworthy.

For my interview at the offices of the Tata Trusts near Flora Fountain in the heart of South Bombay, the office district of Raj-built city, I went with Mala in her mother's chauffeur-driven car.

Mrs Vesugarh was a diminutive Parsi lady who, with her shock of white hair, resembled Bertrand Russell. I was shown into her large office where she sat, looking tiny behind an ample desk. She was small but formidable. Asking me to take a seat, she immediately launched into questioning me.

'Why Cambridge, Mr Dhondy?'

I wasn't expecting the question, but said, 'I suppose, wanting to study physics and … er … Cambridge has and had … um … some of the best minds in the world in the subject is why I …'

'That's as may be,' she said. 'But one goes to Oxford or Cambridge in order to make acquaintance with people who will be useful in later life.'

'Yes, I suppose.'

'Look,' she said, pointing at a door at the far end of the office. 'There's a lavatory behind that door, go and use it.'

I swerved round and saw the door. What was this about? She wasn't, surely, asking me to provide a urine sample? Some medical test I hadn't passed? I was bewildered but felt I had to do as asked and went along to the door, locked it behind me, urinated, flushed and re-emerged.

'That's good,' she said. 'I merely wanted to check if you'd use the flush.'

I was relieved that I had.

The tests were over. We chatted pleasantly for a while with her telling me about some encounters and mild adventures in her days at Oxford. She asked me to return in a few days' time to be fitted for the clothes that she would have tailored for me.

A tailor and his assistant were in attendance when I entered her office again. They had brought with them wrapped reams of cloth, which were piled upon a side table.

'Mr Dhondy, you are to choose some fabric for some pairs of trousers,' Mrs Vesugarh said and, as I approached the pile of reams, she prompted, 'The grey ones, third from the top, would be ideal.'

Those were, of course, the ones I chose.

'And then, fabric for your suit. We need to equip you with a suit.'

I pointed to a chocolate-coloured ream.

'Mr Dhondy, no gentleman wears a brown suit,' she said and proceeded to choose a navy-blue fabric.

The tailor measured me for the clothes, and his assistant took down the figures as his boss announced the inner and outer lengths of my leg.

By this time, my father had quit the army early in his career so he could get the official pension owed to him in a lump sum and with it pay for an arterial operation of which my sister Meher, ten years younger than me, was in life-saving need. The operational technique and expertise were not available in India, and my mother and Meher had to go to London where she was operated on during my initial days at Cambridge.

The surgeon, Sir Russel Brock, probably treating a young Indian girl for the first time, said he had come across some condition that he had put right and which had given him a new learning experience. He very graciously said he would waive his surgical fees, and the sum my father had obtained from his commuted pension went into providing their airfare, hospitalisation charges and living expenses. Meher's operation was successful, and she led, shall I say, a 'normal', if unconventional, life as a consequence—but I shall leave that for her own autobiography.

Months after leaving the army, Dad took up a post in the steel town of Jamshedpur, named after its founder Jamshedji Tata, who had started the first steel plant in India, exploiting the ferrous and coal mines of Bihar. My father was appointed town engineer in charge of all the buildings in the steel town.

I was with Mala in Bombay through these days, aware that soon we would have to part for years. Of course, we pledged to keep in constant touch by letter and, when we could afford it, by phone—the 'trunk calls' of the day—to remain faithful and resume the relationship when I returned.

She was by then enrolled in Sophia College, a Christian institute run by nuns on a hill in South Bombay. Mala chose to live in the hostel rather than with her mother and mother's husband in their rich flat not far from there. I would visit her in the college, sign some register on entering and wait for her to be summoned. The college had strict hours, and I would accompany her to the entrance in the early evening.

On one of these visits as I left Mala at the college doors, it began to rain. It was the end of June and the monsoon was heavy that year. As I walked out of the gate, there was a sudden downpour and I was lucky to hail a taxi. A few hundred yards down the hill with the blinding torrent coming down, we passed what appeared to be a young white man, walking with an umbrella that would have given him scant protection against the torrent. He waved at the cab. The stormy breeze turned his umbrella inside out. The taxi driver said in Hindi, 'See these goras, they used to rule the world and now they have to get drenched in our rain as the poor have to.'

'It's dreadful. We should stop for him. Stop!' I said.

'You're paying the fare,' the driver said a trifle sulkily, but he brought the cab to a halt by the side.

I shouted at the young man to get in, and with great relief on his long face, he did.

He was heading to South Bombay, round Colaba, where he was to be taken to a ship. We got to making polite conversation. I asked the young man, who was English, whether, since he had mentioned a ship, he was a sailor. He was amused. He had been teaching at a school for several months in Shimla and had gone up to Sophia College to visit his aunt who was a nun, living and teaching there. He was going back to England the next day and was due to go to university there.

On being asked, he said he was going to Cambridge, and I said that I too would be going up there in October. He looked at me as though I had claimed to be the emperor of China.

'What? Which college?' he asked.

Was it a test? 'Pembroke,' I said.

'This next term?' he asked, still bewildered by the coincidence.

'Yes. Reading natural sciences.'

I used the term 'reading' rather than 'doing' or 'studying'—an Oxbridge conceit I had picked up from a novel. He looked at me as though I was playing some sort of premeditated practical joke on him.

'So am I,' he said, searching my face for any clue of someone having put me up to it.

Before he got out of the cab, thanking me for the ride and unfurling his umbrella, he said he would be at Queens' College and we should meet, if I was really going to be in Cambridge.

DELIBERATE DISGUISES

Without telling anyone, I had tried to find novels about life in Oxford or Cambridge. I had discovered and read Evelyn Waugh's *Brideshead Revisited* and found it amusing as it contained the conceits I might encounter. *Lucky Jim* by Kingsley Amis was funny and reassuring. Yes, I would fit in. I was ready for the journey.

The clothes Mrs Vesugarh had had tailored for me were not in the style of the day. The trousers were Oxford bags, the fashion of the 1930s, when she had probably been at Oxford—very different from the narrow, almost churidar-width of trouser leg that we in India were, in imitation of American youth, wearing. But these were what were stitched for me and I went with them to Cambridge. Perhaps England would be different. The style of the bags were perhaps, through some traditional conceit, what they were indeed wearing in Oxford and Cambridge?

Most or all of the young men who got on the train with me at Liverpool Street station were dressed in shabby, old clothes or in the popular fashion of the time—either Mods or Rockers. I felt self-conscious in my tweed jacket and Oxford bags, a worthy oriental gentleman from the 1930s.

The letter inviting me to Pembroke was very precise. It said I should arrive at the college by noon. From London, where I had spent the week before term started, I took a train which would, according to the railway timetables, take me to the college an hour before the specified time.

The train was full of boisterous young men going 'up'. It stopped just outside Bishop's Stortford. The attendant guard passed through the train announcing that the delay was owing to some track or signal failure and British Rail were attempting to remedy it as soon as possible.

An hour passed. The lads in the carriage began singing songs and throwing bunched-up socks at each other. They didn't seem perturbed by the delay. I was in a panic as the hands of my watch came together at '12' and moved on and there was still no movement from the train. No one spoke to me, and for all my Indian street-wiseness and bravado, I didn't know how to approach those seated next to me, who didn't stay seated but joined in the raucous merriment.

We finally reached Cambridge at one o'clock. I was on a budget of two pounds and fifteen shillings as my weekly pocket money and had just that amount in my wallet. I joined the taxi queue outside the station and was approached by several lads announcing the names of their colleges in order to find others to share a taxi with. I joined two of them who said 'Pembroke', and we drove in silence and landed up at the fourteenth-century entrance to the college, splitting the fare three ways as we alighted.

One of the men I had shared the cab with turned to me as we got out, saying I was obviously a 'fresher' and what I should do was line up outside the porters' lodge, just within the gate, and register my arrival. I thanked him and took my bag from the cab.

I joined the queue, and when my turn came, I told the porter, who held a register behind the counter of the lodge, my name.

'Dondy, Dondy, Dondy,' he said, pronouncing the first soft 'd' as a hard one. 'Right, you are on V staircase, and Mr Dewey, your tutor, will see you at 12.30.'

'But it's now 1.30,' I said.

'You're late then,' he said. 'Next!'

The person behind me stepped forward and began his registration. I stepped outside the porters' lodge and waited by my suitcase. Would they send me back to Bombay? It wasn't my fault that the train was held up. To whom should I explain this? The only member of the college staff I could appeal to was, perhaps, the porter who was registering the queue.

At about three o'clock, the queue dwindled and was no more. I went into the porter's lodge and said, 'I was the one who was late, because the train from London …'

The porter was resignedly sympathetic. 'Don't worry. I'll show you to your rooms.'

'What about my appointment with Mr Dewey?'

'Leave him a note in his pigeonhole, and he'll probably reply to yours,' he said and showed me to my rooms.

I carried my suitcase through the quadrangles of Pembroke to what looked like a more modern block which contained the V staircase, a word used by Oxbridge to refer to a set of rooms. My room was on the second floor, and a slatted wooden board in the ground-floor hall had the names and room numbers of each occupant. I decided, after thinking hard about it, as I was let into my room by Mr Johnson, the porter, that this not being a hotel and not being India it would be inappropriate to even think about tipping him.

As I surveyed the room, I wondered what I was to do about Mr Dewey. I didn't know what or where his pigeonhole was and how I would leave him a note without any notepaper. Just then, there was a knock on the door. A tall young man walked in and introduced himself as Michel Beresford Summers and said I should call him Berry. He was in the room next to mine on the landing. While my room faced the quad of the college, from where I could imitate the character from *Brideshead Revisited,* quoting Eliot at late-night rugger buggers, his overlooked Tennis Court Lane behind the bicycle sheds along the rear wall of the college, from where he threw rotten apples at students who tried to climb over the wall and sneak in to see a lover.

Finding the first friendly face, I explained my dilemma. He told me that the pigeonhole would be Mr Dewey's mailbox in the senior common room, which he offered to help me locate, but first we should both go down to the junior common room, where all three hundred or so undergraduates would each have their own pigeonholes.

We went down together and, sure enough, there was one with my name in the alphabetically arranged wooden slotted board on the wall. It was packed with solicitations from Cambridge societies informing me about what they did and asking me to join. There were also some important notes about lectures and the names and locations of my subject tutors.

I asked Berry where I could get notepaper, and he said he wasn't very familiar with Cambridge, but happened to know, from his last visit with his parents, that there was a Wooly's in the centre of town which was straight out of the main entrance, turn right, down to a church and again right to the town centre. I couldn't miss it.

I couldn't miss what?

'What's Wooly's?' I asked, and he couldn't suppress a contemptuous smile.

'It's a shop called Woolworths and it'll sell you a writing pad cheap,' he said. 'Don't bother with envelopes, the dons don't expect them from us.'

I composed the note to Mr Dewey, attempting to explain and apologise for my dereliction. I drafted it several times and finally decided on the briefest version:

> Dear Mr Dewey,
> I have arrived and will contact you whenever suitable.

I folded it and walked to the senior common room, which undergraduates seemed to access without knocking. I walked to the pigeonholes, found Mr Dewey's and left my note.

I went down from my room every fifteen or twenty minutes to the junior common room to see if he had replied. Nothing for three hours. Then a note in a neat hand:

> Dear Dhondy,
> You may have arrived, but the verb 'to contact' has not.
> I shall see you in my rooms at 7.15.

It was signed Meredith Dewey.

I went to the first sitting of dinner in the 'hall', which was at six. An undergraduate sitting opposite me asked my name and offered me his, John Hay. He said we were both new and both obviously foreigners. There was nothing obvious about his being one, until one heard him speak—he was Australian. I said I had to meet my tutor after dinner, and he said he would see me in the junior common room afterwards. He was meeting some other 'foreign students' there and I should join. It was, after Berry's kind advice, the first friendly gesture.

I went to Mr Dewey's rooms at the top of the building and stood on the staircase for a minute outside his oak door, wanting to be precisely on time. I could hear him playing Chopin on the piano. I knew the piece, as Khurshed mamu had a huge collection of Western classical records and played them every moment he could. This Chopin sonata wasn't a particularly unpopular one.

At precisely 7.15, as appointed, I knocked at the door which was ajar by a few inches. The piano continued playing. I waited half a minute more and knocked again, a little harder, thinking he couldn't have heard me the first time.

I tried a third time when there was no response and the piano continued with the same sonata. Was he deliberately ignoring me? A punishment for having missed my afternoon appointment or having used 'contact' as a verb? I put my head round the door. Mr Dewey was seated at a miniature grand piano on the right, a few yards into the oak-panelled room.

'I'm Farrukh Dhondy,' I said.

Mr Dewey looked up, but his fingers kept playing. 'How very interesting,' he said.

Was I being punished? I withdrew my head from the door.

He must have relented because he stopped playing and came towards me saying, 'You'd better come in then, Dhondy. I believe your train was delayed at Bishop's Stortford. It's that fellow Beecham. Tampering. Licensed tampering. They've cut all the village services, you know.'

I had no idea what he was talking about so didn't venture a comment.

'Do sit, dear boy,' he said, indicating the sofa under the ample bookcase. 'So, you arrived in England when?'

'In London a week ago, sir.'

'Ah! And don't call me "sir".'

'Very well, Mr Dewey.'

'Good, and what will you have to drink, Dhondy?'

'Oh, anything, Mr. Dewey.'

He came up to me and, lowering his voice, said, 'Don't say "anything", say "dry sherry".'

I caught on. 'I think I'd like a dry sherry, Mr Dewey, if I may.'

He leaned over to me. 'Dhondy, you're a man of taste,' he said and with a wry smile went off to his drinks' cabinet to pour us each a glass of dry sherry.

'Are you happy with your rooms?' he asked, even though it was a single room.

'Perfect.'

'We put all the wogs in the new block because it has central heating, so they feel warmly at home.'

I hadn't heard the word before and didn't know what it meant. I gathered soon enough that it was an insulting term for people of colour, black or brown. That was strange as Mr Dewey gave no indication of having the slightest race prejudice—he was just using the term. In that day, he got away with it.

And we got on well through my three years at Pembroke. At the end of the third term, the end of the academic year, Mr Dewey, on one of our dry-sherry jaunts in his rooms, asked if I would like to join his group who were bicycling to Jerusalem. They would go through the continents, visit the holy city and return by plane in time for October's Michaelmas, or the autumn, term. He had already recruited eight fellow travellers. I said I would give it a thought.

My second night in college posed a sort of dilemma.

All through my life, heat, cold or monsoon, I had slept in pyjamas. When I was ten years old, my aunts took me to the cloth merchants to select the material for a new pair. I chose a jaunty floral pattern, and we took the cloth to the tailor, who measured me up, and the next day, I had my floral pyjamas. My father threw a fit. He shouted at me and, by implication, at my aunts.

'This is not what boys wear. Get rid of these, give them to your girl cousins and get some decent striped or plain ones.'

My aunts and I thought it best to go along rather than argue, and we got plain light-blue ones made.

I had carried a similarly modest pair to Cambridge. On my first day there, I was told by Berry, who had assumed the burden of instructing me about the ways of England and the college, that I should leave my bed unmade as the staircase's 'bedder', the lady who did the beds and washed the coffee cups, would take care of it.

I hung my pyjamas on a hanger on a hook, left the bed unmade and went to the lectures. Sure enough, when I returned, the room had been tidied, and the bedder, Mrs McNeil, having found that I was an overseas student, had left on a plate on my table a madeira cake with a note saying it was made specially for me as a welcome to England and Cambridge. I was astounded.

That night, turning in, I found that the hanger on which I had put my pyjamas was bare. No pyjamas. Had I had too much beer? Had I hung them up or was I mistaken? Perhaps Mrs McNeil put them in the wardrobe or the drawers? I looked. No pyjamas.

Had someone stolen them? What would anyone do with a pair of second-hand pyjamas? It baffled me. I went to bed naked for the first time in my life.

The next day, I left a thank-you note for Mrs McNeil and resumed being confused about where my pyjamas could have gone.

I had left the window open, and a wasp had flown in. I tried to swat it with a book in vain. I would need something larger. I picked up the pillow from my bed and saw, yes, my pyjamas, neatly folded. Stowing them under the pillows instead of freshening them on the windowsill. Silly British habits!

I threw myself into the activity and life of the college and the university. At the time, Cambridge was still the preserve of the upper-middle classes with a leavening of clever working-class girls and boys who had been to grammar schools and made the grade, as it were. The only ethnic faces in my college, and every other, were foreign students. There were no sons and daughters, back then, of Asian or West Indian immigrants to Britain. On my staircase, there was Matty Kambona, the brother of the then defence minister of Tanzania. He was studying agriculture for a postgraduate degree. And the other foreign student was a young man from the West Indies studying mechanical sciences.

The first people I befriended were the Americans and Australians I met through John Hay that first night in college. Among them was one Clive James, who went on to become a journalist and broadcaster, with whom I had a friendly acquaintanceship throughout my three years. They were all postgraduate students. Clive was what one could regard as a mature undergraduate, and the Americans, Stephen Greenblatt, now a professor of Shakespearean literature, and Sandy Mack, were graduates from Ivy League universities. All of them were academically ambitious and would rush off from dinner to their studies. They weren't the socialising mob, though I did go for a brief drink with a few of them on several occasions, when too they would down their beer and rush off to 'work'.

Acquainting myself with different undergraduates at Pembroke in the first few weeks of that term, I was introduced to the enduring reality of Britain: its class system. Of course, any fool reading English literature, from say Dickens onwards, would appreciate that there is a radical difference in the upbringing and the possibilities of the life of different classes in Britain. At Pembroke, this was visible in the personalities, accents, preoccupations and friendship patterns of my fellow undergraduates. Some were 'toffs' from the top public schools—scholars and intellectuals all, no doubt—and some were grammar school lads from working-class families and whose fathers earned their living as fishermen and factory workers.

The lads in this second category, I noticed through even casual contact, were naturally resentful of the class system. They hated the toffs and their assumption of privilege. There was certainly a challenge to class privilege and snobbery, though in the university, it seemed to stay within the bounds of politeness.

Except in some unique cases. I was approached in my first week by a young second-year undergraduate with a scar on his face. He asked if I wanted to join the revolutionary wing of a socialist party in the university. I said I would have to know more about it, though I was a committed Marxist.

'So, not committed enough,' he said, spat at my feet and walked away.

Although I had socialist convictions when I got to Cambridge, the 'socialist' societies of the university didn't interest me. They were stepping stones to political careers in the Labour Party, and I had no such ambitions. I was convinced, besides, through the arrogant assumptions of youth, that parliamentary democracy could never legislate to achieve a communist State.

Nevertheless, in the holidays and on my visits to London, I would go with my friends to Hyde Park to Speakers' Corner, where several rabble-rousers would interact with us drifters on the contemporary developments in world politics. We—the mostly Indian friends who socialised with each other and Shahid Sayyid, a friend from Poona who was at Liverpool University and would come down to visit—would join the various demonstrations demanding that the British government withdraw all support for America's unjust war in Vietnam.

I was also aware that the challenge to the class system had taken a literary form. Books and plays by writers such as Alan Sillitoe and Arnold Wesker were seen as a literary phenomenon called the Kitchen Sink Movement and featured working-class sons and daughters finding their way through intelligence and grit to university and professional careers and then facing a certain cultural alienation from their parents and their class.

Through my acquaintance with fellow undergraduates I realised, quite consciously, that there was a meritocracy being bred in post-war Britain, which was reflected in the gradually changing profile of Cambridge. On my staircase with other freshers, as Pembroke's policy was to keep us initiates in college rooms for the first year and have second-years move to digs or college hostels in the city, was Paul Danaher, a working-class London Irish lad who was reading English. Making his acquaintance, drinking coffee in his rooms or mine, going down to the pub for half a pint of beer or sharing dinner times together, I began to realise that he and several others with whom I was thrown together were the sons of families whose members had never till this generation got a higher education. Paul's was the first generation to have gone to any university. These lads, and even the lasses as I met later, carried, without exception, an awareness of the class system of Britain, their place in it and their resentment of it.

The crowd I fell in with as the weeks passed were ideologically staunch socialists. Some said they were, through political means, going to champion the rights of their class. They insisted that they had nothing in common with the majority of undergraduates who came from top public schools such as Eton, Harrow, Marlborough and Rugby, or the lesser ones in this hierarchy of snobbery.

Very soon, in imitation of these new friends, I felt I had to get rid of my tweeds and bags that I felt awkward in. I resolved to buy a donkey jacket, the crude wool coat that my working-class friends proudly wore as a mark of their identity. It was the style of cheap utilitarian coat worn by miners and construction workers. I saved every penny of my allowance towards such a purchase.

When I thought I had saved the requisite amount of money to buy one, I went to the town centre to a shop that sported men's wear in its window. I tried on several jackets whose price tags had figures within my budget. The salesman appeared to be helpful and persuaded me to choose a grey jacket with a fur collar. I knew no better. It was shaped like the donkey jackets my friends wore, and the assistant assured me that the woollen collar would be an insurance against the coming winter.

I walked out wearing it. My friends were amused but polite.

'It's the sort of jacket that a smooth-talking second-hand car salesman from the suburbs would wear,' Ian Lamb, a dear friend from another college whom I had met through fellow Indian student Darryl D'Monte, said. He persuaded me to take it back and even offered to go with me to the shop to ensure that it could be exchanged for one he would choose. However reluctant the salesman who had sold me the garment was, Ian persuaded him to allow me to exchange it for a rough woollen one in navy blue.

I had already paid another price for my unfamiliarity with British daily existence. In later decades, Indians, Pakistanis and others have made great play of their 'culture shock' on arriving in Britain. There are even sentimental novels on the theme. I felt no such shock but was nevertheless unfamiliar with several aspects and requirements of day-to-day life.

In my first week at college, I accumulated a heap of dirty clothes but didn't quite know what to do with them. No dhobis or domestic workers to pile it onto. I asked Berry what one did with laundry—was it all to be washed by hand? He told me that under M staircase in the basement was the college's laundry room with machines which washed clothes. There was a drier next to the washing machine and ironing boards in the same basement. He told me to get a carton of detergent to add to the wash.

I went down the stone steps to the basement, placed my clothes as the written instructions on the machine directed and poured in the box of detergent I had bought. Berry had told me I didn't have to hang about. I could return later and transfer my washing into the drier. When I returned a few hours later, coming through and blocking the door to the staircase and spreading over the croquet lawn outside was a huge cloud of soapy foam several feet high. Three or four lads with their bags of laundry stood some distance from the foam cloud.

'Which fucking idiot played this joke?' one of them said as I innocently approached.

I knew, by some prompt of the cultural-ignorance fairy, that it was I who had caused this catastrophe. I didn't know how in that instance, but later reasoned that I had, in my ignorance, put the entire carton of detergent instead of the suggested two spoonfuls into the wash.

As I passed the soaked croquet lawn with my fellow undergraduates standing round it frustrated, with their bags of washing, I pretended it had nothing to do with me and that I was just passing through the court to my staircase. In the early hours of the morning, I went down again to the basement. The bubbles had gone and the stairs to the basement, though wet, were accessible. I gathered my washing and smuggled it back to my room. I didn't dare use the drier or the ironing boards that night. The clothes were still soapy, and I had to soak them in the showers and in the basin in my room.

The 'fucking aresehole who had played the practical joke on the inhabitants of M staircase' became a topic of animated, contemptuous conversation in the next few days. I kept very quiet.

INNOCENCE AND EXPERIENCE

That first term, attending lectures and trying to make sense of them, socialising with new friends, joining our drama society, the Pembroke Players, and generally getting accustomed to being in England and Cambridge, I didn't pay any attention to the coming Christmas holidays.

When my Indian friends, other scholarship boys with whom I spent some of my time, said they were going to work for the post office in London, I discovered that the British postal services took on students weeks before Christmas and New Year when there was a deluge of post to be dealt with and delivered. Darryl D'Monte and Michael Masceranhas, two Bombay boys with whom I hung out, had both secured such employment and arranged for their stay in London in rented accommodation or with friends and relatives.

It was too late for me to do the same, and I realised Cambridge would be empty of students. From the middle of December, parents arrived in cars to take their sons and daughters away. By the third week, the college was empty, as were other colleges. The porter told me I had to vacate my room as it was required for students who were attending international conferences in the college over the holidays.

I had to hire a room for the four weeks before the next term began. I found a room on the top floor of a two-storey terraced house in Fitzwilliam Street not far from college. The landlady lived in her flat in the basement and always had a cigarette between her lips. The rest of the house was, in the holidays, empty.

For the first few days of the break, I spent some time with Pakistani undergrads who lived in a college hostel a mile or so from my digs. Then they, most of them from rich Pakistani families, packed up and left for London and even for Paris and Geneva where they had diplomatic or other relatives.

The stove in my small kitchen and the gas fire in the tiny fireplace had to be activated by feeding coins to a gas meter in a metal box. I budgeted my needs. The gas meter would, to heat the room against the threat of a very cold winter, take up most of my money. I figured that I could subsist on potatoes, eggs, cans of fish and the occasional loaf of bread. The savings had to be on gas, which meant spending as little time as possible during the day in the freezing room. The obvious plan was to spend time in the university and faculty libraries which would be adequately heated. I did just that until, approaching Christmas, the libraries also closed their doors.

It began to snow. Winter was setting in and the streets of Cambridge were by and large deserted. I then hit upon the idea of going to churches. They would be heated to a degree, so to speak, and I could read and write sitting at the pews closest to the radiators.

After doing this for a few days, on Christmas Eve, dressed in my warmest sweater and coat, I set out for the service which had been advertised in St Mary's opposite King's. The church was crowded. From my education in the Anglican Bishop's School in Poona, I remembered some of the words and sang along with gusto. Then came unfamiliar hymns, and as I kept my silence, the person next to me in the pew held his open hymn book up to me so I could sing along with the congregation. He was perhaps in his forties, with a heavy coat and centrally parted thick black hair.

The service ended, and the congregation spilt onto the cold, snowy street. I walked briskly down towards my digs as the snow began to fall again. As I passed the entrance to Pembroke, I noticed footsteps just behind me. It was the gentleman who had kindly shared his hymn book.

'That was a beautiful service,' he said, catching up and walking beside me.

'Yes,' I said.

'You knew some of the hymns. Are you a Christian?'

'I'm not, but I went to a Christian school, and we sang the hymns in assembly.'

'Ah, where was this, in Wales?'

'No, in India.'

'I was just wondering about your accent.'

'I'm Indian.'

'You're studying in Cambridge?'

'Yep. That's my college just behind us.'

The snow was getting heavier now.

'I come down from King's Lynn to Cambridge every year for the St Mary's service,' he said. 'I've got to get back tonight. Restricted service on the trains as always, so there won't be another one for three or four hours. Where do you live?'

I said I lived in college but had a room in an attic for the holidays.

'Ah, there won't be anything open for me to get even a cup of coffee in this snow. It's beautiful but cold.'

I agreed. We walked along.

'That's my street,' I said and turned into Fitzwilliam.

He turned with me. 'That's my way to the station,' he said.

I found the key in my pocket and turned towards the door of the house.

'It's very nice meeting you,' he said. 'I didn't get your name.'

'Farrukh,' I said, impatient to get out of the snow.

'I'm Harry,' he ventured, extending a handshake, and as I took his hand out of politeness, he added, 'I don't suppose you could give me a cup of coffee, could you? Get me out of the wretched snow. The platform will be empty and cold.'

I didn't think I had much choice. He had been friendly, and I hadn't spoken to anyone for the last three days.

'Yes, come in,' I said.

As we climbed the staircase, a young man came out of the basement.

'Ah, you're Farrukh, Mum's lodger, are you?'

'Yes, hi!' I said, turning round.

He was staring with knitted brows at my visitor. I thought it best to hurry up the stairs to my room.

Harry looked round the room. He kept his coat on and, seeing the gas meter, went up to it.

'If we want coffee, I'll have to get the gas going,' I said.

'Oh, don't worry,' he said, and fetched a little cloth purse out of his coat pocket and fed the meter with several half crowns, enough to keep me supplied in gas for perhaps two days.

'Please, what are you doing?'

'We might as well be warm,' he said.

Taking his coat off, he pulled something out of its inner pockets. I didn't quite see what it was and went to the kitchen corner, filled the kettle and put it on the stove for coffee. There were a couple of mugs, and I put a spoonful of coffee in each. Waiting for the kettle to boil, I turned round.

Harry had taken his shirt and vest off, thrown them on the floor and was grinning broadly at me, his eyes dancing with expectation.

'Will you powder me?' he said, his eyebrows twitching.

I now saw that what he had in his hand, which he was extending to me, was a can of talcum powder.

How naive could I have been?

'No, no, please, you'd better go,' I said. 'Please!'

'I've filled your gas meter so we can have a nice warm cuddle.' He was still smiling expectantly.

'I don't … I can't. Please get your stuff and go.'

I thought it best to open the door of the room. Just as I did, the landlady's son, the one who had greeted me, came bounding up the stairs.

'Who is that fellow? What are you queers doing in my mum's house?' he demanded, pushing past me through the door.

'I don't know. He followed me,' I said, sensing the aggression in his voice and manner.

Harry instantly grabbed his vest and shirt from the floor and his coat from the bed and tried to push past the landlady's son, who grabbed him by the throat and dragged him to the landing. Harry stumbled down the stairs to the next landing, and the young man bounded after him and kicked him so hard that Harry stumbled onto the next flight and landed on his face. He scrambled up in a panic.

'I'm gone,' he shouted, crying for mercy. He ran to the front door and out.

The landlady's son came up the few stairs to accost me. 'Why did you bring that filth in here?'

'He followed me from church,' I said. 'I didn't know what …'

'Yeah, yeah, Mum told me you was a bit kinda innocent. I fuckin' saved you, didn't I? Merry Christmas,' he said and turned and went back to the basement.

I went into my room. The kettle was whistling. I turned it off, got my coat, went back down into the street and headed to the railway station in the snow.

It was deserted and the platform was dimly lit. Harry was the only person on it, sitting on a bench, his handkerchief to the bruise on his forehead. I approached him, uncertain as to how he would react.

'I'm very sorry,' I said. 'I didn't know he was going to come up—the landlady's son …'

There was really nothing I could say.

Harry waved his hand. 'Don't worry. Nothing new. Always happening.'

'There's two hours more for the train, and the pub on the next corner is open. Can I buy you a drink?'

'You, buy me a drink? You're hard up for a penny for the gas!' he said, then changing his mind, stood up. 'Come on!'

After a beer, for which I insisted on paying with my next few days' gas budget, and with very stilted conversation between us, I left for my room and Harry for King's Lynn.

When term resumed, I recounted this incident to Berry.

'Good that your landlady's son saved you from the bum bandit!' he said.

Well into the term, nearing Easter, Harry turned up at Pembroke. I remembered, as he knocked on my door, that I had indicated my college to him when we walked past it. He said he thought we were friends now and that he would call on me. I invited him into the room for a coffee and left the door open.

As we sat and chatted about the weather and trains, Berry wandered in, wearing the sports gear of the college rowing team. On seeing Harry, he scowled. Harry glanced at him and there was a flash of panic in his eyes. There was an exchange of subtle cultural signals which I didn't understand, an instinctive flash of recognition between possible predator and prey.

'Is this the bender who tried it out on you?' he said.

Harry hastily got up, putting the mug of coffee down, and made for the door.

'Berry, no, leave him. He didn't mean anything,' I shouted as Berry followed Harry, who headed straight for the stairs. Berry ran after him and landed a kick on his back. Harry took the blow and ran out into the court and out of it in terror.

'He didn't mean any harm,' I said, 'Why the hell did you ...'

'You still don't understand Britain, Farrukh. I know these pillow-biters. He didn't just come here for a coffee. He thinks you are a foreigner and fair game.'

Right through the first and second terms, I had regularly written to Mala, mostly on the blue air-mail letter forms that the post office sold. On occasion, I had written a verse or two of some possibly silly or sentimental but certainly sincerely affectionate profession of love and loyalty. At first she used to reply at once, but as the months wore on, the letters got fewer. They contained peremptory news of who from our crowd was doing what and very little of what could be considered the embarrassingly personal stuff we used to write to each other.

Other friends in Poona and Bombay from our crowd with whom I corresponded hinted that they had seen or heard of Mala doing this or that. When I asked explicit questions, I was told that she was now recognised as the girlfriend of one Darius Ardeshir, another military brat, a general's son whom I vaguely knew in Poona. I didn't know whether it was true, some rumour that my friends had picked up or an innocent friendship which had been mistaken for romantic commitment.

In my letters to Mala, I didn't put the question brutally. I suppose it hurt my ego to so do. Instead, thinking to myself that the Othello syndrome was a brutal waste of emotional energy, I wrote to her saying that since we were not to meet for years, it would perhaps be best to release each other from any vows of faithfulness.

The epistolary gesture was a conscious way of vanquishing my overwhelming, destructive and disturbing sense of jealousy, of being betrayed, and though it wasn't at the time a ruse to feel free to have some unspecified romantic adventure myself, it may certainly have struck Mala that way. She didn't reply in any direct way to my mealy-mouthed proposal to suspend our loyalty to each other. Her replies, now very occasional, seemed to take no notice of what I had said. She wrote to me as though nothing had happened and nothing had been said. Was this then a closed chapter?

A friend did eventually confirm, without my asking, that Mala was now constantly seen in the company of her new boyfriend.

If I was shattered, I was also resolved to see love in a more philosophical way. I nurtured the conceit that love and affections were labyrinthine dimensions with a mystical base as perhaps D.H. Lawrence would have put it.

The admittedly pretentious escape from my twenty-one-year-old heartache—if not heartbreak—seemed to work. I wouldn't prevent myself from expressing my attraction to the young women I met. Through the Pembroke Players, I met Mary Hoffman, a girl from Newham College who was reading English. She was the daughter of a railway worker and was the first generation of their family to have, through grammar school, qualified for entry to Cambridge.

We spent a lot of time together and were regarded as a couple. We talked about literature and the theories of the interaction between men and women inherent in the works of Leo Tolstoy, George Eliot and, of course, D.H. Lawrence, the writer who had made sexual interaction between man and woman a central concern.

Mary was quite fascinated that, as a student of natural sciences, I had any opinions on the books and writers who were her legitimate line of study. I confided in her that I always had an abstract urge to be a writer but had no confidence in my ability to do it and didn't have a clue where to start and how to continue. I would, I said, have chosen to do English at university, but boys in India didn't do that, and even if any university in England or elsewhere had given me a place to study English literature, no Indian scholarship would have paid me to do it. Science and professional studies that would lead to the health and wealth of India was what they wanted.

As the Easter holidays came, Mary went to her South London family home. Before leaving Cambridge, she proposed that we holiday together by hitching rides across England to the west and land up for a few days in the Scilly Isles, off the coast of Cornwall. I didn't know where or what these Scilly Isles were, but the promise of an adventure was welcome. Mary brought me a map and pencilled the route I should take. She would set out from London on the same day, and we would aim to meet in Penzance. If we arrived a day or so separately from each other, the first to arrive was to wait at a pub she named, and if the other didn't turn up, to stay the night there and continue waiting.

I set out on the appointed day with a backpack of sparse clothing for perhaps a week and some saved cash. After several hitched rides from Cambridge, I was picked up in the early evening outside Oxford by a man in a sports car. He said he was going towards Cornwall and would take me some distance before it got dark.

We conversed on the way and I told him I was Indian. He wasn't surprised, but I was when he said, 'Oh, are you?' and pulled over to the side of the road we were on. This was, I discovered later, in a sort of forest in Gloucestershire. The trees were dense on both sides of the two-way road. I wondered what I was in for.

'Open that glove compartment,' he said with a mischievous smile.

I opened it.

'There's a little box, bring it out.'

'This little jewellery box?'

'That's the one.'

I pulled out the box, and he asked me to open it.

'Tell me what that is,' he said triumphantly.

'It's some light-blue semi-precious stone, I suppose. I don't know much about gems or stones,' I said.

'You're right, but where is it from?'

I shook my head and turned to him with a quizzical expression. 'It could be from anywhere.'

'Ah! I thought you'd recognise it. That, me dear Indian, is straight from the Taj Mahal.'

'You bought this from some tout at the Taj?'

'No, no, no, it's from the actual Taj Mahal. I pulled it out of the wall with my pen-knife.'

I didn't know what to say. He picked up the stone and took the box from me.

'You stole that by wrenching it out from a panel in the Taj Mahal? That's the worst bit of vandalism I've ever heard of,' I said. I couldn't help myself.

'Get out of my car. Now!'

I got out, and he slammed the door and drove away, accelerating in fury.

It was getting dark. There seemed to be no traffic on the road, and the forest was all round me. Perhaps if I walked some distance I would emerge from it. I must have walked half a mile before a truck passed me, and when I stuck out my thumb, it stopped.

The driver gave me a lift all the way to Exeter. I determined to hitch through the night. We stopped at a lorry park, and the driver, who had become quite friendly, said he would go into the cafe where the other truck drivers were and find me a lift to Penzance through the night. Another friendly driver did give me a lift all the way, curious as to why I was hitching to Penzance at that time of night.

Mary arrived early that afternoon. We didn't have to stay the night and took a ferry to the Scilly Isles. We compared notes about our adventures and encounters on the way as we spent three days loafing round the island and asking different farmers if we could sleep on the hay in their sheds. Then we hitched back to London together.

Mala's letters said she had moved into a student girls' hostel in Bombay. Her communications mentioned old friends but never once her supposed boyfriend.

Years later, I came across his name again when I heard from friends in Poona that the husband of Darius Ardeshir's sister, one Mr Debu, had set out for a walk from their house across the river from Bund Garden and had not returned. The police found his clothes on the banks and dredged the river for his body for possible clues. They found nothing. Rumour had it that he had planted a change of clothes further upriver, taken off the ones he was wearing, swam up to the spot where he had planted a change, worn fresh clothes and decided to disappear from his life and start another somewhere else and as someone else.

It brought to mind the story of Khasi, who had returned from the dead. Could one really start another life as someone else? Would it amount to having two lives, or would the chain of the past and memory confine the second to a falsity, to play-acting?

Suddenly, Mala's letters became more affectionate, saying she missed me and was desperately fed up of life in Bombay. Our correspondence was not on the same teenage love-track but still read like the exchanges between a committed couple. My letters in reply were intimate but not gushing and desperate as they used to be. I had told Mary all about Mala, and we both, in the zeitgeist of 'free love', accepted that our relationship was not an eternal marriage. I didn't know what exactly I now felt for Mala and would perhaps only find out when I encountered her again.

AMOR VINCIT OMNIA

Johnny said he was going to use the four months of the summer holidays to travel overland to India, partly on a cheap coach route he had discovered which went from Europe to Turkey and then by buses and coaches or hitching lifts through to the country. He showed me the planned route and asked if I wanted to make the trip with him. I thought about it. Apart from the adventure, it would be a way of meeting Mala again. I told Johnny I would go with him. I had to tell Mr Dewey that I wouldn't be cycling to Jerusalem with his flock.

When Johnny first suggested it to me, I had marvelled at this proposal to undertake a difficult and, to my mind, impossible journey, but it soon became apparent that very many of the undergraduates had planned just such seemingly outrageous adventures. Was it this spirit of challenging oneself that led to climbing Mount Everest, settling America or indeed the establishment of the British Empire?

As the summer holidays arrived, Johnny and I moved to London. I was sleeping on bedding on the floor of my poet friend from India, Adil Jussawalla, who was renting a tiny South Kensington bedsitter. After my first night there, I woke up with a painful swollen neck. British citizens are expected to register at a doctor's practice and use the general practitioners at that medical centre as their first port of call. Not being registered with a doctor's practice, I went to the accident and emergency clinic of the nearest hospital and was diagnosed with mumps and immediately incarcerated in a single room. It was the only time I have, in my short and happy life, been forcibly segregated.

I must have spent two and a half weeks in the West Brompton Hospital's infectious diseases ward. The sentence for mumps at my now adult age was isolation and a regular check by doctors and nurses of my testicles, as the disease could turn males impotent. (That didn't happen as my subsequently born children are proof!) Adil brought me a radio and the disturbing book by Truman Capote *In Cold Blood*. I had two or three short visits from friends who had already had mumps in their childhood and were allowed in for short periods.

A Spanish lady pushing a trolley of tea and biscuits would come round each afternoon and dispense these to the inmates. She spoke very little or no English and would repeat 'Cup-o-tea!' a few times as she entered each cubicle. I used to try and chat with her, and she always replied with a smile and some words in Spanish.

One day, inspired by boredom, I said to her, 'Don't say "Capote", say "Truman"!' The poor lady took me at my word and went round the ward offering 'Truman' from her trolley. The head nurse in charge of the ward tracked the mischief down to me, and I was given a severe dressing down for teaching the poor Spanish lady this rubbish. I held up the cover of the book I was reading, and the head nurse broke into a smile, shook her head and walked out.

Johnny was compelled to change the coach tickets from Germany to Turkey, but he came to visit me in the dumpy ward with the good news that there was another trip available as soon as I was out of West Brompton.

We travelled with a small rucksack each with sleeping bags, cans of food, chicken stock cubes and a saucepan. We got to Munich in Germany, caught the coach and went through Salzburg in the country to Zagreb in Yugoslavia. The fellow passengers on the coach who could afford it would, at each stop, book themselves into hotels. We couldn't and found parks and empty spaces in which to sleep. We slept rough, cooked on fires we lit with gathered twigs and ate our canned food in Zagreb, Sophia and other towns we passed through. We drew the attention of the local police on several occasions but managed to convince them, with difficulty across the language barrier, that we were harmless travellers and were running out of time to catch our coach.

Once we reached Turkey, in Istanbul we found lodging for a few nights in a dosshouse in which the beds, two feet from each other in several rows, were rented out in eight-hour house shifts. Getting into the bed at ten at night with the previous occupant gathering his things and leaving, we would be woken up at five minutes to six with the next occupant standing at the foot of the bed.

We crossed the Bosphorus, a narrow strait, and in Ankara, being Turkey's capital city, found beds in a youth hostel. Occupying the hostel with us was an expedition of young American bikers who were as curious about our travels as we were of theirs.

Late on the second evening of the two we spent there, two Englishmen in suits brought in a tall but very emaciated young man. He had a long straggly beard, matted hair and sunken eyes, with the bones of his skull prominent through his face. The suited men asked if we were British, and Johnny said we were. They said they were from the UK embassy and were lodging this young man for the night in the hostel and to please see that he was afforded the facilities to clean up and rest. They would be back in the morning to escort him to a doctor and then put him on a plane back to England.

The entire hostel gathered round to listen to his story. The young man said he had come to Turkey three years earlier to climb the mountains, and he was captured by a tribe of wandering gypsies, enslaved and chained, made to work, starved and randomly beaten. We listened in stunned silence to his account of three years in this captivity, from which he had escaped a few days ago and been helped by villagers to Ankara. He paused, and one of the American bikers was moved to exclaim, 'Yeah, man, gotta watch them gypsies!'

We went over the mountains to Tehran in Iran and found our way in the city to the Sikh gurdwara, which we knew would welcome travellers and give them a space, if only in a courtyard, to sleep. Gurdwaras are known all over the world to feed the hungry, which is what we were, so we readily accepted the Granthi's largesse of rotis and daal.

Here, we met several adventurers. A young, concave-chested Indian with shoulder-length hair and an endearing smile had already spent five or six days in the gurdwara. He spoke in Hindi to me and knew only a few words of English but was, he said, eager to learn. He showed me a dog-eared book from the days of the Raj, an idiotic primer of English phrases translated into colloquial Hindi.

He told me he was reading it backwards. He would find the phrase in Hindi that struck him as useful and then read and memorise the English. I glanced at the book. 'Fetch me another peg of whisky and fill the ice bucket' was, I told him, not the sort of phrase which would be most useful. Nor would 'Take this dog out of the drawing room and see he is chained inside his kennel' find service. He said he hadn't looked at it carefully, but his grand-uncle, who had served in the British Army, had acquired it and gifted it to him as he had set out to traverse the world.

This precious book travelled with the rest of his luggage, stuffed into two saddle bags astride his bicycle, on which he said he was cycling from India to America. Johnny asked if he was aware there was water in between. He didn't understand the question, and I didn't bother to interpret.

He rolled up the left leg of his trousers and showed me surgical scars where his knee-cap should have been. 'No patella,' he said and grinned. It was something he was proud of, and he repeated the demonstration the next day when a Frenchman called Bruno and his Dutch girlfriend, Desiree, arrived seeking shelter at the gurdwara. For the time we spent with him in and about Tehran, he was known to Johnny, Desiree, Bruno and me as 'No patella'.

Our plan was to avoid Pakistan as I couldn't travel through it with my Indian passport. Bruno and Desiree were also on their way from Europe to India, and we decided to travel as a group to Mashhad on the Iranian border and cross over to Afghanistan and then down into India via the more obscure land routes or by my catching a flight from Kandahar to Delhi and they coming through the Khyber Pass and Pakistan.

Even as we planned, the Iranian government announced that owing to a plague in Afghanistan they were shutting the border at Mashhad, with no prospect of its early opening. The four of us therefore set off instead for the southern port of Khorramshahr. We spent a night there and, on enquiring about passages by boat to India, were told to go a few miles west to the port of Abadan.

Here, we found one small ship which was heading for Bombay. We spoke through an Indian Iranian worker in the dock to the captain, who said he couldn't take any Europeans on board his vessel, but the one with an Indian passport could travel. Something to do with the legal restrictions on his small ship, he tried to explain, but the Indian Iranian thought it more likely that he was afraid of a crew of pirates posing as hippy passengers.

I decided I would go alone, and the others would follow, either by a boat that was willing to take them or by travelling across Iran to the southern Makran Coast of Pakistan and thence through Karachi into India.

The boat trip was hell. The ship itself, carrying some minimal cargo, was going to pick up Indian exports to Iran and the Gulf. It was disgustingly dirty, and the turbulence of the Indian Ocean made me horribly seasick. But I kept telling myself I was heading to India and to Mala.

I hadn't told her I was. I wrote to her and to my family saying I might be travelling here and there and possibly in Europe and so the letter-writing would be erratic or there could be postal silence for a few weeks. They weren't to write to Cambridge as I wasn't there.

Of course, she was surprised to see me. Or perhaps surprised is not the word—unbelieving would be more accurate. And when she had absorbed the shock, she started jumping up and down like a child and hugging and kissing me.

I had turned up at Khurshed mamu's door and received the same shocked reaction but the usual warm welcome. Mami wanted to know if I had been thrown out of Cambridge, but I reassured them that this was a holiday.

In a week, Johnny, Bruno and Desiree arrived. They had come via Pakistan, and Bruno was impatient to get to Goa where he could be with more Europeans. They journeyed south.

After a week or so, Mala, Johnny and I set out for Jamshedpur where my parents were. My parents, while welcoming Mala as my girlfriend, would not countenance her sleeping in the same bed or even bedroom as myself, and so she slept in my sister's room, while Johnny and I were accommodated in the guest room of the spacious bungalow.

By the time we returned to Bombay, it was evident that I didn't want to be separated from Mala or she from me. I was twenty-one and she was eighteen, but we were determined to make a life together. I couldn't give up on Cambridge, I had to return. Mala said she would go with me.

There was no official way she could get a visa to enter Britain. It was 1965, and the UK government was cutting down on immigration. Britain wouldn't contemplate a random application for entry from an eighteen-year-old female who wasn't enrolled in any university and had no nursing certificates to justify her entry as a potential worker in the National Health Service. Neither could she, as we found out from the British consulate, travel as my partner or wife as I had a student visa.

It was Johnny who came up with a solution. He volunteered the idea that he with his British passport could marry Mala, and she could as his wife apply in Bombay for a British passport and have unrestricted access to the UK. Once she was there, they could settle for a legal annulment of the marriage, but she would retain her citizenship.

It seemed foolproof but for the fact that the three of us were foolish enough to endorse such a stratagem without any consideration of the qualms we knew our parents would certainly have, 'qualms' being a euphemism for a fit of forbidding severity.

But it was planned and so was it done. Johnny and Mala went through a Hindu temple ceremony as Johnny thought that would be adventurous, and they converted the religious wedding certificate into a legal one and registered Mala's claim to a British passport with the embassy, which said it would take a few months to process.

I had a Jawa CZ motorcycle in Poona, which my mamu, having no use for it in Bombay, had given me. It had been rotting in the backyard of the Poona house for a year. I went to Poona, sold it to a second-hand motorbike dealer and gave the money to Mala to buy her air ticket to London when her passport came through.

Johnny and I were in London when it did. It was during the first few days of the Christmas holidays, and we had come down from Cambridge to live with Dolly Rawson, my Kanpur friend who had a flat in Kensington High Street where we were camping. Mala phoned. She had her passport and her air ticket.

She arrived and told me that her parents were unaware of her flight, but that she had told her friend Sunita to inform her mother and then her father after she was beyond their preventive reach in London.

After Christmas, I went back to Cambridge, having settled Mala in a basement bedsitter in South Kensington, close to where Adil Jussawalla, Dara Cama and Ratnakar Kini, a writer friend, had their rooms. She would have company. In the next week, Mala found a job in Sarees Centre, a shop in Soho selling Indian garments.

We would meet every weekend when I came down from Cambridge or when she took the train up. One weekend, Mala came and stayed the night in my room.

Cambridge undergraduates used all manner of ruses to dodge these rules against sharing beds. Every college knew escape routes through which there was constant traffic, comings and goings of girlfriends and boyfriends in the night. In Pembroke, when the gates shut for the night, one went round to the back of the college, where a telegraph pole allowed one to climb onto the wall and thence to the roof of the bicycle shed, going round the building with V, W and X staircases and thence to the rest of the college.

In the second year, I wasn't allocated a room in the college. Second-year undergraduates had to live in houses in town which had been requisitioned as 'hostels'. My hostel, run by the wife of one of the college porters and with equally strict rules against overnight guests, had no such access, so the subterfuge we had planned was for four friends to turn up in the morning and for six of us to leave together.

The plan didn't work. The housekeeper had diligently counted the number of people who came in and left, and she challenged me about the 'extra' girl who had emerged from my room. Despite having attempted the subterfuge, I considered it demeaning to lie and openly admitted that my fiancé from London had to spend the night with me as she had missed the last train back. Mrs Porter was having none of it. She said I had to leave forthwith and that she would inform the college of my precise misdemeanour.

On returning to college, I found a note from Mr Dewey asking me to see him as soon as I could. I went up to his rooms. He said he had heard the complaint, that I had had a woman in my room overnight. I said I did. He asked if I was aware that I was no longer welcome to stay at the college hostel, and I had to say I had been told. He was more solicitous than admonishing and seemed to take my breaking this rule in his stride.

'Where are you going to go?'

I said I had no idea but would start looking for digs which would have me.

'You'd better move into the college guest rooms, my dear fellow, just till you find something,' he said. He would instruct the duty porter to give me the key to one of these.

The guest rooms were reserved for visitors to the college, mostly academics and personages of some import. They were rarely, if ever, handed out to undergraduates, so the porter who escorted me to one was supercilious. But the word of my expulsion from the hostel and interim occupation of the guest rooms had got round the college and given me the aura of a defiant hero.

Staying here for a few days, I looked for suitable digs to move into. My friend Mathai Joseph, one of the first computer science postgraduates, lived in a room in Churchill College. He had heard of a house for rent at a cheap price from an agent and asked if I wanted to share the place with him.

We went to see the two-up-two-down property at the end of tiny Trafalgar Street, situated behind the college boat clubs on the other side of the river Cam. It was filthy. It had been occupied by two undergraduates, a boy and a girl who were well known as stars of the Cambridge theatrical circuit and would go on in later years to make their name in national theatre. They had left the place in a decrepit condition. Doors swung off their hinges. Gutted mattresses lay about with their innards spilling out in the rooms and on the landings. Kitchen cupboards were greasy. Seats and fittings in the toilet and bathroom were shattered or missing. We thought it was fantastic. Just right! After two years in Pembroke, I had my own digs.

Mathai would have the back room on the first floor and I the front one facing the street. We would clean up and repair the bathroom and kitchen and buy second-hand furniture from the shop round the corner—desks, chairs and mattresses.

Years later, I wrote and published this poem:

ON FINDING NOTES IN OLD BOOKS

(for Mathai Joseph)

We fought our Cambridge house together,
The ghost of a locked-up bat-wool smell
Lay down for smoke injections from
Our almost panacean spell
Of joss-sticks,
Stale, three years from home

When neighbours gathered in a head
Like onlookers at accidents
With shrugging raincoats, playing dumb
And wishing that we hadn't come
We set about to mend the fence
And hung our washing line indoors

'Foreign students' we played our parts,
Whispering when we stayed up late
With drunken friends to celebrate
Sergeant Pepper's Lonely Hearts.

By winter the neighbours thawed their looks
We shivered like sparrow-hearted lovers
Our scholarships kept us cold in books,
We stacked them on the floors,
Took notes in their covers
Inscribed the dates on the frontispiece,
A pretence we'd look at them again,
Remembered that we'd fooled ourselves
Packing and nailing and mailing them when
The house like a corpse gave up its lease.

Again these books demand their shelves,
To gather neglect in this Indian town
Where the buildings fall away in steps

(Like a queue of pilgrims walking down
To the river) becoming tin-roofed shacks
And where
The highway packs its dusty trucks
Off to less religious places,

Where kites like demons mock the roofs
And the urchins never wash their faces.

The front room on the ground floor was unoccupied. We used it, with the kitchen behind it, as a place for friends to gather, unrestricted by college or hostel rules, and occasionally, close friends who had visiting girlfriends would come and stay as weekend guests. When Mala turned up on weekends, we would cook and have drunken dinners. She remained in London in order to work and earn the money which paid the rent for the bedsitters she lived in and which I would share for the six months of the year when the university had holidays—four in summer and one each during Christmas and Easter.

I was sad, at the end of the one and a half years I had spent there, to leave 4, Trafalgar Street.

A few weeks after Mala came to Britain, Johnny and Mala signed affidavits to say that they had not consummated their marriage and through a magistrate's court obtained a legal annulment of it. They didn't have to appear. The papers they signed through a solicitor were legally sufficient.

Mala's mother had, in the few weeks after her daughter had left Bombay, traced through questioning her friends and mine how Mala had made her way to Britain—the marriage to Johnny, the sale of the motorcycle to pay for the ticket and the rest. She called upon her friend who frequently had business in the UK—an ex-army officer and part of the close circle of high-ranking army families who socialised and brought their children up in friendship groups—for assistance. This retired officer, a brigadier, was now one of the trustees of a Tata company and, obviously, could call upon the officials and board of the Tata Endowment for the Higher Education of Indians, which had granted me the scholarship to come to Cambridge.

One day when he was in London, he phoned my college and spoke to Mr Dewey, who called me and said I was to go and see a brigadier at a given address and time. The brigadier had told the professor that he had to discuss a serious matter with me which could put my scholarship in jeopardy. Mr Dewey seemed quite disturbed by the call and asked if I knew what this was about and why this person had used a threatening tone. I told him that the brigadier was a good friend of my girlfriends' parents and that they disapproved of our relationship.

Mr Dewey nodded and said, 'Why is it any of his business?'

I knew he wanted to show me that he was on my side.

I got to London and told Mala about who I was going to meet. She said she was expecting him to threaten cancelling my scholarship, as her mother had informed her just that through her sister Kum.

Mala had grown up with his children and with the daughter of another family in their circle. This girl, now in her late teens and deemed startlingly attractive, was very close to Mala and they confided in each other. She had revealed the details of her dangerous, secretive and illegitimate 'affair' with the brigadier, who was forty or more years older than her.

I went to the Mayfair address I had been given.

The brigadier was curt in his greeting. He said he had an unpleasant but just duty to carry out and that I was obviously a person of dubious character. He had known Mala from the time of her birth, he went on. She was young and impressionable and I had obviously taken advantage of her naivete.

He hadn't even asked me to take a seat in the drawing room of this Mayfair apartment. I stood there and tried, perhaps unsuccessfully, to seem penitent. I said I was fully aware that he had known Mala from her infancy. I also knew that she was a close friend of his daughter's and of her friend, whom I shall call X, and that they shared all their secrets.

The brigadier looked as though he was on a Second World War battlefield and a grenade had exploded in his face. He turned pale.

'Sit down, Farrukh,' he said. 'Please ... please sit down.' He was shaken.

I sat, while he paced the room.

I thought I would rub it in. 'Of course, Mala doesn't keep anything from me,' I said. 'But I don't think she shares these secrets with anyone else. And I think X treats her as her best friend.'

He stopped pacing.

'I'm sorry, would you like a drink?' he asked. He seemed in need of one. 'A whisky?'

'If you are.'

He went to the drinks cabinet and poured two whiskies. He handed me one and, standing by me, drained the other.

'Look, Farrukh, we are both men of the world.'

I didn't reply but sipped his whisky.

'I ... I will tell Babli ... er ... Mala's mother and, of course, her father, that we met, and I found you to be ... a perfectly intelligent and honourable young man and ... that you intend ...'

I felt sorry for him. He was devastated by the possibility that if the truth were out, it would destroy his family, his reputation, his friendships, his life. I wanted to reassure him.

'Of course, Brigadier sir. Mala and I intend to get married as soon as I graduate, get a job and can support her.'

'Yes, yes, of course, I shall say that,' he said and poured himself another drink.

'Mala would never want either of us to betray any confidence that her good friends pass on,' I said.

I could see from his expression that he wanted to know if that was a promise, but he was loath to ask. So, I volunteered it. 'That's a promise.'

He touched my shoulder as he came up to me. There were tears in his eyes. 'Thank you, thank you. God bless you,' he said.

We talked about the weather, and then I left, the blackmailer of Mayfair.

BYLINES BY LINES

I passed my second-year exams with advanced physics as my special subject. Cambridge deemed the second-year exams in natural sciences, uniquely, as the qualification for a Bachelorhood of the university. In other words, one needn't do the second part of the 'tripos', the third-year exams, as was necessary in every other subject, to be awarded a degree. Nevertheless, one had to spend the third year in Cambridge and either read a further course in science, switch to some other faculty who would accept one, or indeed do nothing except eat the requisite number of dinners to 'keep terms'.

Mr Dewey suggested that I study 'something easy like archaeology or anthropology'. I was sure that would have been interesting, but wasn't sure it would be easy. However, I told him I wanted to do English in my third year. He said that would probably not be possible, but he would speak to the English faculty.

He came back with the proposition that they would let me do English for the third year with a proviso and a concession: I was to do a 'fourth term', in other words, forego the summer holidays and catch up, under severe and fast-track tutelage, with some of the curriculum I missed in the two years I had done natural sciences. This would mean all of Shakespeare's plays, Chaucer, Milton, the modern novel—by which they meant nineteenth-century works in the main—and the concession was that instead of Anglo-Saxon literature, I could do a paper in the history of the English language.

I avidly embraced the conditions and was introduced to several tutors who, the other undergraduates having gone off for the summer break, I had to myself. At the end of this fourth term, I was examined on what I had 'caught up' with and was admitted to the English faculty's final year. I passed the third-year exam and got an 'unplaced second' as a grade.

Just before graduation day, I received an unexpected letter from the Atomic Energy Commission of India. The letter congratulated me on graduating from Cambridge, obviously pertaining to my natural sciences degree, and offered me a job in the institution. At the time, India was engaged in joining the arms race and manufacturing a nuclear bomb and destructive nuclear capability. I was a firm supporter of the Campaign for Nuclear Disarmament at university and wedded to socialist ideals. It would have been hypocritical to participate, even in some oblique way, in the manufacture of weapons of mass destruction. I wrote back declining the offer.

The exams being over, the traditional round of celebrations began. The colleges held 'May Balls', which were always in June. They would invite prominent pop bands to perform, and the parties would go on all night until dawn.

A group of probably fifteen or sixteen of us, boys and girls, set out to our respective May Balls together and appointed to meet at dawn to punt down the Cam to Grantchester. Cambridge was alive with young men and women in dinner jackets and gowns. The streets and the river resembled a carnival rather than a sombre university.

After the festivities, our company got into three punts and made its way downriver. All of us were sufficiently fortified with the night's champagne, some merrier than others. As our punt passed under the bridge of Trinity, a tall young man with three cameras hanging from his shoulders was standing on the bridge taking photographs, clicking in rapid succession. One of the girls in our punt stood up and took her dress off her shoulders and unstrapped her bra to reveal her breasts.

'Here you are,' she said to the photographer. 'If you want any more, you'll have to pay!'

The young man clicked away, and someone from our punt shouted at him asking what he was doing. He shouted back that he was taking photographs of Cambridge madness.

The punt had paused before the bridge.

'You've found the right crowd,' one of us said.

The young man came down to the riverbank.

'Can I interview you?' he asked the girl who had now covered herself. The other two punts drew up alongside ours.

The photographer said he worked for an international news agency based in Germany. They wanted these photographs and also a write-up, but he couldn't find a writer.

'You've just found one,' one of my friends said and pointed to me.

Andrew Whittuck, the young photographer, was immediately interested.

'Are you a writer? Can you do it?' he asked.

'Let's discuss it,' I said.

'We're all having breakfast at Farrukh and Mathai's at about ten o'clock. Join us there,' one of my friends volunteered and gave him the address and directions.

Andrew came to breakfast, and I had my first professional post-Cambridge writing assignment.

In my three years at the university, I had written various articles for Indian newspapers about the racism of some Cambridge landladies and about other aspects of university life from an Indian undergraduate's point of view. The *Times of India* had published some of these.

Andrew and I struck up a partnership. He would initiate the assignments and call me.

On one occasion, Andrew called to say I should be at a basement venue in Tottenham Court Road to listen to a pop group who had just issued their first record, predicted to rapidly climb the charts.

When we got there, the group had set up a 'psychedelic' light show of colours round the basement room, which was now packed out with fans. The band played its heavy rock numbers, and after the gig, Andrew stayed behind to offer them a free professional photographic session at his father's mansion in Hampstead.

His father was Admiral Whittuck of the Royal Navy, and Andrew lived with his parents in a large detached house. He photographed the band in a room he had set up as his studio. I interviewed them and wrote my piece for the agency.

The band rocketed to fame, and after the success of their first single, *See Emily Play*, Pink Floyd put out their first album in 1967. I have always claimed that some of the sentences in the blurb on the back cover of the album were taken from my writing for the German agency—but, of course, the designer of the sleeve was not obliged to acknowledge this petty borrowing.

The assignment that followed was exciting. Andrew rang to say that the Beatles were meeting a guru called Maharishi Mahesh Yogi to whose Indian mystical philosophy they subscribed and that we should report the encounter.

The Beatles were to meet the Maharishi at the Hilton in Park Lane where he was staying. We turned up there that evening and stood outside with literally hundreds of reporters, photographers and TV crews waiting for the famous four to turn up. There was a heavy police cordon keeping us reptiles at bay as the Hilton had banned all journalists and crews. Or perhaps it was a request from the Beatles to have an unmolested darshan with their 'spiritual guru'. Andrew said we could at least get snaps of them as they got out of their cars and that I could write about the crowds. But fate proved kinder.

The late 1960s was the era of flower power and hippydom, and I had gladly adopted wearing kurtas over my jeans, growing my hair down to my shoulders and allowing my black beard to flow.

George Harrison, a purported devotee of all things Indian, stepped out of his limousine fairly close to us. Andrew rushed to snap him, and I pushed my way towards them. Spotting me in the differently clad reporter-crowd, George grabbed my wrist and pulled me through the police cordon. I, in turn, grabbed Andrew's wrist, and the cops made way for us as part of George's entourage.

George turned to me and in his Liverpudlian accent asked if we wanted to report on the meeting. He took us in and we were the only reporters there, standing behind Yoko and John Lennon, who garlanded the Maharishi and talked in unmemorable platitudes about peace and love.

As we emerged from the meeting, several journalists and editors accosted me. Could I write a report for them? The best and most independent offer I received was from the *Listener*, a weekly I subscribed to and admired.

I wrote up the encounter that night, and it was published a few days after. It wasn't kind to either the Beatles or the Maharishi. I was doggedly sceptical, and remain so, about claims of Indian 'spirituality' and was mildly contemptuous of the Beatles falling for a possibly unintentional cultural confidence-trickster. The quest for spiritual enlightenment by the very prosperous always struck me as pitiable if not unselfconsciously hypocritical.

My article was accompanied by a cartoon by Barry Fantoni, showing the Maharishi muttering about frugality and hailing a London cab. Not very spiritual or ascetic then. Unless, of course, luxury hotels and spirituality can, as some of those who have acquired Buddhist practices as a luxury pastime believe, go well together with renunciation. Many indeed chant for the achievement of worldly wishes—meditate to accumulate.

Andrew called me early one July morning to say he would pick me up at Regent's Park station in about an hour. We had an appointment to interview and photograph Allen Ginsberg.

I had first heard of the poet five years ago in India, when Adil suggested that I read his work. Months later, while I was enrolled in Bombay University, Adil called to say that three of the Beat poets, Ginsberg, Peter Orlovsky and Gary Snyder, were visiting the city and were going to meet Indian poets in a gathering on the terrace of the famous theatre director Ebrahim Alkazi's apartment. Adil had been invited, but I was told it was strictly by invitation.

I thought of gatecrashing the party, but given I would have to fight chowkidars and possibly be repulsed, alongside other intruders, I didn't attempt it. Adil described the events of that night the next day.

The Beats had turned up, Orlovsky with an outrageous crop of hair and a beard that covered his face like a moon peeping brightly out of storm clouds or like a large hole in a dark woollen blanket. He read a poem which, Adil said, was a plea to the almighty to 'make him different'. How much more different did he want to be?

Then, rather impolitely, the Beats said they were not really interested in the poets gathered there, who wrote in English, but would want to hear recitations from native-language poets. In the middle of the night, emissaries were dispatched to find Hindi and Marathi poets, wake them up and bring them there.

They did arrive, but what Ginsberg et al made of the Marathi verses, which they apparently loudly applauded, couldn't be gauged.

The next year, when I quit the chemical engineering course halfway and returned to Poona, my friends and I took to reading the US-based *Mad* magazine. It featured a lampoon of the opening lines of Ginsberg's 'Howl':

'I saw the best minds of my generation destroyed by madness ...'

The lampoon went on: 'and I laughed because it got rid of the competition!'

My friends and I, callous teenagers, thought it funny. It became a gang shibboleth, a phrase to qualify as one of the crowd.

And here was Ginsberg again. Andrew and I drove to Regent's Park where Ginsberg was living for a few days in the annexe of one of his friend's large Regency-style terraced house. The annexe was a cottage at the back. We were greeted with casual and familiar American courtesy.

I questioned him about the conference he had come for—the 'Dialectics of Liberation' convened by anti-psychiatrist R.D. Laing—and Ginsberg talked about radicals changing the world. Andrew clicked away.

At the end of the interview, Ginsberg asked why London was so sleepy. We gathered that he hadn't been out of Regent's Park with its zoo and impressive Regency terraces.

'Where's the action?' he asked. 'Take me!'

I looked at Andrew, who immediately said we should drive him to where he might find the sort of action he was looking for.

We drove Ginsberg to Earl's Court, parked the car and walked with him to a famous gay pub and pick-up joint called the Coleherne Arms. Andrew bought the beers. Ginsberg looked round. He wasn't recognised. Several of the drinkers at the bar and on stools and tables were eyeing us.

'This is Earl's Court, right?' he asked. He named a restaurant a friend had told him about.

We walked out of the pub and took him to the basement restaurant. He was pleased but wanted to venture in alone. He said thanks and asked us to leave him.

I would meet him again years later. It was the early 1990s, the hippy era was long past, and Ginsberg had shaved his beard and cut his hair short. I was by then a commissioning editor at Channel 4, and Uri Fruchtmann, a friend of mine, was making a documentary on Ginsberg for us. I had told him about my brief but memorable encounters with the poet, and Uri invited me to be filmed talking to him.

Ginsberg vividly remembered the night in Bombay on Alkazi's terrace but corrected me on some of the details Adil had relayed to me. He also recalled our sojourn to Earl's Court.

'That was a useful outing,' is all he said.

My next break at journalistic writing in Britain was again the result of a chance meeting. I was in a South Kensington pub called the Denmark with Adil, who was meeting a Sri Lankan academic and writer called Wignesan. Over beers, we talked about writing, and Wignesan asked if I had thought of syndicating the articles I had been writing for the Indian and British newspapers. I didn't know what syndication meant, and he very helpfully explained. Adil had shown him some of my pieces, he said, and he could introduce me to a syndicate which would possibly accommodate my work.

A few days later, he got in touch and asked me to bring along some of my pieces to a meeting with the editor of Forum World Features, a journalistic syndicating agency based in Lincoln's Inn Fields.

At the agency's office, Wignesan introduced me to John Tusa, to whom I presented my freshly typed samples of work. They were in the main about my time in Britain, and some were opinion pieces against American foreign policy in Vietnam and even Pakistan.

Mr Tusa asked me to come back in two hours, in which time he would have a read and decide. This seemed unusually efficient, if not kind. Wignesan left me, wishing me the best of luck, and I walked round the square, anxiously passing the time. When I went back to Mr Tusa as arranged, he, surprisingly, said he liked all the pieces and would use them one by one in the packs that the agency sent to various newspapers and publications round the world, who would then publish them if they chose to.

He asked me which ones were unpublished, and when I offered him two such, he chose one. He was going to pay me twenty-five pounds for it, which he was commissioning straight away, and then, if I wrote one each week, he would consider it at the same price. I had never had so much money for any journalistic piece and thanked him profusely.

EENUK-A-POLE HAI HAI!

Having graduated, I continued to write articles for Indian magazines and newspapers as well as for photographic features with Andrew for international publications. The magazine *Debonair* in India commissioned me to do a regular monthly column on any topic of my choice. It was an uncertain and certainly meagre living, but Mala's wages were regular and paid for food, rent and heating.

I was surprised to be invited, only two weeks after the article was published in the *Listener*, to a party at the magazine's offices. There, I got into conversation about literary values over a glass of wine with a gentleman who told me that he was a professor of English at Leicester University. I had been talking about my attitude to Rudyard Kipling when he asked if I would like to perfect my notions and perhaps write a piece on it. I said I didn't have any forum in which to do this, and who would be interested in a piece on Kipling from the likes of me?

He would, he said, and concluded by offering me a scholarship to do an MA in contemporary literature and write a thesis on Kipling as part of it. Luck again—the right place at the unanticipated, unexpected, right time. I accepted his offer on the spot and asked what I needed to do to enrol.

He said, 'Come to Leicester, find a place to live, get to the university on the first day of term, go to the university office and they'll have your name and form to fill in.'

When I told Mala this, she said she was delighted and would find a job, any job, in Leicester and earn the money for rent and food, which my scholarship, though generous, wouldn't cover.

In the following days, I went down to Leicester a couple of times to look for a place to live in for the year and a half I was to spend there. I went to estate agents in the town centre, who would send me to houses which had advertised one or more rooms to let. On visiting at least four of these places, I was turned away at the doorstep by the landlords or landladies who protested that the rooms had just, half an hour prior to my arrival, been let. The repeated excuse was obviously subterfuge.

I wasn't polite when I spoke to the estate agent who sent me to the last place where I had been rejected. I stormed out of the agent's office and started on my way to the railway station to take the train back to London, frustrated at having once again wasted the rail fare. The secretary who worked at the agent's office, with whom I had exchanged smiles on entering, came running behind me. Catching up, she said, 'Sir, sir, can I tell you ...'

What could she want?

'Sir,' she said. 'I know what's going on, and I'm really sorry. I know you've been to ten places, and I know, because I work here, that going through my agency or any other here won't work.'

'I can see that,' I said, not knowing what she was getting at.

'What you can do, and please, I'm sorry to say this even, is go to the ... Asian district of the city ... Narborough Road and thereabouts and look on the notice boards outside the newspaper and grocery shops. They advertise rooms, and you'll definitely get something. I have Indian friends there. I went to school with them ...'

She was unsure as to how I would take the advice. Of course, I was grateful. I took her hand in both of mine.

'Thank you so much. I'll do exactly that. Right now. Where is this Narborough Road?'

She seemed relieved that I hadn't taken offence and gave me perfect directions.

'Thank you. Buy you a drink when it works,' I said.

'It will work, and I've got to get back to the office. I think they know I ran after you.'

'Tell them you only wanted to tell me to go back where I belonged.'

She laughed and waved as she hurried back.

I went to Narborough Road and did as she had advised. I took down a few phone numbers and, sure enough, was shown a couple of rooms. Two young white men had converted a house they owned on a street just off Narborough Road, and they offered me the room at the back of the ground floor.

A door under the stairs in the main hallway led into the bedroom and another room served as the kitchen. The door led out to a yard in which the lads had installed a perfectly functional toilet and shower. Great!

I put down a deposit and phoned Mala in South Kensington on the house phone we shared with four other tenants, who knocked on each other's doors to inform about calls they happened to pick up. That was the communal convention.

We moved to Leicester a few days later. I started my course at the university, and Mala got a job issuing bills at the gas board. She earned enough for us to pay the rent and buy food, and as a treat, on one day of the week we would go and have half a pint of beer each at the local pub. It was called the Pack Horse but was universally known as the the 'Paki Horse' because of its largely Asian clientele.

One Friday, the pub was crowded with Indian men, who I noticed were speaking Punjabi. They occupied several tables, with many pints of beer spread out before them. Mala and I sat on the bar stools and ordered our half pints. As we sipped them, one of the men came up to us with a smile.

'Are you Indian?' he asked. Mala was dressed in a salwar-khameez.

We said we were. He introduced himself as Sain Chaudhuri and said his friends were all dying to make our acquaintance. Would we join them? As we walked back to their tables with him, a couple of them immediately got up, went to the bar and fetched us each pints of beer. Both Mala and I had three pints each set before us.

'I can't drink more than one,' Mala said.

'Slowly, slowly,' one of the hosts said. 'Drink mine first!'

I drank a couple or maybe all three. We talked about what we were doing, and they said they worked in different factories, but most of them were in the same factory making typewriters. And yes, they were mostly Punjabi and Indian, and though there were a few Pakistanis and Bangladeshis in the factory, they didn't openly come to pubs.

When we left, they said they celebrated payday every Friday by coming to the pub and pressed us to meet them again the next week.

Slightly embarrassed at not having enough money to buy a round for the company, we debated whether to go or not, but we did go the next week and were received as long-lost friends. At eleven o'clock, when the pub was to legally shut, the white landlord bolted the doors with most of the clientele still there. The story, after hours, was that we were now all the landlord's guests and no money would pass over the bar. There would be a tally of what we drank, but it wouldn't be registered on the till. It would then be paid as a lump sum the next day, shared evenly amongst the drinkers—excluding us, despite our protests and to our embarrassment. We wondered if this was strictly legal, and were quite surprised when, round midnight, we were joined by three policemen who were known to and were guests of the Indian workers' Friday-night, or now Saturday-morning, gatherings. They came in regularly for a nightcap, we were told, and were greeted heartily, joining the crowd and drinking shorts rather than beer.

On one of the Fridays when we stayed late, the landlord evicted us at about half past two, and as the company left the pub, they invited us to go to one of their houses for a meal of makki ki roti and sarson ka saag. Apparently, each Friday the women of one of the families were alerted that eight or ten guests would turn up for such a meal. One of the men would volunteer on the previous pub evening or perhaps at work, to honour the informal rotating roster of generosity.

We sat in the front room of Keval Singh's house, and his wife, sister-in-law and mother or mother-in-law got out of their beds and, without the least resentment, provided the meal—which could, at past three in the morning, be called 'brinner'. It was embarrassing, and Mala insisted on going in to help the women but was vociferously barred by the women themselves. It didn't occur to the host, to the company or to the women, with whom Mala had several conversations, that this was a tyrannical segregation. It was tradition and accepted practice by all.

One evening as we gathered in the pub, there was a sullen atmosphere. I asked Sain what it was all about. Those five, he said, pointing to a group of men sitting silently, had been dismissed from the factory, just that day.

'Why?'

'Oh, one of them argued with the supervisor over going to the toilet too often—that was Jarnail there. He is quite hot tempered, so when the supervisor said something rude to him, he abused him and it came to a slap and a physical fight. The others joined in, then the other supervisors came, and the five were told they were sacked.'

'So, what are you going to do? What are they going to do?'

'Who knows? Find another job? But the management will stop them from doing that also. They are bastards. The supervisor started it. They are bloody Hitlers.'

'Didn't you say you were all members of the Indian Workers' Association?' Mala asked.

'What fucking association?' Keval said. 'All the association does is fight over bhangda costumes and organise some party on Baisakhi. That fellow there, Gurvinder Singh, is the secretary.'

Sain shouted across the tables to Gurvinder.

'Oi bey, Bhangda Costumes, what are you going to do about us?'

Gurvinder knew he was being addressed and came across. 'What can we do? I will do whatever you say!' he said.

'Have you never taken any political or industrial action?' Mala asked.

'What action to take?'

The entire contingent of Indians in the pub had gathered round now.

'Aren't you members of a union?' I asked.

They looked at each other. Sain was contemptuous. 'Union came to us, but none of the workers wanted to pay the fees.'

'How many Indians or Punjabis are there in the factory?'

'Nearly all the workers.'

'Then appeal to them to strike,' Mala said.

We left the pub in a crowd and drove in several cars to the university student union building, which stayed open till late. I composed a pamphlet, an appeal to all the workers to fight for justice for the 'Leicester Five'. We ran off a few hundred copies on the student union's cyclostyling machine. Sain was sparkling with excitement. 'The shift starts at six o'clock, so twenty of us will be at the gates at five,' he said.

When the workers, men and women, came to the factory gates at six the next morning, they were met by Sain, Keval, Gurvinder and twenty-five others who addressed them, urging them not to cross their picket line. No one did. By six, the entire morning shift was outside the gate, and Mala addressed them in Hindi standing on a wooden crate. Gurvinder introduced her as an honorary secretary of the Indian Workers' Association (IWA) of Leicester.

The local press had been alerted overnight, and their photographer and reporter landed up outside the gate.

Mala said the arbitrary action of the management, which had only listened to the supervisor's account of the incident and moved immediately and unjustly to sack those involved, was racist. If we let it pass, the management and supervisors could do that to any worker on any excuse. She was met throughout the speech with strident applause and shouts of approval.

At round half past nine, a member of the management team came out and asked if the striking shift had any representative they could negotiate with. Sain stepped forward with Gurvinder and asked Mala to join them. In an hour and a half, they re-emerged and announced that the workers had been reinstated with immediate effect and that the entire workforce would get a weekly pay rise of 4 per cent. Sain waved a piece of paper at the crowd. There were loud cheers, and the shift poured through the gates to their workstations.

The action and victory transformed the Leicester IWA into a radical organisation. Sain finally told us that in India he had been a member of the Communist Party (Marxist), but when he had come to Leicester, he had met with fairly right-wing views among the other Punjabi workers and so had not tried to proselytise at all. He was glad he had come across us and now Mala and I must be honorary secretaries and help plan other actions.

A month or so later, we took two coachloads of supporters to an anti–Vietnam War demonstration outside the American embassy in London, marching under the banner of the Leicester IWA. At least a hundred members of the organisation had, through these two actions, become interested in political agitation and were willing to follow the leadership into them. Mala and I didn't have to recruit them to left-wing causes. At least three of the workers there, including Sain, had been members of the Communist Party in India, and after the successful strike action, began to propagandise the other members.

After joining the demonstration in London and generating an interest among the Punjabi community—most of whom had joined the IWA as a social organisation, if not political—in the international protest against the US war in Vietnam, we became aware of the release of a film called *The Green Berets*, which had been internationally criticised as pure propaganda for US heroism in that unjust war. Forming an alliance with the radical students of Leicester University, the Leicester IWA bought tickets for the first show, clandestinely invited the press telling them there was going to be an incident and, as the film got underway, stood up and protested with slogans to shut it down and ban it. We were a majority in the theatre, and the management stopped that first showing. After we threatened a boycott of the theatre by the Asian and student communities of Leicester, the management agreed to withdraw the film completely.

There was no stopping the IWA now. They started to have political strategy meetings. With Sain, Keval, Gurvinder and the rest, we decided at one of these meetings to take action against a Leicester pub which regularly hosted meetings of the neo-fascist National Front in their first-floor meeting room.

By this time, an alliance between the radical socialist society of my university and the strategic committee of the Leicester IWA was so firm that the students were called to a meeting.

We jointly decided that on the night of the National Front meeting, several white students would attend it at the pub, posing as citizens interested in joining the Front. As the meeting progressed, they would interrupt it, and a few of us, who would pose as innocent Asian drinkers in the pub downstairs, would join the students and provide the numbers to ensure that the Front's members and speakers would surrender without a fight and leave.

The planning committee designated six members—Sain, Keval, Gurvinder, Jarnail, Mala and me—to pose as the drinkers. Any more Asians turning up casually to drink at that particular pub would seem suspicious.

But somehow word of the plan leaked, and eighty Indian workers turned up at the bar on the appointed day, all pretending that they had dropped in for a casual drink to a pub which rarely entertained any Asian clientele. Having come in separate groups, they decided not to acknowledge us or each other but to just settle down with their pints or pegs. The landlord and bartenders must have wondered what the hell was going on, but on the principle of 'business is business', they were happy to sell this flood of unusual customers a drink and take their money.

The meeting upstairs, which had placards in the pub publicising it, went ahead. Twenty minutes into the meeting, we heard shouts and furniture crashing upstairs. We left our drinks and rushed up, and so did fifty others. There was chaos. The students had challenged the speakers, and then the opposing sides had thrown chairs at each other. We came in as the battle raged and by sheer dint of numbers overwhelmed the National Fronters, whom the students now held down for all the world as though they were defeated wrestlers.

The landlord had called the police. The stairway, which was now packed with our IWA supporters who couldn't get into the first-floor room, had to be vacated to let them in. The leaders of the Front, fearing adverse publicity, said they didn't want to press charges. They left under police escort. The landlord protested that he had nothing to do with the Front and would welcome any clients who paid for their drinks. It was either a statement of good pragmatic sense or of surrender.

The Leicester IWA, invigorated by its triumphs on home ground, decided to join the protest called by the Birmingham chapter, an openly Maoist organisation run by the Indian Communist Party (Marxist-Leninist). They had called a demonstration against two political developments.

The first was the notorious racist speech by Tory minister Enoch Powell, who, using classical Latin allegories, had said he 'saw the river Tiber foaming with blood' if immigration from the ex-colonies was allowed to continue. Labelled 'The Rivers of Blood', his speech was a bid for the leadership of the Tory Party. It nakedly asked for an end to immigration and perhaps the repatriation of the existing immigrant population. The bid failed miserably as no one in his own party and no associations of the working class supported his hysterical appeal. In the following weeks, he was forced out of his British working-class constituency of Wolverhampton and ended up as a candidate for some obscure Ulster unionist protestant seat in northern Ireland, as marginalised as Cinderella in her stepmother's house.

The second issue was that the Conservative prime minister James Callaghan enacted a law restricting entry to the UK of Kenyan Asians, part of the former colony, who held British passports.

As the Leicester IWA contingent, we gathered men and women into a fleet of coaches and drove to Birmingham to join the national demonstration, marching and shouting slogans in the centre of the city. The only problem was, despite Mala, me and others rushing down the demonstrating columns in an attempt to correct the pronunciation of the slogans, the ones our phalanxes were shouting made little sense to the general public: 'Eenuk-A-Pole hai hai!' and 'Challaa Ghunn hai hai!', the first of which lampooned Enoch Powell and the second Callaghan. The population of Birmingham must have been justifiably bewildered. What was this orderly crowd so passionately denouncing or demanding?

The Leicester IWA now had a reputation for inventive radical action in the city, unlike other branches of the organisation which were fronts for Indian communist factions to gather funds from immigrant supporters. As a now reputedly militant immigrant collective, we were invited to a conference of black and Asian organisations in Alexandra Palace, London. Parties and organisations from all over Britain would be represented, and the aim was to thrash out, if at all possible, some common aims and strategies representing the social and political rights of the new and ex-colonial immigrant communities—Asian, West Indian and African. We took several coaches of our membership down to London and had a good day out.

The conference was noisy and well attended but, despite the radical speeches and uncompromising standpoints of the speakers, wasn't planned or destined to have any practical results. The one benefit I derived from it was noting that some of the demagogues who posed as leaders of the new communities were fools, confidence-tricksters, Stalinist degenerates or pure opportunists making a living out of the plight and hopes of the communities they purported to lead. The second realisation I took away from the conference was that the organisation calling itself the British Black Panther Movement (BPM), despite its imitative appearance and boy-scoutish membership, seemed to be a serious, incorrupt and politically engaged entity.

By now, I was near the end of my time at Leicester, having passed the written papers and completed my thesis tracing the influence of Indian myths and ancient texts on Kipling's literary oeuvre.

Professor Fraser invited us seven MA students to dinner at his house to meet Lawrence Durrell, whose work Fraser had written about and who was staying with him for a few days. I couldn't believe it! I had read every work of his, which inspired me to become a writer.

Among the seven students in our course who had gathered at Professor Fraser's house was a girl of Persian origin, a graduate of Cardiff University, and a Greek gentleman, a mature student. There was also Paddy, Professor Fraser's wife, and Professor Graham Hough.

As we drank and talked, I ventured to tell Durrell that I had read the *Quartet* in Bombay and it had made me quit chemical engineering studies and aspire to be a writer.

He said something like, 'Wrong decision,' but smiled and added, 'Perhaps you'll regret it.'

After dinner, Durrell proposed we all head to the pub. The company agreed and, getting their coats, set off down the road.

I offered to help Paddy clean up before joining the others. As she loaded the dishwasher, she realised that someone was still upstairs.

She shouted, 'Hello?' from the kitchen.

Professor Hough answered from the upstairs landing.

'It's me, Paddy. Graham!'

'You didn't go to the pub?'

'No, I'll give it a miss,' Professor Hough said. 'Too many wogs!'

Paddy turned with a look of absolute terror on her face to see if I had heard that last remark.

I had, but I smiled. She stood open-mouthed as she looked at me for a reaction.

'Relax,' I said. 'Let him say and do what he wants?'

'I ... I'm so sorry ... I ...'

'Paddy, I don't give a shit. I'm quite happy with being a wog. A cuss is on the tongue of the abuser. Forget it. We're finished here, let's go to the pub.'

We walked down the road in silence as we made our way to the edge-of-the-town pub, a few hundred yards away.

'Where's Graham?' Professor Fraser asked Paddy when we reached.

She turned to me, looking miserable.

'He said he wasn't joining us because there were too many wogs in the company,' I said.

'He didn't say that?' asked Professor Fraser, looking shocked. Paddy nodded. There was shock all round.

'Fuck him,' Durrell said. 'I wouldn't want to drink with him anyway.'

BLACK IS A POLITICAL COLOUR

Mala and I moved to London and resumed life in boarding houses and bedsitters. I got in touch with the leadership of the British Black Panther Movement, assessed them as serious and inspiring individuals and was accepted as a 'candidate' member who had to prove his commitment by participating in the propagandist and agitational activity of the 'collective', as they called it.

Altheia Jones, the Trinidadian-born, uncrowned but undoubted leader of the organisation, a PhD student of medical science at London University, explained that they called it a 'movement' and not a party because despite drawing inspiration from the Panther Party of the USA, the British political circumstances were different. Though some junior members of the movement sported American-style black berets, the leadership didn't indulge any symbolism apart from a flag with a panther on it, which they carried on demonstrations to identify the phalanx of marchers who loyally followed the banner.

I served my apprenticeship by going on demonstrations, standing outside the British courts in protest at unjust arrests, attending 'history' classes in which books by the US Black Panthers were discussed and composing pamphlets at the North London 'base' of the movement.

Though most of the membership were West Indian, there was no racial bar, and the movement had several Asian members and a few Africans. Altheia was from Trinidad, an island whose population was half Indian and half Afro-Caribbean, and this necessity for political cohesion must have influenced the BPM's policy of including Asians under the 'black' label. The slogan, often repeated, was 'Black is a political colour!'

One of the first assignments the BPM gave me was drawing up an account in simple English of an important and dramatic trial in which Altheia was one of the nine defendants. This would become famous as the Trial of the Mangrove Nine.

The Mangrove, a restaurant in Notting Hill owned by the activist Frank Crichlow, was a meeting place for the Caribbean community of West London. It was victimised and raided by the Notting Hill police and Harrow Road police on several occasions. The raids were purported to be about illegal drugs, but no charges were ever brought because nothing was found. It was, for all purposes, police racist bias. The community, sick of the raids and harassment, launched a demonstration in the early 1970s to protest against this. It wasn't a huge demonstration. Perhaps two hundred supporters and sympathisers marched through Portnall Road to Harrow Road police station, carrying banners and shouting anti-racist and anti-police slogans. The police cordon that was deployed to block the access to the front of the station confronted the demonstrators, and when they tried to force their way through, a tussle ensued. Nine demonstrators were arrested.

The public prosecutors had never, in recent times, been confronted with a demonstration of this sort and with such determined resistance. The nine were charged and put on trial at the Old Bailey, the Central Criminal Court in London. The charges were absurd and over the top. Apart from charging them with riot and affray, they were accused of conspiracy to overthrow the British State. It was a clear indication of panic by the British establishment.

Altheia, who defended herself, labelled it a political trial. Darcus Howe, one of the more colourful and outspoken defendants who had qualifications in law, also defended himself, vehemently attacking and picking logical holes in every police argument. Darcus was playing to the gallery and perhaps the British establishment's appreciation of debate and drama. The nine were acquitted of all serious charges, and only minor charges against two defendants were upheld.

My role was to attend court and take notes of the proceedings and, at the close of the trial each day, to get to the Panther base and write up, from my notes and those of others who had been in court, the events and significant arguments of the day. Precising the events and arguments of a whole day's proceedings into a couple of pages was not simple, but the journalistic self-training came in useful. Writing these up in a bulletin each evening, we sent them to the media and supporters in Britain and in the Caribbean.

My main profit on it was making the firm acquaintance of Darcus, who remained a friend, close comrade and fellow fiend from then till he died in 2018.

I had encountered Darcus once before. On an underground train with five companions returning from Speakers' Corner in Hyde Park one evening, this tall, handsome black man had approached us selling a political rag called the *Black Eagle*. He offered my friend Shahid a copy, which he bought. The man then turned to me.

'You want to buy one?' he asked.

'I'll share my friend's,' I said.

'Will you share the same jail sentence?' he said and walked off, apparently pleased with himself.

As the trial ended, Darcus joined the BPM and became an active member. One of the roles both he and I were assigned was to lecture to the movement's youth group, which assembled, perhaps a hundred or more strong, at the community theatrical space called the Oval House opposite the cricket ground of that shape and name in Lambeth, South London. Darcus would talk about Caribbean history, and I lectured them on E.P. Thompson's *The Making of the English Working Class*. We wanted the classes to go beyond propagandic purposes, and the youth membership which came to the classes was eager to absorb the knowledge, political understanding and the purpose that the movement generated through its activities.

DOLLY MIXTURES

All through this, I continued to write for Forum World Features, faxing them my articles, which they duly and flatteringly put at the top of the pack they sent out to the world. They paid me regularly and, what I considered, handsomely.

Through my membership of the BPM, I became aware of events in the black struggle in the USA and used some of the material in my columns for the Forum. For the first time, the Forum rejected my articles. They didn't inform me immediately, but when I rang up and asked why the last two pieces had not appeared, a secretary told me that Mr Tusa was not available and that the pieces had been rejected because the writing was not up to my usual standard. This was, to say the least, puzzling.

I had come to rely on the occasional, at least fortnightly, income from this source and, after the third rejection, concluded that it had dried up.

A friend advised me to go to the Inner London Education Authority (ILEA) and offer myself as a 'supply teacher', one who would be sent to different schools to fill the temporary vacancies left by regular staff on sick leave or other absences, something he too did.

'Why would they accept me?' I asked

'They are desperate, they take anybody,' he said.

I followed his suggestion and went to the ILEA offices. I listed my academic qualifications, and the interviewer, impressed apparently by a Cambridge and a Leicester University degree, said I could be hired from that afternoon and gave me a registration number and then the address of a school in South London which could use my presence in the next hour. I went there and taught a rather unruly class some poem that the absent teacher had set them.

The next school to which I was assigned asked me, at the end of a full and tiring day with several classes, if I wanted to stay the full term or even more and join the English department. It would be perfect. The school was relatively easy to get to by the tube, and the job would give me guaranteed earnings for several months.

The school was in Clapham, overlooking the Clapham Common Park and had been named Henry Thornton after the eighteenth- to early-nineteenth-century philanthropist, member of parliament and campaigner for the abolition of slavery.

The year before I was recruited to teach there, it had been a grammar school, a selective State-funded institution which used to have exclusively white middle-class boys with a few sons of Asian doctors and the like. Under the Labour government's recent educational policies, Henry Thornton had become a 'comprehensive', by amalgamation with two other schools of the borough called Aristotle and Tennyson. In contrast to the Thorntonians, the Aristotelians and Tennysonians were from areas less gentile and almost exclusively black. The pupils were the sons of Caribbean immigrants with a smattering of white working-class lads.

As a result, the school, operating from three buildings and miles apart, was chaotic. The grammar school teachers who had inherited, or been compelled into, this comprehensive structure were overwhelmed. They were used to obedient and eager classes and were now faced with a majority of boys who were neither obedient nor eager.

The school had resolved this problem in a way antithetical to the principle on which comprehensive schools were founded, that is, children of all backgrounds and abilities would be taught in the same institutions and would be allowed to find their own academic and scholarly levels. It was the Labour government's attempt to abolish the earlier practice of selection and separation of students at the age of eleven into those who were academic and those who were less so. It was a gesture in the direction of abolishing the privileges of birth and establishing those of a meritocracy which, in theory, equalised opportunity. It didn't work and wasn't structured to work in the school I joined.

I had never taught in a school before and didn't know how a British one worked. As I began my regular appointment there, I was given a timetable by the head of the department and had to ask one of the other teachers what the numbers and letters in the squares meant. Steve Ayers, a teacher, explained. The school had ten classes in each year, divided by their tested academic ability. So 3.1 would be the 'cleverest' class of the third year of mostly thirteen- to fourteen-year-olds and, going down the numbers, 3.10 would be those deemed the least academic. And the same with the other years.

There was a preponderance of the lowest classes of the third and fourth years in the squares on my weekly schedule. They had awarded me one class, 5.1, in which I would teach some part of their literature syllabus for their final school exams. But dotted about the week were also classes called 3.X and 3.Y. What were these? Something to do with chromosomes?

'Ah, no!' said Steve. 'These are the unruly lads from each year, extracted from, say, 3.8, 9 and 10 and placed into X and Y. You seem to have them quite a lot of the time.'

Steve was sympathetic. He had been a teacher at one of the other schools and didn't agree with the stratification of this one and the separation of the almost entirely black boys into what he called the ghetto classes.

'Most of the teachers who are assigned to these classes just take them out to the indoor football pitch and let them kick the ball about and tire themselves out. But I am sure you will try something with them. Hope you do,' he said.

These classes were a riot. The boys were not inclined to learn, and their defiance was fuelled by the consciousness that they had been marked out as beyond any possible achievement. I didn't resort to taking them to the football pitch and persisted in trying to get them to follow a story or even the lyrics of a pop song. It worked for a couple of boys who ignored the hubbub of the rest, but it was not in any sense more than a detaining exercise from which, at the sound of the bell, the class would push past each other in a scrum to get out.

The ringleader of the disobedience I was offered was one Colin Cumberbatch, a young lad of diminutive stature from a Jamaican family. And yet, he was the undoubted kingpin and instigated the banging of desks or the collective insouciance of the rest. On the second day I was assigned to that class, he egged on the rest to shout 'Koolybasha' at me each time I turned to write on the board.

At first I didn't understand what this meant, and most of them didn't either. Then it dawned on me that Colin must have picked it up from some older Jamaican relative. On sharing that his English teacher was an Indian, he must have been informed that Indians only spoke 'coolie bhasha'—the Jamaican racist term for the language of 'coolies', the Indians who formed a minor proportion of the Jamaican population. I retaliated by pretending I didn't know what was being said, and when the provocation didn't cause me to react in any way, it died down.

The second thing Colin asked me a few times was whether the shirt I had on was a 'Ben Sherman'. The shirts I wore were, I thought, decent, and some may have been tailored in India as every holiday I used the opportunity to get cheap bespoke-tailored shirts and trousers. I didn't know what a Ben Sherman was, till I asked and was told that it was a designer brand of shirt favoured by young black men.

Then one day, things changed. I was on supervisor duty in the playground when Colin, followed by a group of his friends, came up to me and respectfully asked, 'Dhondy, you've gone for a Panther, yeah? I know!' He grinned at his friends as though he had openly imparted information which was secret or dangerous.

One of his group, not realising that this question and encounter marked a change of heart and attitude, said, 'Koolybasha,' and grinned. Colin turned on him, viciously asking him to shut his mouth.

In class after the break, Colin took charge of the class.

'No one fuck with Dhondy, right?'

No one did. They sat at their desks in silence waiting for what I had planned to teach.

I was puzzled, thinking at first that it was some sort of practical strategy whose impact would be soon sprung on me. Or was it because they mistakenly thought I was wearing a Ben Sherman?

Taking advantage of the subdued class and asking them to read and write in the course of the lesson, I got to know that most of them couldn't do either.

That evening, the mystery was solved. I was lecturing at the Oval House gathering of the BPM, and after a session on the formation of the Labour Party out of the political struggle of the white working class of the nineteenth century, a young man and his friends came up to talk to me.

'I am Colin brudder. You ah teach him, right?' the young man asked.

I said I did.

'Him have fey be displin' wid you bro! Seen? You jus' tell me what I'm ah do, right?'

I didn't know whether he was affecting the Jamaican Yardie idiom, but I was told later by one of the senior BPM members that the young man had come out of jail and had resolved to go straight. The Cumberbatch family was known as a rough-and-tough Jamaican clan, and Colin was the youngest of several brothers, all of whom had acquired convictions and a reputation for commanding 'respek'. This brother had joined the BPM and was diligently reading George Jackson, Bobby Seal and other black US radical writers at the suggestion of our BPM classes. He had told Colin to afford me 'respek' or face his brotherly discipline.

If their inattention and riotousness arose from their inability to read and write and their effort to disguise it, I had to, as their teacher, deal with it. I set out to teach 3.X how to read and write. I didn't know how to do that but was directed to evening classes run by an English inspector called Geoffrey Thornton on how to teach literacy to older children who hadn't been initiated into it at the infant stage.

I picked up from him what I called the method of phonics by context. It entailed begging other teachers to arrange exchanges of supervision with me and taking out six to eight of the 3.X students onto the streets of Clapham with a pad and pen each. I would point to a pub sign and ask them what it said. They would know that it was The Windmill. I would get them to copy the pattern of lettering, and then we would repeat together the consonants and vowels. And so with other public lettering, such as the names of supermarkets, banks, shops, road signs, underground stations and any writing they could 'read'. It worked.

At the end of the year, I was called in on the last day to the headmaster's office to be told that I had been detected as having used my position to propagandise senior students into radical politics. I said it wasn't true and that I kept my teaching and my politics separate. Mr Heaton Page, the headmaster, told me and an Australian teacher, also summoned on the same charge, that we were dismissed and would never teach in the ILEA again as he had seen to it that we were listed as subversives and unsuitable.

The Australian, a tall fellow who had shoulder-length hair and a beard and was known in the playground as 'Jesus', unbuckled his trousers, pulled them down and, turning his back to Page, declared that he wanted to introduce one arsehole to another.

I left hastily before the police were called.

That source of income was dead. And though I had interesting stories to tell and perhaps articles to contribute, I had nowhere to publish them. My old contact Andrew Whittuck had left the agency and had successfully turned to purely photography.

Forum World Features had also decidedly shut its doors to my opinions. Very many years later, at the occasion of John Tusa, the former editor of the Forum, being appointed head of the BBC World Service radio, an investigative report in the media said that the Forum was financed and controlled by the Central Intelligence Agency (CIA) in the US as a front for their anti-communist propaganda. Tusa maintained that he knew nothing about the connection.

It was disappointing to learn, even so many years later, that my articles with their left-wing and even Marxist biases were perhaps used to front the weekly bulletin bundle to dupe the recipients into believing it to be an ideologically balanced forum. The articles that followed, though I never studied them with any care, were straightforward CIA-inspired propaganda. And there I was, harbouring the conceit that my writing had been commissioned for its quality and clarity.

After being dismissed from Henry Thornton, I spent my blackballed term without steady employment or income and did odd jobs to eat and pay the rent.

A colleague of mine at Henry Thornton got in touch and asked if I wanted another teaching job. I told her I had been blacklisted by the Education Authority, which hired and paid teachers. She said the prospect of employment was at a church school and so fell outside the board's jurisdiction. It would be the head teacher's decision to appoint.

I was desperately interested. She had heard that at the Archbishop Temple's School, where she used to teach, the head of English had quarrelled with the head teacher and resigned in the final term of the year. This head teacher, a clergyman, she said, was not a pleasant person and had caused her to quit the school too. Now the school was desperate to recruit a teacher who could take over the A and O level classes, whose exams were coming up at the end of the term. The head of English had left the school in the lurch by resigning at this crucial time, and the parents of the boys and girls in the exam classes were exerting extreme pressure on the unpleasant head.

'You have the degrees and the experience. He'll beg you to take the job and save his bacon,' she said. 'Just one thing. He can't offer you the head of English job to replace my friend who's left, because a junior school teacher, who happens to be the mistress of the very domineering deputy head of the school, has, through internal political manoeuvring or perhaps even blackmail, been given that job and the salary.'

'I don't care. I just want the job. And wow! Teaching exam classes will mean desperately attentive students and reading books I love!'

I called Mr Helft, the head teacher, and he asked me to come in straight away. I found my way to the small two-form entry school—two classes, around sixty pupils in each year—in Archbishop's Park in Lambeth.

A short, round-faced, partially balding man with shaded spectacles and a dog collar, Mr Helft greeted me as though I was the Messiah come to save him from eternal damnation. I did tell him that I had been unjustly blacklisted by the ILEA without any investigation into the truth …

He interrupted me. He wasn't interested in any of that, he was sure I was innocent, and then he began an awkward explanation about how my timetable included exam classes but, despite carrying the responsibility for these, the post of head of English …

Now, I interrupted him, pretending I was relieved to hear this. I didn't want to take charge of any department of teachers or do any bureaucratic paperwork, I told him. I just wanted to teach.

He looked at me as King Midas might have looked at the first thing he touched that turned to gold. Could I start that afternoon? I said I would have to look up the syllabuses to know what I was teaching. He went to the filing cabinets in his office and pulled out some pamphlets.

'This is the one we do,' he said.

The top class was doing *Macbeth* and some Henry James. The O level class was studying Orwell's *Animal Farm*.

'I can start straight away,' I said.

He took me to where the sixth-formers were being 'covered' by a teacher who could only ask them to read by themselves. Dr Helft, as he told me he preferred to be addressed, introduced me to the class. The physical education teacher who was standing in looked me up and down and, without a word, packed his things and left.

I asked the ten pupils in the class their names and then, where they were with the books they were to be doing. They were a wonderful class, as were the O level boys and girls of the fifth year.

After a week, a girl called Kim came up to me after class and handed me a letter from her mother.

It said:

> Dear Mr Dhondy,
> Thank you for taking over our Kim's exam class. She and her classmates say you are a wonderful teacher and they are learning fast. I am writing this letter to ask a favour. Several ladies and I run a youth club for young girls and boys on our housing estates in Kennington and next week are having a prize-giving ceremony to reward the winners of the competitions we have held during the last month. It has been a vast display of real talent. We would be absolutely delighted if you would consent to be our guest of honour and compere at the prize-giving ceremony which, by the way, is called The Dolly Mixtures.
> Please say yes ...

She had signed the letter and added within brackets 'Kim's mum'.

I read it and asked Kim, who stood expectantly by, 'That's very sweet, but why me?'

'You'd be perfect, sir. I told my mum you make up good jokes.'

'Tell your mum I am flattered to be asked. I've never been a compere at a "Dolly Mixture" before. Of course, I'll do it, and just hope I don't let you all down.'

'Don't get all nervous, sir! You'll be a big hit.'

I tried to practise some clean jokes, which I was told was expected of a compere.

On the evening of the event, I dressed in my most flamboyant outfit—a maroon velvet jacket and chocolate-coloured flared velvet trousers. A reception committee of ladies, dressed for the occasion, waited for me in the car park as arranged and escorted me to the improvised artist's entrance of the hall. It was packed with people of all ages, from infants to their great-grandparents. The stage was crowned with the name of the event.

I had done my homework and found that Dolly Mixtures was a collection of differently flavoured and shaped sweets. Kim's mum introduced me to the crowd, which cheered enthusiastically at my entrance. As a member of the BPM, I had lectured and ranted and raved and held forth in front of all sorts of audiences, but here was a purely non-political white working-class, council-estate audience of all ages. My gut tightened with nervousness, but I ventured my first few jokes about what I initially imagined Dolly Mixtures might be. I kept it clean. The response was encouraging and emboldening.

I had watched a few stand-up comics on television and knew that their stock-in-trade was spinning narratives out of personal observation. I launched in, saying we Indians didn't have double-barrelled names. I had only come across someone called, for instance, Heaton Page, when I came to England.

'He was the first headmaster I worked for down the road, and he threw me out for being a dangerous person. Me? Me! Dangerous person?' Even that got a laugh.

'It, of course, boosted my ego but cost me my job. Never mind, I am happy being a political danger to your wonderful kids.'

I thought I hit the right register.

'Double-barrelled names come about because someone who thinks they are very important marries someone who is equally important, so they keep both their names. For instance, if the philosopher Immanuel Kant or his daughter married the great cricketer Ranjit Singh, the couple could be called Kant Singh—which, now that they have passed away, would play hell with their heavenly choirs.'

It worked on that audience, at any rate, on the older individuals in it.

After the first round of prizes, Kim's mother said, 'Go on, make them dirty. I'm sure you know some.'

None of my dirty ones were original and certainly not for that crowd. But I still ventured, when she prompted me from the wings: 'Go on, Farrukh, some risky stuff.'

'What did Robinson Crusoe look forward to on Thursdays?' I asked.

'Doing Friday,' someone shouted and got the response he wanted, leaving the infants and the young bewildered.

A few of the teachers next day at school said, 'Believe you've launched a brilliant new career and will be leaving us soon?'

FIRE

Both Mala and I were invited to join the central core of the BPM. It consisted of about eight to ten self-selecting members who were judged to be the most dedicated and capable of leadership.

In my judgement, either Darcus or Barbara Beese, beautifully imperious with her tall stature and Afro hair, would have been ideal candidates for the central core.

The electors to the central core labelled Darcus a populist demagogue whose personality was at odds with the movement's aim of collective leadership. We insisted the BPM was not a political party and had no ambitions to contest a parliamentary or council seat. Besides, they said, with some justification, that Darcus was not willing to adhere to any imposed and mutually agreed-upon disciplines and had ideological determinations and, therefore, strategies of his own. Behind these objections was the clear apprehension that Darcus's charisma as a speaker and charmer would propel him to a publicly perceived, if not official, position of leadership. There was, I thought, certainly some jealous guarding of positions. Barbara Beese was, I felt, too closely associated with Darcus and, though she was in every sense endowed with leadership qualities, was disqualified perhaps for just that.

The BPM took over our lives. Mala and I were constantly in meetings; at actions the movement had called for, such as demonstrations, pickets and strikes; and writing up this and that for pamphlets, for *Freedom News*, the movement's newspaper, and for bulletins we sent out to sister organisations round the globe. *Freedom News* attempted some stuff that could be characterised as political rhetoric, along with news and views of the immigrant communities.

Altheia, I think, was made aware that C.L.R. James, the Trinidadian philosopher, activist, Marxist and author of several unique books, was in London and would consent to speak to our organisation. C.L.R., or 'Nello' as his friends called him (it being derived from Lionel, his middle name), was escorted into a very crowded room. He was tall, bent, wearing a hat and dressed in a Western suit. He took his place at the table and, after the niceties, got to the point.

He held up a copy of *Freedom News* and asked who edited and wrote for it. Several hands went up in the audience. He said he was glad to see some of us actively writing for a committed publication, which he proclaimed every organisation dedicated to and inspiring change must have. But, he added, it was unnecessary to indulge in or offer any political rhetoric. The public we were trying to reach and encourage to accompany us in the movement for justice, equality and social and political rights would respond to experiences parallel to or evoking their own.

I was fascinated by the penetrating accuracy of his words. He was saying: devote the newspaper to the experiences that you as immigrants—black and Asian people—in this country have. He went on to describe how to practise this.

Pointing at a young man, he asked, 'What is it you do for a living?'

'I am a bus conductor,' the young man replied.

'Then why not write in this paper about what you experience in the garage and on your journeys at work from the public every day? Be specific and general. Say what happens to you in the garage, how you are seen and treated, and highlight some episodes of what you have experienced on the buses.'

C.L.R. turned to others in the room. Through some insistence of fate, he pointed at me.

'I am a schoolteacher,' I said.

'Then write what you see and what happens to you at school.'

Freedom News followed his guidance, and a broader section of the membership was now invited to share their experiences in life and work as write-ups for the newspaper. I began to write short pieces on events in the school I taught. I wrote about the black girl who was accused of stealing a pen and her protesting that she 'never trouble it!' And then, about the strike by the senior boys against the prescribed length of hair they could wear at school. Subsequently, about the black girl who had won an interschool prize for a painting of her family.

Probably the most dramatic piece I anonymously wrote, always in the form of a short narrative, was about the fifth-form disco at the end of term. I had been appointed head of English by this time. In that capacity, I was implored by my very friendly students to help them out. Mr Aggett, our new headmaster, appointed when Dr Helft resigned, had specified that they could have a disco if there were at least five teachers prepared to supervise it. I was able to persuade several of my colleagues to sacrifice their Friday night for duty's sake, and it happened; in fact, about fifteen teachers turned up.

Round ten at night while the disco was in progress, six boys from Brixton, not pupils of the school, pushed past the assistant school-keeper at the door to challenge a girl, who one of the intruders said was his girlfriend and was two-timing with some other lad from the school. A fight broke out. The lights came on, and the disco ended with school-keepers summoning the police and telling us all to go home.

When the cops did turn up, the pupils and the Brixton boys dispersed, and we fifteen teachers retreated to the staff room to regret the sacrifice of a Friday evening and to gather our coats and things on this last day of term. Someone suggested that we shouldn't admit defeat, and we collectively decided that we would continue the evening and drive to Camden Town to a club called Dingwalls, where we could drink and dance the night away.

We drove in three or four packed cars to the North London club, which was off the main road through a cobbled courtyard. Our company had perhaps eleven women and four men, and I shared dances with four or five of them, holding each other for some moments of a piece as was the convention of the day.

We left the club at three in the morning and were making our way to the cars when three burly men in suits accosted me on the cobbled yard. The men of our company had already gone home in their cars.

'Dancing with our girls? You think you're fucking Haile Selassie?' one of them said, obstructing my path to the car.

'They are not your girls, they are mine.' I said. 'I'm highly obliged, now get out of my way.'

The fellow didn't get out of my way. He swung his fist and struck me in the head. I grabbed him, and his two buddies joined in. The girls from our company got out of the cars and tried to join in the fight but were singly battered and flung aside.

I don't know how long the fight went on for, but a contingent of police arrived on the spot and stopped it. I was bleeding, but so was one of my assailants.

'If you're both bleeding, it's an equal fight,' the senior policeman said.

'Three against one you call equal?' one of the girls shouted.

The policeman shrugged. I felt dizzy and sank to the floor. The policeman said it was just a street fight and they weren't going to do anything about it.

The girls took me to the nearest hospital, where I was admitted with concussion. I stayed there four days.

I wrote the experience up in *Freedom News* but didn't include the racial assault at the club. The story was about the senior school disco.

An unexpected endorsement of the movement came in 1972 when a nominee for the Booker Prize for Fiction, the art critic, novelist and British Marxist John Berger announced that since the prize was sponsored by Booker McConnell whose sugar trade had exploited the Caribbean for centuries, he would, if he won, give half the prize money to the BPM. His announcement came out of the blue. He said he had read *Freedom News* and that the BPM was the one organisation closest to his idea of radical activism.

On the day the prize-giving was scheduled, Darcus and I, by prior arrangement with Berger, stationed ourselves, as delegated by the central core, in a pub called the Albany in Great Portland Street. Berger was going to drive over whether he won or not and, at the least, have a drink with us.

The prize-giving was televised, and Berger's novel *G* won. He came, followed by reporters and photographers who kept an immodest distance as we celebrated his win. He was ready with the cheque and asked to whom he should sign it. I said it had to be to my personal account as the BPM didn't have a bank account yet.

He signed over £2500, and we told him that the money would be turned immediately into a deposit on a property in which members could live and which could act as our North London base. The house in Islington we were using had been reclaimed by the lady who generously allowed us to occupy it rent-free for years while she was abroad.

John invited us to the celebratory party at a house of his friends in Primrose Hill. Darcus went his way, and I went with John. We walked in to cheers from his friends and fans.

The money was deposited with a mortgage company, and this enabled us to buy a Victorian house at 37, Tollington Park, in North London. Since Mala and I had regular jobs, the mortgage of the property was in our names, though we didn't pay the monthly dues as other members of the BPM, principally Altheia and Eddie, moved into the house and managed the mortgage together. The basement was rented out to Abdul, another member, and his family, and several single members, men and women, occupied rooms on the upper floors.

By then I was occupying a squat in South London in what was known in Brixton as the Front Line as it was where street drug-dealers encountered the police, who arrested or made corrupt deals with them. My architect friend Keith Cowling and I had worked for days with friends and other members of the BPM to make the squat, 74, Railton Road, habitable. We installed an operative kitchen and bathroom and created two decent flats, one floor for me and one for Keith.

I was not living with Mala anymore, as the politics of it all had entered our lives in a different way, and she and I had split up.

It was the era of assertion which, having begun with the Civil Rights Movement in the USA, soon turned into black power and 'people's power', turning radicals such as Malcolm X and George Jackson into advocates of a Marxist future, whether they called it that or not. It gave its impetus to immigrant communities from the ex-colonies of the British, French and Dutch empires to demand social equality and to politically agitate for it. It went hand in hand with the new wave of feminism, the inheritors of the suffragette mantle, which became a worldwide and powerful movement. In the British BPM, it gave rise to a 'women's collective', where the female members of the organisation would meet and come to their own determinations.

These determinations entered into the daily lives of Mala and me and then, inevitably, into our relationship and its assumptions, practices, loyalties and limitations. Round us, there was the assertion of women not belonging to men, of marriage being a hypocritical institution which had enslaved women since Adam and Eve, and ideological truths and contentions, which at first seemed to be theories to test the ether and then evolved into the possibilities of action.

Mala demanded equality in our relationship, which I never thought to be lacking, and then asserted that being married could not restrict a woman's choices and behaviour. It led to her attending parties thrown by friends she had made in the women's collective, some in far-off North London, and staying out nights, excusing herself at first by saying she missed the last train and later openly asserting, without any hint of it being a confession, that she was free to have any sexual liaisons she chose.

Of course, she said that the same applied to me and reminded me of the sentiments I had expressed in my earlier letters in my first year in Cambridge. There were all manner of arguments at home and a growing distance between us, till finally, perhaps mutually, we decided to separate after thirteen years of being together since we first met in college. She wanted me to move out so she could have her 'own space'. She was going for a break to India any way, she said, and this could be a testing time, a period away to see how things work out.

This is when I came to move out of our South Clapham flat and, coincidentally, found that the BPM needed someone to take over the Railton Road property, which Keith and I then fixed up.

By then, I had also been promoted to head of English. The previous head had resigned so she could run a chain of laundrettes with her lover, the deputy headmaster, or so the rumour went.

I had gone to India for the holidays. Not being able to get a flight in time for the next school term, I was a couple of days late. When I went to work, I was immediately waylaid by Mr Agget and informed that he had appointed a new teacher during my absence to fill in for another sudden resignation.

I met the new teacher in the staffroom when she returned from a class. We looked at each other, both of us trying to recall where we had met before.

'You're Ian Lamb's friend. You came to my flat in Notting Hill,' I eventually said, recognising her. Mala and I had shared a basement flat with Ian right after we had moved back from Leicester.

'Yes,' she said. 'I remember I came there with a few friends, and I sat in your room and argued over something. I'm Margaret Peacock, but everyone calls me Piki.'

As we worked together, I struck up a friendship with her, which evolved over the months into an open relationship. There was no need to call it an 'affair' as I wasn't with Mala by mutual consent. Neither was it in any sense a clandestine relationship. The zeitgeist was with the idea of consent and choice rather than patterned or traditional commitments.

It is impossible to say what makes people 'fall in love', though it is quite possible to trace the reasons they fall out of it. Both attraction and the subsequent atrophy of passion or respect are instinctive, though we can articulate reasons for the presence or growth of the latter. The idea that people see reflections of their future selves and some avenue of development for themselves, instinctive and elusive even, through contact with another person is perhaps the key. When this growth in a relationship stops, mutually or for either of the parties, the couple look for projects to engage themselves collectively in—the house, the child, the small or large enterprise, social or material.

Even while I was with Piki, in a non-conventional mode of commitment that both of us accommodated, I remained in deep friendship with Mala. Yes, the passion of the teenage romance had passed, but we understood each other, and to the end of her life, I would do almost anything if she needed me to. Despite her occasional bouts of bitterness, I know she would do the same for me.

The ground floor of the Railton Road building was to become the bookshop of the BPM—the Freedom News, named after the newsletter. Its glass front was cleaned up, shelves were erected, a proud sign announced the bookshop, and volunteer members operated the shop in rota; the movement was in biblio business. We did a deal with the local council Lambeth, which supported the idea of the bookshop and agreed to charge us only a nominal rent.

Some time after Keith and I moved in, a young black man, not a member of the movement but a friend of Eddie's, was allowed to occupy the basement. He would play the drums late into the night, and his single chant to a monotonous tune was 'Aaaaa ... free ... ka! Aaaaa ... free ... ka!' We didn't know his name because he would say, 'Jus' call me Afrika!'

One morning in the early hours when I was asleep on my mattress on the floor, Afrika knocked at the door.

'Faroot,' he said. 'How do I go to Manchester?'

I didn't think the question merited being awakened at two in the morning.

Nevertheless, propped up on my elbow, I said he could take a train from Euston station.

'Me 'ave a dream,' he said, echoing Martin Luther King. 'There's the best weed there. I goin'.'

'Go after six in the morning. There won't be any trains now,' I said.

Afrika was gone, and the next night, Keith didn't return from his girlfriend's flat.

Providence perhaps. At four the next morning, I felt like I was being smothered in my sleep. I opened my eyes and couldn't see, but the stinging in my eyes told me the room was full of smoke. I clambered through its thickness to the fireplace at the other end of the room to see if I had left the gas fire on. I hadn't, but I had to get out. I couldn't breathe. I dashed to the door leading to the staircase and attempted to open it. As I did, a roar of flames coming up the staircase hit me. I slammed the door and rushed to the window above my mattress and opened it. It was the first breath I had taken in all that time.

I grabbed my boxer shorts from where I had thrown them and climbed out of the window. Below me, the flames were storming out of the ground floor as the glass front of the bookshop exploded outwards with bangs and crashes.

An old woman standing on the pavement opposite shouted, 'Oh god! Oh god!'

The few seconds I hesitated standing on the ledge outside my window seemed a long time.

'Forget god, call the fire brigade,' I shouted and then decided to take a chance and jump. There was burning glass on the pavement and I might break a limb, but I had no alternative. I didn't jump straight away. I bent down, grabbed the ledge with my fingers and, hanging from it with my extended arms, lowered my body. This would cut the impact of my fall by eight feet.

I let go of the ledge and kicked the wall to get me as far as I could from the front of the building. I fell backwards onto the road, landing on burning glass and twisting my ankles, but I didn't break them.

The small crowd that had now gathered there—neighbours who had heard the explosion of the glass—pulled me by my arms to the opposite pavement. A neighbour brought me a coat, sat me up and draped it round me.

'I'm OK,' I said as people gathered round.

'Is there anyone else in the building?' a young neighbour asked. He seemed to be indicating that he would be willing to risk his life if there were.

'No one,' I said.

The fire brigade turned up and went to work hosing the building. Black smoke billowed out as they poured water.

I was sitting on the steps of the house opposite when the fire chief came up to me.

'You have enemies?' he asked.

'Not anyone I can name,' I said. At the time, I hardly felt the pain in my ankles and the agony from the burns on my feet. The shock may have overtaken everything else.

'We've called the police,' he said.

'Do you know how ...'

He had anticipated the question. 'Yes,' he said. 'Someone had thrown a fire bomb, a burning bottle of petrol, through the ground-floor glass.'

I remember wondering how he had concluded this so quickly.

I called Piki from the neighbour's phone. Someone had alerted the BPM members who lived three streets away in Shakespeare Road, and they now came running to me. Two of Piki's flatmates, who hadn't woken her up to tell her about the incident, came and picked me up in their car. None of the BPM members who had rushed to assist owned a car. The couple who shared Piki's house and had kindly hurried to where I was waiting, took me to St Thomas' Hospital, where the staff of the emergency department dealt with the now painful burns, tied my sprained ankles and gave me a pair of soft bedroom slippers.

Archbishop Temple's, the school where I taught, was situated in a park just across the road from St Thomas'. In an hour, I limped across in my underwear, wrapped in the coat I had been given and wearing the bedroom slippers over my blistered and burning feet, and got to school an hour before anyone turned up. I sat on the steps of the single-storey Victorian building till the school-keeper came to open the doors.

Barry Simner was one of the first teachers to turn up. My flat, clothes, books and records were all gone. Barry said he would take me to his flat on Lavender Hill right way and that I should stay there, rest for the day and use it as my home till I made other arrangements. The teachers gathered contributions and sent me three sets of clothes—jeans, trousers, shirts, underwear, socks, shoes and even a pair of pyjamas.

The next day when I insisted on going to school, the English inspector of schools brought a cardboard box with a record player and a voucher which would buy me at least ten albums of my choice, and said, 'We can't have a head of English without a record player.'

The kindness was overwhelming.

The police response was less so. They didn't bother to interview me. The next day, the newspapers reported the burning down of Freedom News in an item which said five black and Asian houses were fire-bombed in different parts of London that morning. There were no reported fatalities. One report said that a witness had seen a helmeted man on a scooter hesitate in front of my address round the time of the incident. Though the fire brigades claimed they were clearly cases of arson, no one was pursued or charged with the crimes.

The date stays significantly in my memory because it was the Ides of March.

BIG AS DE 'OUSE

Soon after, my commitment to and membership of the BPM was to come to an abrupt end. I was informed at short notice that an emergency meeting of the central core was to be held at Tollington Park.

Mala, who had been visiting India, had returned, and I moved back with her into our old flat in South Clapham till I could find alternative accommodation. We remained fast friends, though we were both aware that we had moved on from our relationship as a couple. I was seeing Piki, while Mala had cultivated a relationship with a fellow in Bombay who was a prominent environmental activist and campaigner. She told me all about the endeavours of his group to stop the government from building dams, which would ruin agricultural land owned by thousands of poor peasants. She wasn't anxious for me to move out, so I stayed there for several weeks before I moved into a flat with a friend in the same locality. Mala and I continued to stay in touch most days.

On the Sunday of the emergency meeting, we went together on the tube to the Tollington Park house. As we gathered and came to order, Eddie outlined the agenda of the meeting. This was to be a trial of Brian, a young member of the movement who occupied a room at the top of the house, for sneaking a white girlfriend into his room and having sex with her. Almost immediately, Brian was escorted into the room by a central core member. He was crying. Eddie said he was to be subjected to questioning about his behaviour and disrespect for the collective and 'exposed' to the community.

I was astounded and protested. What the hell was this about? Some kangaroo court on what was nobody's business but Brian's?

'He pays the rent, he hires the room, he has his private life, and he hasn't committed any crime,' I said.

'This is a commune and there have to be rules,' one of the core members said.

'It's not a commune, and what members of the movement do in their private lives is none of the movement's business. This is the central core of a political movement, and I won't participate in turning it into what is nothing but a punishment committee of a cult.'

I said my piece and walked out. Mala didn't walk out with me. Perhaps she agreed that Brian should be interrogated, punished, 'exposed' and expelled.

Walking down Tollington Park, I found a phone booth. I had promised to tell Darcus what the mysterious emergency meeting of the central core was about.

'Oh my god, oh my god,' he said. 'It's turned into its opposite!'

Darcus had picked up the notion that Marx had written somewhere that institutions turn into their opposites, doing what they set out to undo. I haven't come across this Marxian maxim but thought it was an appropriate observation.

I spoke to Mala later. She said she could see my point of view and would have walked out with me, but thought I had been hasty before hearing all the arguments. She joined Darcus, Barbara and me for a chat that evening.

Darcus said the movement had turned pseudo-religious, policing morals, and had to be destroyed. That was possibly melodramatic, but the four of us decided to formally leave and to make known to other members why we had chosen to.

Several members of the movement, individually and in groups, contacted us to ask us why we had dissented and quit. When we told them, they asked if we were setting up a dissident group. If so, some of them said, they would join it. Our leaving led to the disintegration of the BPM, which didn't have the strength or the organisation to continue any activity that could be called political.

Before the BPM fragmented, the movement had within it three opposing ideas of what the organisation should do. We had members and associates in several cities of Britain and contact with radical organisations internationally.

The central idea and the one that appeared to prevail was that the organisation was a distinct part of the British working class and ought to coordinate and organise into direct action the demands that the black communities had for equality, recognition and advance in employment and education, and resistance to the racism of British institutions across the board. It was or could be called a derivative Marxist perspective as opposed to a black nationalist and separatist one.

A second body of opinion wanted to convert the movement into a black self-help organisation, inspired by the example of the black Muslim separatists of the USA. These brothers and sisters would favour delivering breakfasts to poor children and old people.

The third section wanted us to turn into a militant organisation like the Irish Republican Army and raid banks and surreptitiously murder racists. One of the young men in this faction was Wesley Dick, of whom we would all hear about a few years down the line.

There were formal discussions at constituted forums between the leadership of the BPM and those who wanted to move our membership and efforts either towards social service or militant violence.

Social services, we argued, was the responsibility of the State, and we should campaign for their provision, not substitute for what the State should be doing.

To the militant camp we said that the IRA was engaged in a factional war for control of the State through religious allegiances, a war that had gone on for centuries. We had no such targets and could formulate no goal as immigrant workers in this country of claiming a separate State of Brixton and Handsworth in Birmingham, Moss Side in Manchester, Southall and Wembley in London, and I threw in Narborough Road in Leicester. The irony eluded the likes of Wesley Dick.

Having quit the BPM, Darcus, Barbara, Mala and I now discussed the possibility of setting up an alternative formation. Left-wing parties, and even right-wing ones all over the world, had a well-attested record of disagreements, splinters and splits. Yet, after years of active participation with these same members, it seemed daunting.

And what would happen to 37, Tollington Park, which Mala and I still nominally owned as per the formal mortgage papers?

A few days after I had made known that I was no longer a member of the BPM, Eddie, accompanied by Reginald Beckles, who fancifully called himself 'Shaka', and a fellow called Lloyd, who always reminded me of Dickens's Uriah Heep, came through the gates of Archbishop Temple's, openly carrying two large machetes. They asked some pupils in the playground to call me. By the time the bell rang for the end of the period and I went out to confront the trio, the news had gone round the school, and a bevy of students crowded excitedly round, anticipating some drama.

As I went up to the three to ask what they wanted, several of the senior boys of the school, most of them from white working-class estates and no strangers to confrontations, gathered behind. Eddie waved a piece of paper and said, 'Sign this or you'll see what we do.'

The paper was typed out, and if it was something Eddie had drafted, would be some benighted document purporting to transfer the ownership of Tollington Park to him.

'I think you should leave,' I said. 'I am not the sole owner, and I can do this after speaking to the lawyers. Now just go.'

Eddie pulled out the machete from under his arm and, though pointing it at the floor, shook it menacingly.

One of the lads behind me said, 'Shall we have them, sir?'

I gestured with my hand, forbidding any such thing.

'If twenty of us jump them, machete or no machete, they don't stand a chance. Peter's brought some fucking cricket bats,' the boy insisted.

'Don't talk rubbish. Get back,' I said. 'Please! Now!'

Someone in the school office had called the police, and two squad cars came screaming through the red-brick arches at the entrance to the compound, fifty yards from where we were. Eddie and gang hid their machetes and hastily moved in the other direction, walking through the park. The police jumped out of their cars, and four of them ran behind the trio and spoke to them, just as Mr Aggett and other teachers emerged from the building and ordered the children back to their classrooms.

I went to Mr Aggett's office and explained what had happened. He was more bemused than annoyed.

'You do get yourself into all sorts of scrapes, my boy,' is all he said, shaking his head.

In the weeks that followed our departure from the BPM, a revolution of sorts was taking place in an outfit called the Institute of Race Relations, which had its offices in a building off King's Cross and was led by a Sri Lankan called A. Sivanandan. With a small permanent staff and contributing writers, mostly academics, it published a quarterly periodical, *Race and Class*, and a monthly magazine, *Race Today*, which was financed by the World Council of Churches.

The editor of *Race Today* was a genial and gifted white British Anglican priest. Late in 1973, the predominantly black staff of this magazine collectively decided that it needed a new and more radical direction and a reputedly radical black editor. The founding and long-standing editor agreed with his staff that it was time for progress. He would voluntarily step down.

Some of the staff, notably Leila Hassan Howe, had been or were members of black activist organisations such as the Black Unity and Freedom Party, a group which had aims parallel to those of the BPM. The staff of the magazine invited Darcus to take on the post of editor, and he enthusiastically accepted.

The magazine was, under Darcus's editorship, clearly searching for a new direction with the ambition of being a national force, if not international. Darcus discussed the direction with those of us who had left the BPM with him and with C.L.R. James. For one of the first editions, he invited the US feminist and social activist Selma James, also C.L.R.'s wife at the time, to contribute a piece on sex, race and class.

Darcus commissioned me to write an overview of the black presence in British schools, not in any academic vein, but through the prism of my experience teaching in several London schools. This piece, published in early 1974 and titled 'Black Explosion in British Schools', attracted the attention of the national press, and for the first time in my life, I was invited onto TV news and current affairs shows to defend its radical contentions.

Darcus and the staff of *Race Today* determined to take the magazine in an 'activist' direction. They wanted it to report on what the new communities of Britain were politically, socially and culturally doing and to contribute to the organisation of that activity if needed. It meant that campaigning went hand in hand with reporting. This stance was at variance with the arguably sterile, academic approach of Sivanandan and his associates. Essays from universities and polytechnic institutes on the 'dialectics of class' and recondite arguments about the cultures of race might have had a function, but whatever the pretensions of its writers, they were contributing nothing to social and political change.

Apart from the ideological differences, there was the division of the grants which the World Council of Churches gave to the institute. Their representatives backed the new direction that *Race Today* was taking and allocated funds accordingly.

It had come to an impasse. Under the previous editor, Sivanandan had been used to dictating the stance and even the content of the magazine, something he couldn't do with Darcus in charge.

But it was more than a clash of egos. The institute was a factory for academic complaint. It assembled statistics about the evils of colonialism and was dedicated to an idea of blacks and Asians as victims of a racism that would or could never end. Darcus's vision was the opposite. Victimhood was the mantle of losers. We ex-colonials were here to stay and here to fight. He decided that the magazine had to sever all ties with the Institute of Race Relations.

Darcus asked me to drive him and two others in my dark-green, rattletrap, ex-post-office van to King's Cross at midnight. From the *Race Today* office, we emptied out and loaded into the van all the equipment, photocopiers, typewriters, library of books, stationery and everything else apart from the furniture and drove to Brixton.

At the time, the landlord of the flat I shared with my friend Andy wanted us out as he was moving his own family back into it. So we had moved into another squatted property on Railton Road. Every day, I would pass the dark skeleton of 74, from whose window I had leapt to escape the fire.

We stored the *Race Today* equipment we had pirated (or 'liberated' as some said) on the vacant ground floor of this new squat and, in a week or two, shifted it to a property further down the road, which a brave young activist called Olive Morris had negotiated for *Race Today*.

The next day, Sivanandan and crew turned up at King's Cross and found the magazine's office stripped.

During the three days of the British August bank holiday, the Notting Hill Carnival takes place. The West Indian community, in particular immigrants from the islands of Trinidad, Grenada and the eastern parts of the Caribbean, have established this as a national event in London. It entails the making of floats—small, cart-like vehicles. Companies of costumed players, under the aegis of an institution or a 'club', dance behind these themed floats on the streets, and a steel band bangs out tunes of popular songs and even movements of symphonies.

Darcus's friends and neighbours in Trinidad came down for the festival. One of his friends, known universally as 'Doctor Rat' because of his narrowing skull, sparse Rastafarian dreadlocks and long nose and chin, was staying in Darcus's house in Brixton. He hadn't been to Britain or indeed anywhere outside of Trinidad before this visit. He ventured out into the centre of London in his first days here, escorted by some members of the Race Today Collective. Then he refused to step out of the house for days.

When I turned up there and asked Leila, Darcus's partner, what our guests from Trinidad were doing, she said Doctor was still up in the guest room and refused to leave the house.

Why, I asked. Didn't he want to see the London sights?

'Upstairs. Ask him,' she said, shrugging.

I went up and indeed asked Doctor.

'Too much beasts,' he said.

Downstairs, I asked Darcus whether Doctor, the fierce warrior of the drug wars, who reputedly had a bullet still embedded in his spine, was afraid of the dogs he saw being walked on the pavements?

'No, man, Dhondy. When he says "too much beasts" he means white people!'

My mother too had come from India. In preparation for her stay, I had ventured to my local, second-hand furniture shop and bought a double mattress, loaded it on top of my car and set it up as her bed. The first night she was there, I heard her pacing about at two in the morning and got out of bed to see if everything was all right.

'The mattress is full of bugs, Farrukh,' she said.

I asked her to sleep in my bed, hauled the mattress onto the pavement and accommodated myself in the front room.

In the morning, I loaded the bug-crawling mattress on top of my car, the way it had arrived, and drove back to the shop. I unloaded the mattress on the pavement and told the proprietor that he had sold me a bug-ridden mattress and asked for a refund. He was a burly Cockney, backed by two other assistants of the same stature. Raising an eyebrow, he told me to fuck off, in these words. He wasn't taking the mattress back or returning what I had paid. His manner was quite aggressive, and I thought it best to cut my losses and leave.

I went that Saturday afternoon to the *Race Today* offices, as was routine. Darcus, Doctor Rat and the others from Trinidad were sitting round and, as they called it, 'liming'—meaning, as a later US generation would call it, hanging out. They asked what I had been doing, and I told them the story of the mattress.

'Le' we go, den!' said Doctor.

'There's three big guys in that shop,' I said.

''Ow big? Big as de 'ouse?' asked Doctor, standing up.

Five of us drove to the shop. The mattress was still on the pavement outside. Doctor, Darcus and the two others stepped out of the car as I parked. They sauntered up slowly to the entrance of the shop, their attitude meant to look menacing. The proprietor who had told me to fuck off came out.

'We come for the money,' Doctor said.

The shopkeeper spotted me and, looking at the array of black men at his door, was in an obvious funk.

'We've left it out there to clean it up, gentlemen,' he said. 'Ah, yes, yes, yes, the refund.'

I followed him to the till, and he gave me what I had paid.

Big as the house, indeed!

Archbishop Temple's was amalgamated with another school called 'St Michael's and All Angels' to become Archbishop Michael Ramsay's, and we moved into new buildings. In a freshly conceived structure by Mr Aggett, who was now the head of the amalgamated schools, alongside the English department, I was also made the head of the humanities faculty, which meant nothing much apart from feeling superior to the heads of departments such as history, geography, religious education and others.

Frustrated with the narrow perspectives of the teachers' unions at the time and their demands for wage increases, although legitimate and welcome but with no attention to or regard for the wider issues of education, some teachers, including Piki and me, formed an organisation called Teachers' Action.

The most militant union to which we all belonged was the National Union of Teachers (NUT), which had by far the largest membership within the profession but was fraught with leadership disputes and grabs from supposedly Stalinist and Trotskyist far-left parties. These enclaves of ideology constantly attempted to dominate the boring regional NUT meetings, which a few teachers bothered to go to, and get their members elected to decision-making posts. Their 'ideology' was all about the pay and working hours of teachers. They said nothing and seemed to care nothing for what schooling was about, why it had become a nationalised institution and where the voiceless pupils of our schools stood in the power equations of education.

Teachers' Action, which had some of the colleagues I had worked with and other like-minded teachers from schools in London and elsewhere, formed a central collective and published a magazine, also called *Teachers' Action*. Its central contention was that schooling was, in the Marxist matrix, the institution which produced the working classes, grading and giving them the skills appropriate to their futures. Of course, schools pretended to offer 'equal opportunity', by which they meant they supported a meritocratic view of class. The publication attempted, apart from carrying articles of ideas, to represent the realities of the school system. We explored the experience of pupils in their own words.

One of the articles that hit the headlines was about a lad, with a Nigerian father and an Irish Catholic mother, who was sent after an 'incident' from a comprehensive school to a school for children with 'special needs'—a euphemism for those who were perhaps neurodiverse. This lad, David, was interviewed by the magazine about his experience. He had thrown a bench in the art class at his teacher.

''E was gettin' on mah tits,' is how he described the provocation.

He was sent away, and he and his mother were summoned to the educational assessment unit, where they went through the child psychiatrist's diagnostic routine. David gave us his description of the encounter, which we published verbatim in *Teachers' Action*. It went:

'I went in with ma mom into the geezer's office, right? And he said, "Take mah hand." So I took his hand. Then he says, "Do de bricks," so I done de bricks. Then he says, "Right, you're mad, your whole family's mad."'

So, we asked him, 'What did you do, David?'

He said, 'Mah mom an I, we began to laugh, right, so he sent me to the idiot school.'

The assessment was probably a practical intelligence test and a written report days later, which may have said genetic factors were involved in what they diagnosed. However gentle and scientific the efforts of the doers, such was their perception of the done-to. This was one of the dimensions—the experiences of the schooled—that *Teachers' Action* sought to explore.

RIGHT TIME, RIGHT PLACE

On a day after school had just ended, a young man in a grey suit, directed to the staff room by the departing children in the playground, knocked at its door. One of my colleagues said I had a visitor, and I went to the door.

'Are you Farrukh Dhondy?' the well-groomed man asked.

'Does he owe you money?' I said.

'No, no, I just want to talk to Farrukh.'

'You're not from the police?'

He knew I was being frivolous, and I relented and asked him in.

'I'm Martin Pick, an editor at the publisher Macmillan, and I wanted a word with you.'

'With me? What about?'

He said he had over the previous year been buying copies of *Freedom News*.

'That stopped publication some time ago,' I said.

'Yes, but the stories you wrote about the school and the children you taught remained in my memory, and I've been trying to track you down.'

'How do you know I wrote them; they were anonymous.'

'I asked the fellows who sold the paper, and eventually one of them said they were written by a teacher. He only knew your first name. I knew there couldn't be many Farrukhs in Inner London schools, so I did my research. I was first directed to Tulse Hill

School and went there, and the English department fellows told me it was the wrong school, but they knew you and directed me here. So here I am, I've tracked you down.'

'Why?'

'Because we want to publish your stories,' he said. 'As a book.'

I didn't know what to say. I could hardly believe this was happening.

'Those pieces? As a book? But they are perhaps 500-words long, and there aren't enough of them, surely?'

'You could write some more. You see, we think, we know, there is an audience out there for what you won't mind me calling "multicultural literature", but there's no multicultural literature. We are convinced the readership exists, but the books don't.'

'Those were written for a purpose,' I said.

'They'll serve ours.'

I thought a bit and said, 'Would you be interested in my writing a book of entirely new, proper stories with literary, narrative structure, say?'

'For young readers, about young readers? Absolutely. We'd be delighted. When can you finish?'

'Wow, Macmillan! I can start tonight.'

He grinned. He had a charming, disarming smile.

'I asked when you could finish. When can you hand us the manuscript?'

He opened his briefcase and pulled out a thin file and from it a piece of paper.

'In case you said yes, I brought along the standard contract we offer to authors of this series.'

He handed the single-page contract to me. I was to give Macmillan, by a date which had been left blank, a manuscript of short stories. They would pay me £200 for the rights in perpetuity.

My hand was itching to reach for my pen to sign the deal.

'The date?' I asked.

'When do you think? Six months from now?'

That seemed a long time. Surely, I could write each story in three or four days and if I wrote perhaps six or seven ... I made a quick calculation. I could write six stories in a month, so I would ask for three.

We settled for four. I signed.

I wrote the stories. Martin and the editor of the Macmillan series, Aidan Chambers, professed themselves happy with them.

East End at Your Feet, named after the title of one of the six short stories in it, was published, and Martin was right. There was an audience for this genre of work. The book began to sell well.

Martin woke me with a phone call at seven-thirty one morning, saying there was a picket of parents, perhaps thirty or forty strong, outside a South London school protesting the use of the book in English lessons. Their banners said the book was obscene and ought to be banned.

'The newspapers are down there,' he said.

'Shall I get down there and check it out? Maybe argue with them?'

'For god's sake, no!' he said.

'All publicity is surely good publicity. It'll increase sales.'

'I'm not sure it will.'

Obscene? The only word they could possibly object to was the inclusion of a line from a Rolling Stones song which went, 'You're a starfucker, starfucker, starfucker, star!'

The next day, the *Daily Telegraph*, the nation's right-wing broadsheet, wrote an editorial attacking the book and advocating its withdrawal from schools. The teachers of the school at which the protest had taken place issued a statement saying they would continue to use the book in classes.

A television chat show rang me up that day and asked if I would appear with William Deedes, the editor of the *Daily Telegraph* who had written that editorial. I agreed and armed myself with the discovery that the person who instigated the picket in Kidbrooke was the parliamentary candidate for the neo-fascist, anti-immigrant party the National Front. I couldn't believe that a national newspaper was unaware of the fact, but certainly believed that the *Daily Telegraph*, even if they were aware of it, wouldn't have publicised it.

Throughout our exchange, Deedes attempted to patronise me before the cameras. He had a peculiar snobbish accent with idiosyncratic pronunciation, which the satirical magazine *Private Eye* regularly parodied, featuring him as a character worthy of ridicule. His speech was easy to parody as he pronounced even his own name as 'William Deedishsh', and the phrase the *Private Eye* attributed to him when correcting some journalist's error was 'Shurely, shome mishtake?'

Even having read this parody of Deedes for years, I was unprepared for his saying: 'My dear fellow, itsh shurely a queshun of balansh!' in response to something I had said.

I didn't catch on, until he held out both his hands, palms upwards, in a demonstration of weighing scales. I got it. He was indulging his conceit to say 'balansh' instead of 'balance'.

It appeared that his editorial, I said, supported the stance of a National Front candidate, who would certainly have some antipathy to a book of short stories about black and Asian teenagers, regardless of the fact that I had quoted a line with the F-word from a Stones song.

Aidan and Martin called me two weeks after the book was launched and said it was being republished in a second edition and then probably several others. When was I writing the next one? That too came as a surprise.

If I was to write another, I thought, it ought not to be an extension of the first—more stories of a similar sort (was it a question of 'balansh'?). There was a world of my own observations and experiences to explore. The one that came to mind was the incident in 1975, about a year and a half after I had left the BPM.

The incident was named, by the national media, the Spaghetti House Siege. On 28 September, three black men, one carrying a sawn-off shotgun and the other two wielding pistols, walked into the Spaghetti House restaurant in Knightsbridge, where one of them had previously worked. They knew that at that hour the managers of the other London branches of Spaghetti House would gather there with the week's takings to deposit them in the safe of the parent branch.

The gang demanded the week's money and announced to the customers, workers and management of the restaurant that they were being held hostage till the briefcase with the money was handed over to them, with an assurance of safe passage in a plane to Algeria.

One of the managers of the Knightsbridge branch was not in the room where the hostages were being held and managed to get out of a rear fire escape and call the police, who arrived in a matter of minutes and surrounded the restaurant.

The desperadoes, under immediate threat of a confrontation with the police, herded their hostages into a basement room and barricaded it. They were thrown a walkie-talkie so the police could communicate with them, and they said they would kill the hostages if their demands weren't met. They wanted to go to Algeria because the fugitive US Black Power radical Eldridge Cleaver had sought refuge there when he was about to be arrested and prosecuted in the USA.

Wesley Dick, one of the three hostage takers, had been a member of the BPM, and I had had several conversations with him, friendly and argumentative. The other two gunmen were radicals who had moved in and out of the black organisations of the day.

While the siege was on, a police officer called me and said he knew I was a leading member of the BPM and that I had argued against the sort of action that my pupil and acolyte Wesley Dick was involved in. I said that Wesley was not my pupil or acolyte and I just knew him as a member of the BPM, which was a legal and sensible organisation. He asked if I knew the two others. I said I didn't and that my contact with Wesley was at least two years old. He enquired if I would agree to speak to the hostage takers and ask them to surrender. I was being told to use my supposed authority, as a former political mentor, to sit in a police van and persuade Wesley that he and his companions were politically mistaken in what they were doing.

I told the policeman that I had no such authority and that Wesley and the others would have nothing but contempt for my opinions if I approached them with a police-sponsored plea on a police walkie-talkie. I added that I was certain my intervention would be counterproductive as the likes of Wesley had always been at odds with my point of view. The cop said he understood what I was saying and would call me again if the circumstances changed.

The demands of the gang were ignored, and the siege lasted nine days, when finally the police invaded Spaghetti House and freed the hostages. The three militants were tried and jailed.

This episode, in the short history of this phase of black radicalism in Britain, was, in a fictionalised form, the story of my second book. I titled it *The Siege of Babylon* and dedicated it to the Race Today Collective, who seemed resentful that I was making my way as a published writer. Not one of them acknowledged the dedication or admitted they had read the book, if they had. I was taken aback by the studied indifference but decided that my participation in the collective was more important than my disappointment at not being acknowledged by my closest associates.

IN THE BEGINNING WAS THE WORD

Why does anyone want to write?

George Orwell asked himself this question and answered it in his famous essay 'Why I Write': 'I do not think one can assess a writer's motives without knowing something of his early development. His subject matter will be determined by the age he lives in … but before he ever begins to write he will have acquired an emotional attitude from which he will never completely escape.'

He goes on to say that the motivations for writers may differ in their proportions but they are basically: sheer egoism, aesthetic enthusiasm, historical impulse and political purpose. He could have added the need to earn some money, but he didn't descend to this, perhaps because materialism wasn't ever part of his noble psyche.

In some proportion, all of the above apply to me, so let me count the ways.

In my case, it was not having any other means to draw attention to myself or show off. Not being good at sports, telling stories, using words and cultivating techniques to make them alluring became a subconscious ambition.

I spoke Gujarati, Marathi of sorts, Hindi and English by the time I was five. The first three of these I grew into naturally, and though I can't assess the proportion or ratio of usage of one or the other in the multilingual household and world of my childhood, I don't think I ever confused one with the other. I do remember, though, learning to write each of them. At the age of four, for example,

I recall Miss Chinoy, my primary school teacher, instructing us on the rule that adding an 'e' at the end of a word changed the preceding vowel to its capital sound. So 'tim' became 'time' and 'rat' became 'rate'.

When at the age of seven I came back to Poona from Madras with my sister, our parents decided that it was time to get us to learn written Hindi. A tutor came to the house twice a week, seated us round a table on the front veranda and made us write the phonetically spelt words from the alphabet and table of verbs of the Devanagari script.

I began to write bits in English for the school magazine at the age of nine or so. The magazine was a cyclostyled rag called the *Mitreite* and mostly written by the masters of Bishop's because the pages had to be filled, but I submitted accounts of funny episodes and occurrences in the daily life of the school, which were gratefully accepted.

In my teens, I wrote verses for the Nowrosjee Wadia College magazine, submitting them to Miss Katy Shroff, the editor. The only one I remember was called 'Symphony in Steel', about the creaking of machines in one of Poona's small but rusty and noisy ice factories in the middle of our neighbourhood. I couldn't have been fastidious about accuracy as the machinery was certainly wrought iron and not steel, but the alliteration was compelling, and 'Symphony in Wrought Iron' would have seemed too prosaic.

When I was sixteen and in college, a businessman of our town started a newspaper to rival the *Poona Daily News*. It was named the *Poona Herald*, and its editor was a Goan gentleman called Able David. They put out the word that they would be interested in recruiting part-time reporters, presumably college students proficient enough in English to write simple reports. I applied, was interviewed in the first-floor offices of the *Herald* by Neelkanth Jadav, a young Maharashtrian who was the assistant editor, and was given an assignment to test my abilities. It was to do with a police boxing tournament to be held that night.

I cycled to the hilltop venue to report on it and submitted my piece by midnight. The editors professed themselves pleased. I was paid ten or so rupees and hired as a part-timer.

The other college-going part-time reporter hired by the *Herald* was Dileep Padgaonkar. Dileep was at the academic and 'serious' Ferguson College, having been to St Vincent's School, a Jesuit school with high academic standards and dedicated to educating the male population of the town. Whereas most of the pupils of Bishop's were from prosperous families, very many of the pupils of St Vincent's were poor. The record of achievement however speaks. St Vincent's produced high-level professionals, politicians and national figures much more so than our school. Although Dileep and I had been acquaintances during school days, it was while we were both part-time reporters for the *Poona Herald* that we became friends. Our assignments, for which we were paid by the column-inch, were carried out on our bicycles, with writing pads and pens in our pockets, and on most days we compared notes about the copies we had filed.

Then the Profumo scandal broke in England. John Profumo, a Conservative minister for defence, was using the services of a sex worker called Christine Keeler, who was also the professional lover of the naval attaché of the Russian embassy in London. Christine's pimp was one Stephen Ward, a self-styled osteopath who was the centre of these controversial arrangements. Ward was reported to have served in India during the Second World War.

That triggered an idea. Dileep and I speculated on the possibility that he could have been injured in his service in Burma and sent, as many soldiers were, to Poona Military Hospital. We cycled to the hospital, identified ourselves as the press and searched the records of war-time patients. We found several soldiers by the name of Ward, but none of them, disappointingly, called Stephen or even S. Ward.

It was, I protest, entirely my idea to proceed with a report of Captain Stephen Ward's confinement in the Poona Military

Hospital. Dileep and I shared the responsibility for the picturesque detail of the report, which included a nurse who recalled how flirtatious he was and attempted manoeuvres on the female staff. The report was given pride of place in the *Herald*'s pages.

The next day when Dileep and I cycled to the *Herald* office in East Street, a relatively quiet street in the central cantonment area, we saw several cars parked outside—an unusual scenario. One of the cars was an Oldsmobile convertible, and a tall, bulky gentleman with a handlebar moustache stepped out of it on seeing us and accosted us, asking if we were Dileep and Farrukh. We said we were. In a commanding voice, he introduced himself as Captain Colabawalla from the *Blitz* newspaper, Bombay's bestselling scandal sheet.

He invited us to ignore the others, presumably representatives of national newspapers, and to get into his car. His inducement was to wave two hundred-rupee notes about. I had never seen one before. He put one in my shirt pocket and gave the other to Dileep.

We got into the car. He said he wanted us to sign over our article to his newspaper, and he would give us the appropriate contract when we got away from 'the vultures'. We saw our advantage and asked him to drive through Mahatma Gandhi Road, where we would be seen riding in style in the open-topped Oldsmobile by friends and the public.

He drove us up and down, and we waved to our astounded friends, who were loafing round as they did every evening. Captain Colabawalla then produced the simple contract. We said we were hungry and a Chinese meal would be appropriate. He was more than willing, and we stopped outside Kamling, Poona's only Chinese restaurant.

The article appeared in *Blitz*, and I vaguely recall that it carried Colabawalla's byline, who had elaborated our story even further.

Such was Dileep's and my first big step in journalism. I went on to study in the UK, and Dileep, who spoke and wrote French from his schooldays, went on to study at the Sorbonne. We met during our holidays in London and Paris, and Dileep, on returning to India, joined the *Times of India* and eventually became its chief editor. In our European days, he was my guide to French films and wine. He never lost the ideals of liberty, equality, fraternity and the Indian secular ideal. I miss him.

I have lived with the suspended and even slightly amusing guilt of having misled Dileep, the future editor-in-chief of the *Times of India*, into the dishonest journalistic escapade about Stephen Ward being in Poona. Partly to tell a funny story and partly to assuage this guilt, I wrote about our fabrication in a memorial tribute to Dileep in a weekly column I write for the *Asian Age*. I insisted that he was Faust and I the devil, though we both profited from the invention.

Lo and behold, I received two emails in response to my column, one from my old and great friend Adil and the other from the distinguished cricket commentator and writer Gulu Ezekiel. They both said the same thing. Stephen Ward was indeed in Poona at the time we had claimed he was. He wasn't at the hospital as he hadn't been wounded in active service, but he was using his skills as an osteopath.

Both Adil and Gulu directed me to biographies of Stephen Ward, one of which claimed that the English establishment had framed him and that he didn't do what the newspapers had libelled him with. In Poona, it seems, he went to the nature-cure clinic of Dinshaw Mehta. It was perhaps at the clinic or elsewhere that he was apparently brought into the presence of Mahatma Gandhi. It was Gandhi's day of fasting and silence, the story goes, but on being introduced to Ward, he excused (or 'recused', as we Indians say!) himself from the vow of silence and said, 'It's refreshing to be introduced to a British officer who hasn't come to arrest me.' Ward's biographers claim that he went on to treat Gandhi's neck for stiffness. Much more interesting and real than our gossipy fabrication.

As I have said earlier, those five months in Delhi when I was in between colleges was a time of intense, if indiscriminate, reading. I read everything from volumes of Lenin's collected works to almost all the novels of D.H. Lawrence, the travelogues in the Mediterranean by Durrell, the works of Charles Dickens and very many more. As with my earlier reading at the Albert Edward Institute, I had no idea that there existed a body of academia called literary criticism which distinguished between books, writers and their achievements and pointed out how poems or other writing 'worked'. I was, of course, aware from reading a few Shakespeare plays at school that his writing was considered a class apart from any other, but I was unaware that novels were diligently divided into the high, middle and low-brow or the worthy and the merely popular.

I was certainly aware that the Erle Stanley Gardner series of books about the lawyer-detective Perry Mason or the Westerns I had borrowed from the Punjab Bookstore on Main Street in Poona, written by Zane Grey and Max Brand, shouldn't be compared to Hardy or Lawrence, but that was the extent of my gradation of literature.

Durrell's *The Alexandria Quartet* was full of words I hadn't come across, like 'palimpsest' and 'obsidian', and I would note these down mentally and diligently look them up in the university library's dictionaries the next day. If Durrell could write this fascinating and layered story with its tricky play on chronology and set it in Eqypt, why couldn't I do the same for a narrative of equal complexity set in Bombay? Durrell was stylishly English. Would anyone read such a book by an unknown Indian?

Was it Durrell who tipped the balance in my head between a profession and an impossible ambition?

Back in Poona, happy to rejoin the friends I had left and completely engaged with the physics and even the math and chemistry I was studying, I came across a book that changed things. I say came across, but it was famous—or rather, from the reception it received from my professors and from the newspapers, questionably infamous. It was called *An Area of Darkness* by one V.S. Naipaul.

This wasn't an English or even European name. The book was in English—a very personal journey and discovery of India by a Trinidadian of Indian descent. I read it avidly. So, Indians could write famous books. They could even perhaps write the *Bombay Trilogy* or the *Quartet*.

As I read, I realised that the writer was telling the truth about things that were evident but had not been put into words before. The book noticed and made much of the fact that Indians excreted everywhere—in the fields, on the streets, by the railway lines. More devastatingly, Naipaul told stories of Indians suffering from double-think, holding contrary universes in their heads simultaneously, as when a nuclear scientist calls astrologers to predict the most auspicious day for his daughter's wedding.

The book was critically received. India was wounded by the truth. In the days of the Raj, British and American writers had written travelogues and books about their findings in the country. The most infamous of these was *Mother India* by the American historian Katherine Mayo, in which she noted the degradations of caste and poverty. Her critics claimed that she had been sent at the height of the movement for independence and as part of a conspiracy by the British to prove to the world that Indians were not ready to govern themselves and would descend into barbarism if given their freedom from the benevolent British rule.

Critics of Naipaul compared his work to Mayo's. They wrote books and essays denouncing him. The nationalist orthodoxy either blamed the rule of the Raj for exploiting India and causing its debasements or turned its face away from the degrading spectacles of poverty, injustice and superstition. Here was a voice with no tinge or taint of the Indian nationalism and could look beyond the patriotic mirror. I thought every observation Naipaul made was justified and were truths every reader should acknowledge, but I kept my mouth shut or, at any rate, only mentioned my approval of the book where it wouldn't cause a rift in friendship.

The fact that an 'Indian' writer who was not Gandhi, Jawaharlal Nehru or Rabindranath Tagore could venture into this territory was a boost to my considerations of being a writer. But I didn't want to write like Naipaul. I wanted to invent the kind of web of intrigue that Lawrence Durrell wove. The ambition would have to wait—and through the waiting, change, evolve or disappear.

It's only with hindsight I realise that the desire, however naive at the time, for social revolutionary change in my growing years was entwined with the ambition to be a writer. They were two strands of realisation and activity which came together like the double helix of DNA. There wouldn't be one without the other.

And again, it is looking back at events that forces my realisation that the political convictions I acted on gave rise to and created opportunities for writing and being published. These political convictions led to experiences that formed the subject and substance of several writings, those which prompted the editors of journals and then of a publishing house to tolerate and invite my writing.

The convictions towards 'leftish' thoughts began early. Perhaps they began in revolt against the Zoroastrian religious tradition which required the suspension of understanding. Let me explain.

The Parsi prayers one is taught to repeat by heart in order to undergo the Zoroastrian investiture or thread ceremony—the Navjote—are in the Avestan language, and no Parsi child even vaguely understands what they mean. Neither do the adults who teach these. The language has been painstakingly translated over the centuries, and yet there is no definitive version of the prayers we offer. We are told it's our conversation with god and necessary for preserving life and good thoughts, words and deeds.

I was inducted into the religion at the early age of seven, because my sister, with whom I shared the ceremonial and joyous induction, was nearing nine. Girls were to be presented for the ceremony before the onset of puberty as the families didn't want priests touching the pubescent breasts of young girls during the rituals.

I still believed in god then; it had been drummed into me. But something seemed wrong with the world. In Madras, every day on the way to school, we passed destitute people who lived on pavements. Some, like Mr Wokoo, suffered from leprosy without hope of any help or a cure. There was abject poverty all round. It was apparent that there were very many who went hungry and had almost nothing. Then there were the taboos. Even in our by-and-large liberal household, my grandmother assigned mugs and metal plates to the domestic workers in our house. They were not to put their lips to our cups. And the workers accepted this as the natural order.

There were other trivial observations, which nevertheless weighed down on my growing mind.

In my grandad's house in Poona, the cook Hukam Ali would spend the mornings buying fresh produce from the meat and vegetable markets and bring the stuff home for the family's lunch and dinner. On some days, I noticed two or three ragged-looking children standing at our gate, having followed Hukams from the market.

'Why are they following you and why are they hanging around outside?' I asked Hukams.

'They saw me buying bhindi, Farrukh, or maybe French beans, and they are waiting for me to start preparing the food.'

'Why?'

'Because they want the tops and tails that I chop off from the bhindi or the beans. Instead of chucking them in the garbage, I give them those bits, and they take them back to their families to cook and eat.'

He deliberately chopped larger bits of tops and tails, he said, so they could have more of the vegetable, while our family wouldn't notice any missing bhindi in a vegetable medley.

Through observations and experiences like these, a vision of this imperfect, disappointing world grew. With it grew the idea, though it was never at that tender age formulated as such—call it an inclination—that this poverty and degradation were connected somehow to the belief in the irrational, in the superstitious, which abounded all round. I was ripe for recruitment into a faith, a new way of seeing the world, an ideology.

In a partitioned house about twenty yards down from ours lived Aspi Khambatta, the first part of his name a short form for the very Parsi Zoroastrian name Aspandiar.

In the 1930s, the Khambattas, Aspi's mother and her husband, had owned and run a bookshop called the English Book Exchange. It was a thriving business patronised by the British officers and by Indians interested in English reading. The Khambattas had a son and a daughter and were expecting another child. The boy was born to Mrs Khambatta, but her husband and mother-in-law took one look at the new-born baby and disowned it. The infant had fair skin, blue eyes and blonde hair. Mr Khambatta said he had suspected all along that she was having an affair with a British sergeant who frequented the English Book Exchange under the pretence of a love for literature. It was obviously his child that his wife had given birth to.

Mrs Khambatta denied the charge. It was her husband's baby, she insisted. She had never been with another man. The evidence against her assertion was the new-born's clearly European or mixed-race features. Mr Khambatta threw his wife out of the house, and she came to live in the two rooms of the partitioned building opposite our house on Sachapir Street.

The central rooms in the same partitioned house were occupied by the Cama family and the third division on the other side of the Cama's three rooms by Mr Hodywalla, who made a living showing films to indoor and outdoor gatherings on a mobile projector and screen.

Mrs Khambatta named her allegedly mixed-race child Aspandiar and brought him up on her own in abject circumstances. Her older son and daughter, it was said in the neighbourhood, visited her and kept her and their half-brother alive. How else could she have survived, no one knew, though there was a rumour that some money trickled in through compassionate and possibly guilty transfers from a very-married army sergeant in Britain.

When Aspi was nearing ten, Mrs Khambatta arranged for his Navjote. A priest performed the ceremony in the front room of the tiny accommodation, but a demonstration of a few score Parsis, instigated by Mr Khambatta, gathered outside with black flags to denounce the boy as a non-Parsi and to stop the ceremony.

My grandfather, who was trained as a Parsi priest and was of ultra-liberal views, watched from our veranda the hubbub of protest as the ceremony progressed. He believed that anyone of any parentage could be inducted into the Zoroastrian faith. It wasn't a matter of blood; it was a matter of belief. But Grandpa was in the progressive, ignored minority.

Mrs Khambatta, known as 'Bootki', meaning 'shorty' in Gujarati, led a sad existence. She would visit neighbours before dinner time and wait to be invited. My aunts, whom she visited on these rounds, would not only invite her to eat at their table but also pack cooked food for her and Aspi's next meal. Other neighbours may have done the same.

I encountered Aspi, the unusual-looking Parsi, when he began gathering four or five of us lads from the neighbourhood. I was twelve or thirteen years old then, and Aspi was eight or so years older than me. He wanted to preach 'communism' to us. He didn't quite define what this term was but said it would abolish superstition and poverty and usher in equality and prosperity in the country. I was willing to listen. He was eager to tell us who Karl Marx was and what he had said about the future of the world. It was the first time I had encountered such an all-embracing idea.

Aspi was a charismatic eccentric. He rode a bicycle whose brakes had fallen off, and so he stopped it by putting his foot on the front tyre. He never had any money and would join us for a cup of tea, for which one of us would pay in exchange for an ideological discussion. We were willing to enter into this bargain so as to listen to the conclusions that Lenin came to after the Eighth All-Russia Congress of Soviets. Not that we understood a word of it, but it sounded like the sort of discourse that would set us apart from the uninitiated, and it always promised to be fascinating. The more contemptuous neighbours, knowing that Aspi preached to the younger lot, dubbed him 'Jesus Christ'.

He used to come to our house to take the daily newspapers every mid-morning, after my grandfather would have perused them. Aspi was studying politics and economics to sit for the recruitment exam for entry into the prestigious Indian Administrative Service. He passed the exam with distinction and was assigned the deputy collector of a district in Maharashtra, with a salary which made him bold enough to send his mother to our house to ask for my sister Zareen's hand in marriage.

My aunts, who received the proposal, thought this was a joke. Shera masi called Zareen and said, 'Jesus Christ wants to marry you!' My sister considered Aspi a figure of fun and far from a potential husband, and so poor Mrs Khambatta was sent away from the house with a contemptuous rejection.

Aspi used his new-found position of authority to attempt revenge on those whose wealth he grew up envying. He walked into Dorabjee's, a prominent Parsi-owned grocery store—the equivalent, or even first, of the later supermarkets—and accused them of stocking smuggled goods. He had called the police to carry out arrests, but the coppers who were in the pay of the owners had alerted the store about the imminent raid, and there were no smuggled foreign goods to be confiscated as evidence.

In a few years' time, after I had left India, I was informed that Aspi had been sent on an Indian Civil Service delegation to America to represent Indian trade unions and had defected, married an American dentist and become a citizen there.

Many years later, when I was a commissioning editor at Channel 4, I received a long letter from Aspi. He introduced himself, recalled our firm association in those childhood years and went on to tell me that he was now a born-again Christian and had changed his name from Khambatta to Come Better.

The letter went on to say that since I now commissioned TV programmes, he would like to propose a documentary about Satan walking the earth, firstly in the guise of Hitler, then in the avatar of Yasser Arafat, and lastly and contemporaneously in the person of someone I'll call Joe Bloggs, who was, the letter went on to explain, the leader of a rival born-again Christian cult in his town in Minnesota. The letter also said that his mother and sister had joined him in America and were all dedicated to being born-again Christians. I replied saying I was happy to hear from him but the documentary proposal about the three incarnations of Satan didn't convince me.

That Aspi had strayed from the straight and narrow, or even broad and labyrinthine, communist commitment and into the nonsense of an American Christian cult didn't come as an absolute surprise. I have no way of tracing the trajectory of that conversion but am sure that the early commitment to an ideology of egalitarianism and revenge on the bourgeoisie arose out of the struggle against poverty and his mother's attempt to preserve some pride against her abject circumstance. How he was elevated to his second birth as a cult Christian I can only guess.

Nevertheless, it was Aspi who, back in Poona, pointed my curiosity in the direction of reading Marx and even bits of Lenin and Stalin. The communist parties of India, which seemed bureaucratic and stubbornly short-sighted about Stalin's murderous historical contribution, never impressed me enough to seek membership. It was much later, after my years at Cambridge and Leicester, that I came to the conclusion that a proper reading of Marx and Engels would lead one to infer that a predominantly peasant, feudal society can't be converted through an armed insurrection into a socialist one. The peasantry has to be converted, however painfully, into a proletariat with nothing to sell but their labour power.

Lenin and Mao's revolutions were historically inevitable and initially inspiring, but in no sense did they lead to or even open the door to the communism that Marx describes. Succeeding Lenin by murdering other comrades, Stalin slaughtered millions of Russians to set up a State-capitalist, imperial enterprise. China, through precisely the pressures of the productive process which Marx and Engels describe, has become the most powerful State-controlled capitalist country in history.

These convictions and understanding came to shape my political thought and actions, and through them, my writing.

HOUSES FOR MR AND MRS BISWASES

The new *Race Today* rapidly established itself and soon had thousands of subscribers. The Race Today Collective was founded round the magazine and the political initiatives we undertook from 1974 onwards. The collective was predominantly black and Asian but had white members too. Some worked as the permanent staff of the magazine, while others who had employment elsewhere, such as myself, attended meetings, submitted articles and assumed other responsibilities.

One morning, the offices received a phone call from a Bangladeshi gentleman who, in faltering English, asked if we were the people who assisted Asians. The colleague who attended the call said we weren't quite that and asked why he was calling and what assistance he required.

He said he lived in a house with other Bangladeshi immigrant workers and that they had been unjustly threatened with eviction by some men who said they were from 'the government'.

Darcus referred the call to Mala and me, and we decided to go down to the East End address the caller gave us and find out what was going on.

The East End of London, principally the Borough of Tower Hamlets, through the late 1950s and throughout the 1960s and early 1970s, had been settled by what were East Pakistani immigrants, whose country was, after a revolutionary war in 1972, called Bangladesh.

It was historically a poor working-class area, neighbouring the prosperous business district of the City of London. It had experienced waves of immigration, from Europe at first. In the mid-eighteenth century, the Huguenots, fleeing religious prosecution in France, settled in the East End and brought with them the expertise and even the capital to set up a silk trade. In Brick Lane, the centre of the immigrant East End, they constructed their weaving factories and built a church. The silk factories gave way to textiles in the nineteenth century when the Huguenot population, through growing prosperity, moved out to more affluent parts of London and Britain.

The settlement of Jews from Eastern Europe, again fleeing from persecution, progressed from the time of Oliver Cromwell in the seventeenth century through the early twentieth century and the rise of Nazism. The poor Jews who settled in the East End worked in sweatshops manufacturing cloth and leather garments. The church in Brick Lane was converted into a synagogue.

In the late 1950s, the immigrants from East Pakistan began to displace the Jewish workers, and very rapidly, the sweatshops of Spitalfields and Bethnal Green became the exclusive preserve of East Pakistani labour.

The Jewish synagogue was consecrated as a mosque. The community, most of which came from the rural district of Sylhet in East Bengal, worked almost exclusively in the rag trade and in 'Indian' restaurants as cooks, waiters and bottle washers. They had no access, at the time, to housing on the council estates, which were owned and administered by the local Tower Hamlets Council or by the Greater London Council (GLC) and were almost exclusively occupied by white working-class families.

Mala, Leila Hassan and I went that evening in 1976 to find the address we had been given. It was off the Whitehorse Road, where the single-storey brick terraces on either side were boarded up, their windows and doors barred with plywood. It was a desolate street with only one door of a house in the centre accessible. We knocked at it.

The gentleman who had called us came out. Several men peered over his shoulder as he talked to us on the doorstep.

The front room into which we were ushered had four beds. We soon learnt as we sipped tea, through questioning and through the eagerness of the men to explain their problem, that twelve of them occupied that house. They were all workers in the rag trade.

They had each contributed a sum and bought the house from a Bangladeshi official called Abu Bhuiya of the local Community Relations Council. It had been in a decrepit state when they purchased it, and Bhuiya had sent in his partner, a West Indian named Farron, to fix the toilets, kitchen and other basics. But the workers had been taken by surprise when, a few days ago, some officials of the GLC had knocked on their door and told them that they were squatting in property that belonged to the GLC, as did all the houses in that terrace. The officials asked them to vacate the premises forthwith as the entire terrace of the uniformly built one-block houses was to be demolished. When the Bangladeshis protested that they had bought the house from Bhuiya, they were told that the property had never belonged to anyone but the GLC.

I asked to see any evidence they had of the purchase of the house from Bhuiya. One of the men went to his trunk and brought out a piece of paper which said something to the effect that they had contributed a sum to Bhuiya's charitable foundation and that this also covered the costs incurred by Farron in carrying out repairs to the property. The men hadn't got it checked by anyone as Bhuiya was a respected member of the Bangladeshi community and an official of the government. We promised the men to get in touch with Bhuiya.

When we did, Bhuiya was evasive. He said the money was for the repairs he had helped them to contract from Farron. We tracked Farron down, who said he was paid to do a job and that's what he had done. He knew nothing about the sale of the house. It was a clear confidence trick.

We published a story in *Race Today* accusing Bhuiya of fraud and of blatantly cheating his fellow immigrants and taking advantage of their illiteracy in English, despite being an official of the Community Relations Council. Bhuiya threatened to sue us for libel, and we jauntily replied that we would love to encounter him in court. We followed up by publishing in the next issue more details of the fraud. Bhuiya didn't return the money as we had demanded but disappeared from the East End. Perhaps he returned to Bangladesh fearing criminal prosecution for fraud.

On behalf of the occupants, we got in touch with the GLC and explained the situation. Speaking to a bureaucrat in their Housing department, it became clear that the council wanted to erase the terrace and possibly sell the land which, in its proximity to the City of London, was fast increasing in value. We petitioned the elected politicians of the GLC: Would they rehouse these occupants, who had been cheated out of their hard-earned money, in council property? The answer was a clear no.

On an afternoon, when the GLC brought in a force of officials, or bouncers, to evict the occupants, perhaps five of us, the members of the Race Today Collective, determined to be present.

At the time, we were naively unaware of the laws governing the squatting of houses. As the arguments between us and the officials of the GLC proceeded on the pavement, a burly, young Irishman passed by on the opposite pavement. When he enquired and was told what was going on, he confronted the GLC officials.

'What do you think you're doing? You can't evict these fellows; they are squatting and legal occupants of the house.'

We were struck by this. He went on to explain as much to us as to the GLC bods, 'If you are caught breaking in, that's illegal, but once you are in an unoccupied property and have changed the locks and possess the key, the law says you are a legal squatter and can't be evicted.' He looked triumphant and turned to the occupants, eight of them who had stayed away from work that afternoon, and told them to get back in the house.

'Get in and bang the door shut. They can't do anything, and we are here as witnesses,' he said.

The GLC-wallahs conferred and, without a word to us, left. The Irish instigator, satisfied with having delivered a decisive blow, was about to walk away when we stopped him.

Terry Fitzpatrick, as he introduced himself, said he and some others were squatting at a house not far away and that he was quite willing to help the twelve occupants move from that property to others which were lying empty and boarded up in nearby streets. He was also curious as to who we were and why we were involved.

True to his word, in the next days and weeks, he guided the twelve men to houses he had squatted in Varden Street and Walden Road, affording them whole flats to which they could bring their families, right then or over time.

Terry and the Bangladeshi workers broke the locks, changed them, entered the building, wrenched the boarding off and replaced the toilets and basins, which the Tower Hamlets Council had smashed to discourage just such squatting. There was no formality to it.

The East End was experiencing racial assaults on random brown people at the time. The 'skinheads', a cult of young men and women with crew cuts, jeans with braces and tucked-in, vest-like shirts, had turned their awkward sartorial fashion into an attitude which embraced racism of an aggressive kind. Gangs of them took to attacking random Asian people walking the street and minding their own business. Hundreds of assaults, mostly unreported and unrecorded, took place in the East End. The vicious sport was known to the assailants as 'Paki bashing'.

Together with a Bangladeshi middle-class group of well-meaning lawyers, restaurant owners and the like, who patronised the East End community and assumed themselves to be its leaders, we, as *Race Today* representatives, organised a meeting in the Bengali Community Centre adjoining the mosque.

The meeting was packed. Young and old, exclusively males, from the local community attended, to participate without presuming to venture an opinion. They were there to listen to those 'leaders' and to us. The meeting resolved to call a public rally in protest against 'Paki bashing'. It would be under the banner of the Anti-Racist Committee of Asians in East London.

On the day of the rally, we had booked the Brick Lane Cinema, where speakers would take the stage, and had expected it to be packed. The turnout surpassed all expectations. The crowd flowed in their thousands, filling the length of Brick Lane and its side streets.

Darcus spoke from the stage of the cinema and was loudly applauded. The moderate leaders of the community association called for police action against the assailants. Dan Jones, a stalwart of the Labour Party, introduced himself as representing 10,000 Labour and trade union members. Darcus heckled him from the stage: 'So, where are the other 9,999?' It brought down the house.

Terry Fitzpatrick was there with several young Bengalis who had helped him with the squats of Varden Street and Walden Street. After the mass rally, talking amongst ourselves, we ascertained from the evidence presented by various people that apart from assaults against lone Asians on the streets, the isolated Bengali families, who had been assigned council flats in the predominantly white estates, were also subject to relentless abuse and attack. There were incidents of excreta and burning bundles of cloth being thrown through their letter boxes, of windows being smashed, and of assaults and abuse of the women and children in the estate compounds.

Despite repeated complaints to the local police stations, nothing had been done to accost the assailants, and there was no initiative to tackle these criminal phenomena. The young Bengalis volunteered an obvious solution. They would spread the word to recruit volunteers and form themselves into several vigilante groups, which would gather each evening in the Brick Lane cafes or in the grounds of the council estates as an inhibitory presence.

On several occasions in the following weeks, these groups were provoked into action. On one such, Terry and one of the vigilante groups challenged the National Front members who were distributing their racist pamphlets and selling their newspaper at the top of Brick Lane. The Front members were asked to leave, and an argument ensued. Terry and the lads attacked and administered a thrashing. The pamphleteers scrambled onto their van and didn't ever return to that propaganda station.

The word spread, and more youths joined the vigilante groups. Following reports of this development in the media, the police reacted by saying law and order should be left to them. One police chief issued a public statement that vigilante groups were illegal and that the police were taking the matter of assaults in the East End on Asians seriously.

Whether it was the vigilante action or a forced and renewed attentiveness on part of the police, Paki-bashing died down.

The squatting enterprise, with pressure from hundreds of families and individuals who had heard of the accommodation others had found and were clamouring for a look-in, necessitated its formalisation, or at least organising in some way. We consolidated the random activity as the Bengali Housing Action Group or BHAG, the acronym in Bengali meaning 'tiger'.

As an association, which many young male volunteers joined, we squatted in several more streets and an estate called Pelham Buildings, an old Victorian structure which the council had left empty.

Terry was undoubtedly the leading light and the most active member of the group. On one occasion, attempting to illegally connect the electric mains running under the pavements with numerous flats in Pelham Buildings, he accidentally blew himself up. After spending some time in the hospital with severe burns, he recovered and returned to fix the electricity.

PILGRIM'S PROGRESS

It was clear to me now that my ambition to write may have originated through reading fiction, the *Alexandria Quartet* in particular, but writing anything relevant entails finding one's material. In my case, the material found me.

The political activity to which I wholeheartedly gave myself contributed the experience. I ventured now into other genres of fiction and writing—books, plays, television—which I hadn't earlier, because the task of reflecting what I was experiencing in Britain seemed urgent. It seemed to be what my writing should be about.

When I was doing the rounds of readings in schools and libraries with my first two books, I met other writers who shared platforms with me and had also acquired this 'multicultural' label. One of them was Jan Needle, who said it was absurd that I negotiated directly with the publisher. I ought to have a literary agent. He spoke to his own agent, Jacqueline Korn at David Higham Associates, and she enthusiastically took me on after looking through my books.

My only previous acquaintance with literary agents was during my time at Cambridge, when Marcus Grant, a fellow undergraduate at Pembroke and another aspiring writer, introduced me to the agent who had placed his short stories in magazines. I knew that Lawrence Pollinger and his firm represented no other than D.H. Lawrence. I sent them three of my short stories. I received a prompt reply, words to the effect of 'Never darken our doors with this rubbish again.' Not very encouraging.

My acquaintance with the young Bangladeshis of East End had given me the background for my third book of short stories, *Come to Mecca and Other Stories*. David Higham Associates sold it to the highest bidder, and it did rather well.

In a sense, I had covered the expanse of my recent experience and acquaintance in these three books. It was time to turn to the dimension of memory. These first books found favour with publishers because, as Martin Pick, the first editor who commissioned *East End at Your Feet*, had said, there was a famine of material of this sort.

Knowing there to be very few books, if any, about growing up in an Indian neighbourhood, I began work on my fourth book, *Poona Company*, using myself, from the ages of eight to twenty, as the pivot for, though not the autobiographical subject of, short stories. It was about the people I knew in that neighbourhood and was fun to write.

I showed it to Martin, who said it didn't fit into any genre that he was dealing with, but my agent sold it to a brilliant editor at Gollancz. I knew the firm as one of the left-of-centre publishers who had pioneered the work of George Orwell, A.J. Cronin and E.P. Thompson. I was thrilled, of course.

I didn't realise it consciously at the time, but years later was struck by the fact that I had probably read V.S. Naipaul's *Miguel Street* only five years before I wrote *Poona Company*. It was Naipaul who had opened that avenue for recollections of incidents, people and the neighbourhood of my childhood and teens.

Under the umbrella of Gollancz and with the encouragement of its editors, I then turned my hand to a work of fantasy fiction called *Trip Trap*, which dealt with paradoxes that have always fascinated me, such as Zeno's puzzle about Achilles and the tortoise. Perhaps my earlier scientific study had bred the curiosity. Are all paradoxes mathematical or linguistic? Or are mathematics and language the parents of the inexplicable? Making readable fiction out of them was the task I set myself for my fifth book.

ALL THE WORLD'S A TV SET

My first glimpse of a TV was in the boarding house in which I stayed in my first week in Britain, in a room I shared with my mother and younger sister Meher, who had been brought to London for her heart surgery. Dinner was served in the basement to all the lodgers of the house, and I went down that first evening and was hypnotically fixated on a wooden box on a metal shelf up the wall in a corner of the room.

It was a portable cinema. I knew what television was, but we had never had one in my home in India. It was the first television set I had seen. On screen were four black girls seductively singing, 'Baby, baby, where did our love go?'

I fetched my food from the buffet but couldn't take my eyes off the screen, which the other diners barely glanced at. For me, it was enchantment, for them, background. Television was, I realised, the conversational vehicle of the nation.

In the junior common room at Pembroke, I sat, with fifty others, through every episode of *The Wars of the Roses*, a Shakespearean adaptation of the history plays. On the days when the weekly music show *Top of the Pops* was on, there would be no standing room in the common room with its single TV set. Some undergrads would skip dinner to get a front-row seat.

Later, in Leicester, we bought a second-hand set and diligently watched it for the news and the drama. The rooming houses and furnished bedsitters of London didn't provide TV sets as part of their furnishings, such as it was. Later, in our own flats or houses, you had to have a TV set because without it you excluded yourself from the nation's chatter. TV served a different purpose from the newspapers.

Even though I was an ardent watcher of some programmes, I never thought of TV as a literary or highbrow creative genre. I classified it, in subconscious conceit, as information and entertainment. Coming to think of it as drama and as artistically demanding as anything in prose or on stage meant being nudged to take a quantum leap of insight. It wasn't the most sophisticated transition for me, occasioned by lofty considerations.

I had written and published four books and had resigned from my teaching post and lost my steady income. After four published books, I thought I would take the risk and try being a full-time writer and quit the teaching job. It didn't get me far at first, and while working on my next book, *Trip Trap*, I had to pay the mortgage and eat, so I took on several odd jobs.

I drove a minicab for a few weeks for a firm owned by a Bangladeshi called Rashid. And when that proved dangerous, as some clients ran away without paying at the end of the journey into a maze of council flats and some passengers even resorted to gratuitous assaults before running off, I abandoned it. The owner of the minicab firm, when I said I wasn't doing it any more, asked if I wanted instead to drive a van.

I said I didn't have a van and wondered what he had in mind.

'You got the estate, Peugeot, so if you can exchange it for a van that can carry goods, I can give you good money to deliver vegetables.'

Even as he spoke, I thought of my friend Mehrwan Cama, known to all as Mervan the Van. He repaired cars for a living in a garage in Southeast London and occasionally traded in second-hand vehicles. I called Mervan, and he said he had a Volkswagen van which he would exchange for my Peugeot, and we could adjust the relative prices after he evaluated my vehicle. As it happened, he assessed it as a straight exchange, no money need change hands.

For several weeks after I bought the van, two Bangladeshi boys and I drove to the wholesale vegetable market in Spitalfields at about two in the morning and loaded the van with sacks of onions. We then delivered the sacks to the backdoors of Indian restaurants, mostly located in sordid and pungent alleys. All this was done by six in the morning so the cooks could start chopping and dicing for the eaters of curries.

Then one day, as I slept off the labours of the night came the phone call of destiny.

The caller introduced himself as Peter Ansorge, a producer at BBC.

'I've read your short stories,' he said. 'Have you ever thought of writing for television?'

'I wouldn't know how,' I said.

'Let me tell you why I called, Mr Dhondy ...'

'Farrukh,' I interjected.

'Yeah. I produce a series called *Empire Road*, written by Michael Abbensetts ...'

'I know Michael.'

'Of course. I thought you might.'

'And I have looked at the series. Birmingham!'

'That's right. We produce it from Pebble Mill in Birmingham, and it's very successful. But so far we can't seem to create, or we haven't introduced, authentic Asian characters, who exist and should be included in the drama. Which is why I called. Perhaps you'd like to write those for us. The TV format is not a problem. We can do that, or I'm sure you can pick it up in a few minutes.'

I was taken aback. Was this the knuckle of fate knocking at a closed door?

'Perhaps we should meet. Can you make your way to Birmingham, and we can discuss it? We'll pay all the expenses. And if you can spend a night, there's a lot to talk about if you can do it.'

I took the train to Birmingham the next day and a cab to Pebble Mill.

Peter was waiting for me. I followed him into his tiny office. He was short, handsome and didn't sit down but paced the few feet available, smoking one small cigar after another.

'I must say, I'm still unsure as to whether I can … I mean I write short stories, a novel …' I began.

'It's more like stage drama but faster. Michael has already introduced Asian characters and you need to think of stories round them, and I am confident you can write cracking dialogue and drama for them. And, of course, introduce your own characters. We were thinking, if you can, you should do two episodes.'

A shadow of hesitance or even doubt might have crossed my face because he immediately said, 'We need the first episode in a week and … er … the BBC pays first-time writers £900 or so.'

It took me several seconds to digest that. It was more than four times the buy-out sum I had received from Macmillan for my first book of short stories. Farrukh in wonderland?

All qualms, hesitation and literary snobbery were swept away.

'Right, let's have a look at the episodes in which the Asian characters are introduced, and I can get on with it,' I said. 'Can you show me the format in which TV scripts are written?'

Peter lit another cigar and pulled on it as he produced a sample TV script of *Empire Road*.

He pointed out the obvious format: the scene number, whether it takes place indoors or outdoors—int. or ext.—the location and whether its day or night. Then the stage directions and before each speech the character who speaks. That was about it.

Peter asked if I would prefer to spend the night at a guest house or whether he could put me up in his house. I said I would much prefer the house. We could talk further.

It was a multistorey Victorian building, and Peter introduced me to his attractive American wife, Beth. Over dinner, he said he had the good luck to have engaged one Tony Bicât to compose the music.

'I have come across Tony,' I said. 'Not in the same college, but we were at Cambridge together.'

Peter's jaw dropped, literally.

'You what?'

'I was at Cambridge at the same time as your Tony Bicât. He wouldn't know me, but he was known among the undergraduates.'

Even Beth looked astounded.

'Peter was there at the same time,' she said.

'Pity we didn't come across each other,' I responded.

Peter seemed to be recovering from a mild shock. I knew that he had thought he was recruiting a writer from the heart of the Asian ghetto, not some Cambridge graduate. It had struck him as something of a let-down, but he quickly recovered, and we discussed all the poets and people we knew in common and discovered there were quite a few.

In the following weeks, I wrote the commissioned episodes of *Empire Road*, and then Peter said he wanted to convert six short stories from three of my books into a TV drama series.

No more delivering onions to Indian restaurants, though I stuck with my white Volkswagen van and drove it proudly round London and even, on occasion, to Pebble Mill.

I adapted five of my short stories and persuaded Peter to accept an original TV play, which I called *Romance Romance*, as the sixth in the series.

The plays went out on BBC2 and were successful. *Romance Romance* went on to win the Samuel Beckett Prize for the Best TV Drama in 1983. A publisher of drama also contracted the scripts as a book.

Thank you, Peter Ansorge.

Does luck come in threes? I received another phone call from one Charlie Hanson who said he ran a theatre company called the Black Theatre Co-operative and could we meet?

We did, over a drink at the Oval cricket ground's pub. Could I adopt one of my short stories for the stage? I said I would prefer to write an original piece for his company, which was made up entirely of talented young black actors. They had had successful runs of plays by the Trinidadian playwright Mustapha Matura, and Charlie wanted to involve another writer.

I wrote a reggae musical called *Mama Dragon* with an agitprop political theme. It featured a young reggae band called The Government on stage.

The play opened at a community centre in Paddington and, after its run there, was picked up by the Institute of Contemporary Arts and then transferred for a run at the Arts Theatre in West End.

Following its success, I wrote a two-hander called *Shapesters* based on a Shakespeare plot for the Black Theatre Co-operative. It ran at the Riverside Studios and then at the Cottesloe, the small venue of the National Theatre.

The one disaster I had with the Co-operative was with a play called *Trojans*. This was commissioned by Riverside Studios for their main theatrical space and went into rehearsal enthusiastically. The opening night was packed, and reviewers from very many national newspapers turned up.

I sat, anxious and anticipating, in the back row with a few friends. The play began and seemed to be going well with a silent and attentive house when, half an hour into it, the female lead faltered while speaking her lines, put her hands to her face and began to cry. She began to howl on stage. It wasn't part of the script!

She was saying something indistinct but to the tune of 'Help me, I can't do this!'

The house lights came on, the director went on stage and lifted the poor girl up and took her through the wings back to the dressing rooms. She was having a nervous breakdown.

'I didn't think the play was that bad,' a friend of mine said.

The director, Trevor Laird, entreated the audience to stay. Two-thirds did. Trevor announced that the actor was in no state to continue and had been sent home with her partner, who had confirmed that she had 'stress' issues. Trevor told the audience that he knew the part and craved their tolerance and indulgence as the troupe would complete the performance with him filling the female's role for the rest of it. He did so bravely, and the audience, those who had remained, were valiant and generous in their applause. But as professional West End-ish theatre, the performance was a disaster, and the one 'review' by Nicholas de Jongh in the *Guardian* labelled it such.

Nevertheless, among those who saw it and had earlier seen *Mama Dragon* and *Shapesters*, was Humphrey Barclay, the head of Comedy and Drama at London Weekend Television (LWT), one of the bigger independent television companies of the UK. He had followed the Black Theatre Co-operative's output from the outset and approached our director Hanson with a proposal. Would the actors and the two writers—Mustapha and myself—workshop an idea for a television situation comedy with our young black actors? LWT would pay for a venue and all of us a wage.

The workshop went ahead in a room above a pub in Chalk Farm, North London. Ideas and improvisations came thick and fast, and the company opted for a storyline with five brothers and a sister, aged from late teens to early twenties—close to the real age of the actors—who share a house in West London after their parents have retired to their native Jamaica.

Having decided on the format, Mustapha and I were given an office in a splendid LWT building on the Thames to write the series.

We wrote over the next few months, and when the scripts were near completion, we presented them to Humphrey, who said he was going to approach the newly instituted Channel 4 to finance and broadcast it.

'But it doesn't have a name. Someone suggested that the family's surname should be Hills and the series *The Hills are Alive* as a take-off on *Sound of Music*. It's funny, but it's much too contrived,' Humphrey said.

We agreed that it was.

'Well, you have till the afternoon to come up with a title, OK?'

Mustapha said, 'No problem!' and Humphrey said, 'That's it! Fabulous. We call it *No Problem*.'

It ran for a couple of seasons on Channel 4 but ended owing to my changing fortunes.

With the success of *No Problem* on Channel 4, I was asked by the commissioning editor, Sue Woodford-Hollick, to think of a situation comedy featuring an Asian cast. I came up with a drama of two rival Indian restaurants and named one, in a parody of the popular TV show of the time, the Jewel in the Crown. As the episodes progress, the chef of the Jewel breaks away from his employment with the owner Jimmy Sharma, played by Saeed Jaffrey, starts his own restaurant a few yards away on the same street and names it the Far Pavilions in the pathetic belief that, to prosper, the restaurant should carry the name of a television hit. The series was called *Tandoori Nights* and ran for one very popular season on Channel 4.

The BBC now invited me to write a serious four-part drama set in the Bangladeshi community of the East End and featuring the people in the neighbourhood I had political adventures with. It took me no time to turn my experience of the housing action, together with my perception of some of the narrow attitudes inherent in the Bangladeshi community towards women and non-Muslims, into fictionalised drama.

Called *King of the Ghetto*, in one of the episodes, a character, played by Zia Mohyeddin, puts a ten-pound note in a copy of the Quran. I didn't, at the time of writing, think this was offensive, but a group of twenty or so Bangladeshis, led by three bearded mullahs, demonstrated with placards outside the BBC's offices condemning the play.

The controller of the BBC channel at the time publicly assured them that, in consideration of their protest, he had taken the decision to never repeat the series on the BBC. Scaredy cat!

After *Tandoori Nights* was transmitted and before *King of the Ghetto* was, I received a call from the secretary of Jeremy Isaacs, the head of Channel 4.

'Jeremy would like to have lunch with you. Would Tuesday at The Ivy be convenient?'

The Ivy? One of the most exclusive restaurants in London, and why the hell would he want lunch with me? He can't like my writing that much, I thought, but readily agreed to being hosted to a free fancy meal.

I was there before Jeremy and was ushered to the reserved table. When he arrived, Jeremy asked me what I would like to drink, and when I said a glass of red wine, he perused the wine list and ordered an eighty-pound bottle of Claret. This was 1983.

Over the meal, he got down to satisfying my acute, unspoken curiosity about the invitation.

'Dear boy, you know that Sue Woodford is leaving us,' he said.

'Yes, she told me. Her husband Clive is now Lord Hollick and Sue is Lady Hollick. The USA, I think she said.'

'Buying Charles Aznavour's house in New England with indoor and outdoor swimming pools and tennis courts—but that's what bankers can do.'

'I'll miss her. She's been very kind to me. And a revolutionary in her vision of what to commission, though as a beneficiary, I perhaps shouldn't say it.'

'Do say it. We think it,' Jeremy said.

I sipped the claret.

'And, of course, we shall need a new commissioning editor to replace her,' he said.

'Of course. Whoever it is, I hope they like my work.'

Jeremy was silent for a long few seconds.

'That may not be necessary,' he said at last.

He was reading my face.

'We want you to do the job!'

It didn't sink in at first.

'Me? Commissioning editor?'

'Yes.'

'But … um … an office job, nine to five?'

'Don't be ridiculous, no one at the Channel works nine to five, more like eight to one in the morning.'

'Wow! But, Jeremy, I earn a decent amount writing, for you and the BBC,' I said.

'That could dry up, you realise,' he said with a straight face.

I got the message.

He didn't conclude our encounter by saying, 'Start tomorrow'. He virtually said the job was mine if I wanted it, but he didn't use those words. He was prudent. There had to be a process of appointment, and he said, 'We look forward to your application, dear boy. A simple note, one or two sentences.' His slightly open-mouthed smile, with a dropped bottom lip, tightened the skin of his cheeks.

That evening, I spoke to my friend C.L.R. James in his room above the *Race Today* magazine's office. He was, as always during the day except when he rose to go to the bathroom, sitting up in bed and at the moment was reading William Thackeray's *Vanity Fair*. I told him about the job offer.

Without a word, he put his book down on his duvet cover, pointed his long finger at the book and then shook his finger from side to side to indicate some form of negativity. Then he pointed at the TV, which he had kept on without the sound, indicating that it was the future.

I spoke to Darcus on the phone as he was in Trinidad. He just said, 'Dhondy, take it!'

I didn't write the letter for ten or so days, still wondering what I should do. Jeremy's secretary rang to say they hadn't received my letter and required it immediately. I wrote the three-sentence letter saying I was applying for the job of commissioning editor of multicultural programmes. I received a letter back in two days inviting me to an interview.

I wore a jacket but no tie to the interview. A shortlist of eighteen people had apparently been interviewed, in all fairness, or unfair subterfuge, for the job. Jeremy and Frank McGettigan, the head of Personnel, asked me a few questions and wore expressions which said they knew how I would answer, even though the framework I had worked out for the future of such commissioning was, to my mind, radical.

Frank walked out of the interview with me and privately asked me when I could start. Sue was still officially in the job, but she would hand over to me as soon as I was ready as she was anxious to get away. He said I had to be introduced to the board as a fresh appointee. The board meeting was a few days away, and I was to attend it with three other fresh appointees, who were also to be rubber-stamped by Channel 4's board of trustees.

On the evening on which the new appointees were to be introduced to the board, its chairperson, Edmund Dell, had absented himself, and the meeting was helmed by the deputy chairperson at the time, the legendary actor and filmmaker Richard Attenborough.

The four of us new appointees waited in the visitor's space in the foyer of Channel 4's Charlotte Street building. The board meeting was in progress, and we would be called in one by one to be introduced. I believe I went in third, the two before me leaving with beaming faces at their welcome to the institution from the greats.

Then, I was called. Jeremey introduced me with all manner of flattering allusions. I could see that Attenborough was staring at me with a deep frown. When Jeremy paused, he interrupted.

'Will Mr Dhondy excuse us for a moment,' he said and pointed very demurely at the exit to the room. His frown remained.

Jeremy indicated to me that I should leave, though he looked puzzled himself and wanted to be reassuring. I walked out bewildered and sat in the foyer with my possible to-be colleague.

'What's going on?'

'Attenborough asked me to leave—they want to discuss something without me being there, I think.'

Frank's secretary passed us in the foyer and took the lift. She came back in a few minutes and went into the boardroom.

About ten minutes later, I was summoned. I went in and sat next to Jeremy.

Attenborough was smiling enthusiastically.

'My darling boy, the board is delighted to have you in this all-important post. We all know what a brilliant and distinguished career you have had and are proud and happy to welcome you to Channel 4.'

I muttered as good a thank you as I could, and Jeremy, smiling his characteristic smile, indicated that that was that and I could leave.

It was a few days after I had started at Channel 4 that one of the senior trustees of the board, Anthony Smith, came into my office.

'You must have been wondering why you were sent out of the board meeting while being introduced,' he said, laughing.

I asked him to be seated and said, 'Of course, I was puzzled. I thought something had come up and I'd be thrown out.'

'Something did come up. Dicky recognised you as the critic who had spoken on Channel 4's film-review programme for twenty minutes reviewing his *Gandhi*.'

'Oh fuck!'

'Yes, he sent for the tape of the review programme from the library when he recognised you, saying, "Hang on, isn't this the fellow who commented on my film?"'

'More fuck!' I said. I remembered this review. My central point was that Attenborough had mythologised Gandhi and not quite seen the cunning, pragmatic politician behind the dramatised facade.

'It wasn't exactly an ecstatic review,' I said.

'I know,' said Tony. 'But thank god you used rather sophisticated critical language, because Dicky turned to me as we viewed the tape and said, "What's this fellow saying?" and I said, "Dicky, he is saying you have put Gandhi on the world map, he loves your film!"

'"Does he? Oh well, turn it off, call the darling boy in," he said.'

Tony laughed. So did I. Thank you, Tony.

I began work the Monday after the meeting with the board. Sue had left me a four-foot pile of proposals from aspirant producers, proposals in every genre and category, some very sophisticated and some nonsensical. On my first day, going through these, I sat in the glass-walled office till about eight in the evening. I could hear voices in the adjoining office.

As I worked, there came a banging on the wall from next door. 'New boy, what are you doing,' shouted a voice.

I dropped the file pile and strolled over there. Andy Parke, the commissioning editor for Music, and his producer friend Charles Thompson were in his office finishing a bottle of wine. Charles had his feet on Andy's desk, reclining in the guest chair.

I introduced myself.

'Yes, we know who you are. What are you doing at eight at night?'

'Looking through proposals. Sue has left me a huge pile.'

'Chuck them in the bin, and get producers to do what you want them to do,' Andy said.

'Yes, but before that, get some wine. Let's drink to your appointment,' Charles said.

'Fine. I don't know the area well, so where's the nearest off-license? I'll get the wine.'

They looked at each other and smiled.

'My dear fellow, at Channel 4, you don't go buying wine. Open the right-hand drawer in your desk, and there should be a key marked "Wine cupboard". It's at the end of the offices on the right. Just go in there, get a couple of bottles you fancy and sign for them,' Andy said.

'Don't worry, it's free,' Charles added.

We had a drink that evening, and though Andy Parke left two years into my term there, we got on well in that time, and Charles and I grew into more than fast friends.

Having become the buyer, I had to stop being the seller. There could be no more of my writing *No Problem* or another series of *Tandoori Nights*. Before taking up the job of commissioning the latter, I had begun planning the second series, and now, under some supervision by me, it had to be farmed out to different writers. We did put together a successful second series.

I had two guiding perspectives in the commissioning job. The first was that the new communities of Britain, or the multicultural folks from former colonies who had settled in the UK, had to wholeheartedly and in all aspects join the national conversation and be assimilated through the main medium of national self-awareness, which was the broadcasting industry, TV in particular.

The presence of black and Asian people on screen, until the advent of Channel 4, had been at first an appearance in patronising programmes, instructing, for instance, Asian immigrants in British ways. They had then been patronised through sophisticated programmes of classical Indian culture at bizarre hours—six in the morning on Sundays—and in an era when the overwhelming majority of them would have been fans of Indian pop culture and what has come to be known as Bollywood.

In the next phase, television gave acting roles to black characters as villains or as comic characters with funny accents. Then, in a typically British liberal reaction to that, was born the mission to complain. Programme-makers and heads of channels, in all radical conscience, formulated formats which gave black voices the opportunity to characterise and denounce racism. It became boring, with a restricted field of life's areas to complain about. And it became counter-productive, in so far as the audience it targeted didn't bother to tune in to these programmes.

My department's output had to embrace every genre of TV and attempt to excel in it. It covered a weekly programme on news and current affairs; several series of documentaries in observational, investigative, educational and even polemical genres; chat shows; drama; single and serialised plays; situation comedy; soap opera and, of course, films.

My interpretation of the remit was to bring people of ethnic origin into the world of TV production. They could be guided by professionals who would mentor or pass on their experience, and we would build a sector of production companies with people of various skills from the new communities of Britain.

I discussed an apprenticeship scheme with the head of Human Resources, and we determined that applicants would be vetted through an interview and that I would induce production companies I had commissioned to take on the apprentices and acquaint them with skills of their choice—camera, editing, research and others—which would lead, perhaps, to their ambition to direct and produce.

We didn't set a number to be enrolled to such a scheme but apprenticed the applicants as planned. One morning, when my secretary Eva was away from her desk, her phone rang. I was out of my cabin and happened to be passing her desk and picked up the phone. I said, 'Farrukh Dhondy's office,' and waited for the answer.

The young female voice at the other end said, 'Oh my god! Is that Farrukh Dhondy?'

I said it was.

'Oh god! I've been asking Eva to put me through a hundred times, but you've always been busy.' Her voice was gushing but confident with a London-accented twist.

'Here I am,' I said. 'What can I do for you?'

'You can save my life,' she said.

I was about to say, 'Hang on, you've reached Channel 4, this is not the Samaritans,' but didn't think the witticism was appropriate.

'My dear, how can I do that?' I asked.

'I need a job,' she said. 'You are taking on apprentices. Give me ten minutes, please, to explain, Mr Dhondy!'

I leafed through Eva's diary as I stood at her desk.

'How about ten minutes at eleven tomorrow morning?'

She did turn up. Sometime later, Miss S told me about her circumstances, which were dire. She spoke about being estranged from her family and having to earn her living when she was only a teen. She had put herself through university by doing odd jobs.

I spoke to her about her interest in TV, and her answers were quite perceptive. She seemed just the sort our scheme was meant to accommodate. I said I would get back to her.

I found her an appropriate company, and she went on to work there and make her career as a successful TV researcher and journalist. I would meet her again years later, after she was married and had three children.

Several others who were recruited through this almost informal scheme went on to be presenters, editors, directors and even heads of vast departments at other channels, including the BBC. It was a great part of the job.

The years at Channel 4 were busy. It was a twenty-four-hour job, but it was very rewarding, with the decisions one took having public proof on screen. Every commission entailed an adventure of some sort. To contribute to the aim of bringing black and Asian producers into the industry, I advertised for documentary ideas from existing or even aspirant black and Asian producers and commissioned a series of the best ones. Very many of the companies who were making these were inexperienced, and I appointed a senior producer, Bernard Clark, to supervise the output as an executive producer and get the series into a uniform and overall shape.

I called this documentary series, slightly tongue in cheek, *Black Bag*.

As it began transmission, Alkarim Jivani, a journalist at the weekly publication *Time Out*, came to interview me. It was obvious from the start, from when he opened his notebook in my office, that it wasn't going to be an appreciative or even friendly interview. He said he didn't like the title.

I said it indicated the content and, being light-hearted, cut the insistence on off-putting solemnity that had dogged black and ethnic TV.

He then got onto the role of Bernard Clark, who, he said, was 'a white man'.

I said I had noticed.

Why had I put a white man in charge of black people, he asked.

Very many of the producers were inexperienced, I explained, and I wanted to assist them and impose some uniformity of quality on the whole series.

His next question was posed as a conditional.

'What would you say to someone who said you were acting like a colonial despot, putting a white man in charge of blacks?'

A phrase from my Poona college days came to mind.

'I'd say, "Kiss my cock and call me Charlie!"' A rude expression probably passed on from British troops of the Raj to college lads in India.

Jivani closed his notebook and left my office without a word.

Two hours later, Eva said that the director of Programmes, Liz Forgan, wanted to see me. I went down to her office on the second floor. John Willis, the programme controller and my direct boss, was seated in the office. Liz asked me to take a seat.

'Did you tell Alkarim Jivani to kiss your cock and call you Charlie?' she asked with an absolute straight face.

'No, I didn't!' I replied and told them both that he had asked me what I would say to someone who accused me of behaving like a colonial despot, and I had replied saying that's what I would say. I repeated the riposte with an equally poker face.

John burst into laughter. He couldn't hold it. He nearly fell off his chair.

Liz broke into a huge and alluring grin, as she often did. 'Please, Farrukh, don't say these things to journalists,' she pleaded.

Every time I passed him in the corridors of the channel, John would, sometimes quite solemnly, repeat the phrase.

A TV HACK'S ODYSSEY

I suppose meeting celebrities in one's TV career merits mention?

I met Oprah Winfrey, once. Or shall I say she met me when she was invited to a Channel 4 dinner. It was a very select dinner, and I suppose as the only editor of colour in Channel 4 at the time, I was invited by our boss Michael Grade. We were served cocktails by uniformed barmen and then dinner in the boardroom by liveried waiters. No expense spared.

Oprah was seated at the head of the table with Michael and our beloved Liz Forgan. I was at the other end of the table and found myself sitting next to Oprah's press secretary. We chatted through the first course and she said they had watched a riveting programme the previous evening in which a white South African eleven-year-old exchanged places and families with a black South African lad of the same age. I had to say it was my idea and my programme. She was fascinated and asked what else I had planned.

I said one of the areas I wanted to venture into was to examine Jazz and Soul as the classical music of the USA.

She was curious if not hooked.

'Which Soul and Jazz artists will you feature?'

'Depends on the thesis of the programme,' I said. 'We are working on it.'

'Who are your favourites?'

'Today? I suppose Stevie Wonder, and by far the best for voice and technique belong, of course, to Aretha Franklin. Shame about her dress sense.'

The lady laughed and put her hand on her mouth as she did. Was this sacrilege?

She shouted across the room to Oprah and walked over to her at the other end of the table. Then the two of them came rushing over to me.

'You must tell her what you just said,' the press secretary insisted, the amused shock still on her features.

Oprah pulled up a chair. I repeated my perhaps injudicious remark.

Oprah laughed. 'I won't say that's so cheeky, but right on the ball,' she said, or words to that effect.

Our brief encounter didn't hit the headlines.

An episode in *Black on Black*—a chat show edited by the British writer Trevor Phillips, who would later run for the office of mayor as a member of the Labour Party—featured Mrs Martin Luther King, Coretta Scott, who was visiting Britain many years after the assassination of her husband. The live programme went out on a weekday night, and in my role as commissioning editor, I sat in the control room behind the director and his assistants to view the screen. The large glass window allowed us to look down on the studio and the guests.

The interview with Mrs King progressed with several questions about politics and the assassination and some about King's character. Then the interviewer sprung a decently couched but spiked question about whether King had been faithful in every aspect of his life. The interviewer was obviously challenging Mrs King to say she knew about his adultery.

The answer was as diplomatically subtle as the question. Mrs King said something like there were ups and downs in all relationships and marriages, but these didn't affect her husband's faith in his historic mission.

All was well that ended well, if it had ended there. As I got to my office the next day, my secretary said that our chief executive Jeremy Isaacs wanted to see me straight away.

When I got to his room, all nine TV screens on one wall of his office were tuned to the Test match being played between India and England to an overflowing stadium in an Indian city, possibly Chennai.

'What could you be thinking of, dear boy?' Jeremy began.

I was perplexed.

'Your programme yesterday, featuring the first black lady of America ... your presenter, that silly girl, insulted her with that question about ... you know! Did you sanction it?'

'Yes, I routinely discuss the approach before the programme and take full responsibility. But it was not put brazenly or embarrassingly ...'

I was going to elaborate on my explanation or excuse, but Jeremy wasn't listening. Huge applause from the stadium filled all nine screens. The Indian bowler had just taken an English wicket. Jeremy's eyes were fixed on the screens.

'Did you see that bowling action. The spinner, did you follow the shot?' he asked.

'Not just then,' I said.

'He is sensational, what's his name?'

The bowler was famous.

'It's Laxman Sivaramakrishnan,' I said.

Jeremy broke into a half-smile, his eyes still glued to the screen to catch the next bowl. 'Hunh! His parents weren't taking any chances!' he said, referring probably to the three god names squished into one.

I waited to see what sanctions he would perhaps impose on me, but Jeremy had forgotten about his complaint.

'Thanks, dear boy. I think India will carry this Test,' he said, waving me away back to my office.

Late one night, Aziz Kurta, a young, handsome maritime lawyer who used to be the presenter of a show of mine on Channel 4, called me. He sounded breathless and excited. Without apologising for the late hour, he said, 'I've just caught Jeffrey Archer coming out of the boudoir of a sex worker in Shepherd's Market. Can you put it on *The Bandung File*?'

Jeffrey Archer, writer of popular fiction, was at the time the deputy chairman of the Conservative Party, and *The Bandung File* was a flagship multicultural programme which I commissioned and controlled on Channel 4.

'Aziz, that's not the sort of news one puts on *The Bandung File*. It's not a scandal sheet, but let's find an outlet for this dynamite. But first, tell me how you know?'

'I am at Shepherd's Market right now with some Arab clients, you know, shipping magnates whose legal stuff I handle, and as I was taking them to this classy call girl Monica Coghlan's flat, Jeffrey emerged and went down and then round the corner to his parked Rolls Royce. I followed him and got the number plate. I went back up to Coghlan's boudoir and asked her if she knew who her last customer was, and she said, "He's John Smith from Basingstoke," or some such. I told her it was Jeffrey Archer.'

I told Aziz I would find a way of blowing this gaffe nationally and called my friend Tariq Ali, who was one of the editors of *The Bandung File* and a left-wing political activist.

Tariq too said it wasn't a story for us but that Aziz should take the evidence to the magazine *Private Eye* through a journalist he knew. We gave Aziz the contact.

I later found out that the *Private Eye* journalist persuaded Aziz to take it with him to a national scandal sheet like the *Sunday Sport* or the *Daily Star*, which would pay them handsomely for the story, something *Private Eye* would certainly not do.

The *Daily Star* bid for the story and set a trap to gain foolproof evidence. With Aziz, they approached Ms Coghlan and persuaded her to phone Jeffrey and tell him that a client of hers had spotted him emerging from her place of work and the newspapers were now after the story. What should she do? Jeffrey said she should leave the country and he would arrange for her to have a few thousand pounds to get to Paris and lie low. She was to come to the clock at Victoria station at a given time, where a contact of Jeffrey's would deliver the money.

Of course, the newspaper was recording the conversation and was waiting with cameras when Coghlan went for the rendezvous under the clock.

Jeffrey kept his word, and a flunkey of his turned up and handed Coghlan a brown envelope with £2,000 in it. The cameras recorded the transaction, and the whole affair was featured in the paper on Sunday.

He foolishly sued the paper for libel. He persuaded his friend Ted Francis to provide him with an alibi for the day and time he was supposed to have availed of Coghlan's services. Jeffrey told the court that he had indeed paid her the money but didn't know who she was. He had felt blackmailed by her, he claimed, and wanted to avoid a scandal.

Mary Archer, Jeffrey's wife, appeared at the trial, which was through those days prime national news. The judge's remarks about Mrs Archer being 'fragrant' in contrast to Coghlan became famous. If you had fragrant Mary as a wife, the judge argued, why would you resort to the likes of Coghlan?

Aziz had unwittingly and hastily fashioned a whip for his own back. In his evidence as a key witness, he had to tell the court that he had taken four of his Arab clients to Coghlan. The judge asked if he too had had sex with Coghlan and warned him not to lie and perjure himself as Coghlan had already given the answer to the court. Aziz had no option but to admit that he had.

The judge removed his spectacles and, with a very solemn expression, said, 'Mr Kurta, I am ashamed to say that you belong to the same profession as myself.'

The judge dismissed the case, and Jeffrey was free.

As the trial progressed, my colleagues at Channel 4, aware that Aziz had presented one of my programmes, asked what I thought this was all about.

'Why would he go to the press with this sordid story?' my boss Jeremy asked me.

'I can only speculate,' I said. 'Aziz is an ambitious member of the Labour Party, and he probably thought that if he exposed the deputy chair of the Tories, his party would reward him with a safe seat at the next election.'

They didn't. The Labour Party didn't exactly expel him, but it distanced itself from the sordid scandal.

That was 1987. Aziz and family left their luxurious residence in London's prime district of Kew and went to Dubai, where he established himself as an art critic and gallery owner.

In 2001, Ted Francis fell out with Jeffrey and admitted to a court that his former friend had lied and wasn't with him that night. Jeffrey was arrested, tried for perjury, convicted and sentenced to serve a prison term. His political career was, of course, finished.

I went with Tariq Ali to New Delhi to interview the then prime minister Rajiv Gandhi and others. The main topic of conversation with the prime minister was the Commonwealth conference of that year, 1987, in which Britain under Margaret Thatcher had opposed the idea of sanctions against the apartheid regime of South Africa, a resolution Gandhi was instrumental in initiating.

On the day after the interview, Tariq had invited those I took to be his Trotskyist comrades to the hotel we were staying in. They sat by the pool chatting over their drinks. (I didn't notice what they were drinking, so won't stoop to labelling them 'champagne socialists'.) I had invited the film producer Suresh Jindal, an acquaintance who had been the associate producer on Attenborough's *Gandhi*.

Suresh turned up by the poolside in his modest but stylish khadi kurta-pyjama and slippers, with his distinguished white beard. We talked about our latest projects and the prospect of working together. Tariq's friends spotted Suresh, and two of them, manifestly and outspokenly critical of *Gandhi*, probably from some pseudo-Marxist angle, put the rhetorical question to Suresh: 'Why the hell was this film made?'

Not slow off the mark, Suresh said, 'It was made to prove that Indira Gandhi was not Mahatma Gandhi's daughter.'

I thought that was the perfect answer and an apt ending to the brief interrogation.

Back in London, the morning we landed, I noticed that the other offices on the floor were unoccupied. My secretary said I should hurry up and get to the boardroom as our new chief executive Michael Grade was being introduced to the commissioning editors and senior staff.

I hurried to the boardroom where 'Dicky' Attenborough was presiding.

On seeing me enter the room, Dicky came up and hugged me.

'So, what did you do in India, dear boy. Whom did you see?'

'Ah, I met with Suresh Jindal.'

'What a wonderful man, really gracious man,' Dicky said.

After momentarily pondering over whether to tell Dicky about Suresh's riposte to Tariq's friends, I decided he would take it in the spirit in which Suresh had offered it and proceeded, as best I could, to recount the poolside incident. Dicky, Michael and some of my colleagues who had gathered round listened. There was a moment of silence after I delivered Suresh's punchline. Everyone was waiting to see how Dicky would take this description of his epic achievement.

'That's right,' Dicky said. 'That's exactly why it was made!' Then turning to Michael, he said, 'And, you know, I was invited to show the film at a very prominent house in Washington DC and after the showing my host said,' and here Dicky went into an American accent, '"What a great film Mr Attenborough. And what a great job his daughter is doing in New Delhi!"'

Yes, it was the actor-turned-president Ronald Reagan, famous also for sending paratroopers to displace the government of the island of Grenada, without knowing where Grenada was. Did he ever meet Mrs Gandhi and say, 'Sorry about your dad'?

Another interesting and moderately life-threatening experience was when I met the British pop singer Cat Stevens.

The producers of a show called *Hypotheticals*, which was screened on UK's Independent Television (ITV) channel, rang my office at Channel 4. Would I participate in a programme about the recent controversy and book burnings surrounding Salman Rushdie's *The Satanic Verses*?

It was a hot topic in 1989 in the wake of Ayatollah Khomeini's fatwa condemning Salman to death and protests by Muslims up and down Britain.

I had read the book when Salman sent me a proof copy. He had appended a note saying, 'What do you think of this?'

Long before the controversy broke and obviously before the book was even published, I took the proofs with me on holiday to Portugal, where I was spending a couple of weeks in the Algarve with friends Margaret Peacock and Ray and Di Bruce. After reading the proofs, I gave it to Ray, a theologian and scholar, familiar with the history of Islam, who was keen to see what Salman had made of Prophet Muhammad's story.

Ray's opinion, with which I concurred, was that it was explosive, perhaps a strong Diwali cracker, if not dynamite. When I returned to London, I told Salman, 'It'll cause some controversy, and you'll be shuffling from studio to studio arguing with detractors.' A grievous understatement.

There was poor Salman shuffling not from studio to studio but from safe house to safe house under the protection of the British police.

I agreed to go on the programme and took the train to Manchester, where the recording was to happen. Its format was simple: ten or so participants who might have some involvement in or an opinion about a current controversy would be invited to sit round a rectangular table and be posed hypothetical what-if questions by the host, the eminent queen's counsel Geoffrey Robertson.

As I walked into the large foyer of the hotel where the guests had been put up and where the show was to be recorded as well, I noticed several men and women clad in traditional white Arab Muslim attire and, looking closely, noticed that one of them, now bearded and wearing a white prayer cap, was the pop singer Cat Stevens, who had dubbed himself Yusuf Islam. He was to be on the programme? I had read several comments of his, reported in the press, supporting the fatwa. He had told reporters that the Quran prescribed death for those who insulted the Prophet and that Salman had clearly done so.

This was ironic. In an interview I did later with Salman for a publication, talking about his children's book *Haroun and the Sea of Stories*, he made a remark which he must have reconsidered subsequently. Here it is in this extract from our interview:

> **FD (Me):** There's just been a new edition of *Haroun and the Sea of Stories*. It's not exclusively a children's book, is it?
> **Salman Rushdie (SR):** The book is clearly at one level about serious things—about language and silence. It's about speech and the silencing of speech.
> **FD:** 'From the moment I could talk, I was ordered to listen.'
> **SR:** Who is that? That's a song, isn't it?
> **FD:** Don't you remember?
> **SR:** Oh yes. It was Cat Stevens. A great and wise man ...

I deposited my overnight bag in my room and went to the bar before I was called for the recording. Yusuf Islam was sitting opposite me at the table and next to him was a charlatan known to me as a paid agent of the Iranian Shia state and the leader of a book-burning demonstration reviling Salman.

Let me state clearly that I am not against book-burning, but have one proviso, that the mob buy 20,000 copies of any book and read them before they burn them and that the protest is restricted to the sacrifice by fire of books and no mention of harm to the author. Good for sales and for the penetration of thick-heads and on to further editions—may they suffer the same fate.

The questions began, and I was asked if I would commission a film of the book *The Satanic Verses*. I said the book had three stories running in parallel, and while this was an acceptable format for a book, it would perhaps pose a problem for a single film, but yes, I certainly would commission such a film if the screenplay was powerful and dramatic. I acknowledged no taboos.

As soon as I pronounced this, Cat Stevens and the Shia bagman stood up, shouting, 'Kill him!' They may have said it a few times. I attempted to try and seem as unmoved as I could, without breaking into a silly grin which would betray my consternation. I had thought they would be subtler than that. Above the murmurs and hubbub, I said something to the tune of 'Barking dogs seldom bite'.

After the show, Brian Lapping, the producer, asked if I wanted to change hotels and if I felt threatened. I said I didn't think that I was in any danger, these fellows just wanted to flaunt their sensational convictions.

Even so, that night I pushed the desk in my hotel room against the door before I slept.

Apart from amping up the diversity of the content, I commissioned various feature films at Channel 4, including Mira Nair's first distributed feature *Salaam Bombay*, which went on to win the

Caméra d'Or at Cannes and be nominated for the Best Foreign Language Film at the Oscars in 1989. Mira said I should get to Los Angeles for the Oscars ceremony. With the film agent—I'll call her Jane—we would be two of the five official guests attached to the nominated film. The other three would be Mira, her then husband Mitch Epstein and Sooni Taraporevala, the screenplay writer.

We got to LA five days before the event as instructed. Convention amongst the international nominees dictated that each of them invite the others to a dinner party, one each day on the four days before the actual awards, and perhaps present something of their national culture to the others. We attended these parties and threw one of our own with Indian music to regale the guests. I also used the time to take a tour of the 'city', which appealed to me as a network of large villages connected by motorways rather than one entity.

On the day of the Oscars ceremony, which was scheduled to begin at half past seven in the evening, Mira said she would pick me up at half past two in the afternoon. The city would be gridlocked with the limousines and cars making their way at a crawl over four or five hours through the streets to the venue.

I dressed in my Indian sherwani and tight churidar, formal national costume. Mira's limo drove up. The other guests were already in the stretch limo. Mira and Sooni were in gorgeous saris, and Jane was wearing a striking black brocade ankle-length Victorian dress that had belonged to her grandmother. She sat opposite me. There was a bar with a fridge in the limo and a TV. We didn't bother with the TV as we got going but poured out freezing mojitos from the fridge.

As the limo crawled along, some white powder was brought out and cut into neat little lines on a hand-mirror's surface.

Finding an empty stretch, the limo sped up. I had rolled a ten-dollar note in anticipation and so had one or two of the others. Then suddenly, the driver braked, and the limo came to a halt with a jerk. The mirror flew out of our companion's hands and the precious powder was spattered all over Jane's lap, white and visible on her stretched black dress.

'Don't move,' we shouted and, getting on our knees, snorted as much of the powder we could get through the rolled-up dollar bills. Waste not, want not!

The ceremony went very engagingly, though we didn't win. And then several more parties one after the other, into the dawn.

In 1995, I got a call from the famous and fearless Indian documentary maker Anand Patwardhan, with whom I was acquainted. He said three of his documentaries on radical subjects were being screened at the National Film Theatre in South Bank in a few days' time. Would I come for the screening and perhaps commission them for broadcast on Channel 4? I was very interested and told him I would certainly attend. We arranged to meet at the theatre's bar after the event.

I went to the bar, and soon, Anand, who was probably signing autographs or posing for selfies with fans, turned up with two striking young women. The four of us sat at a table. I was taking their drink orders when one of the women said she had just read a book of short stories of mine and thought they should be filmed. Even as I thanked her for the compliment, I had a nagging feeling I had seen her somewhere but couldn't place her. She spoke to me as though she knew me too.

I was racking my brains when the other woman said, 'I'll have the same as Julie!'

As I walked to the bar, it hit me. Of course, I didn't know her. It was Julie Christie, and I had seen in her *Dr Zhivago, Far from the Madding Crowd* and other films! I kicked myself, bought the drinks and carried them back to the table.

Anand asked me what I thought of the documentaries we had watched. I said I would certainly consider screening two of them but had a small issue with the third.

Such as what, he asked.

The documentary I was alluding to was of two Indian political activists, Dev Nathan and Vasanthi Raman, who as Maoists had been arrested and tortured by the then prime minister Indira Gandhi's police for subversive activities during the Emergency. The documentary highlighted their torture by the police, who placed the activists' hands under the chairs on which the policemen sat while questioning them. Dev Nathan's hands were badly damaged. It was a horrific story.

However, I told Anand, Julie and her friend, I had known both Dev Nathan and Vasanthi in the 1970s in Bombay, when they had been part of a radical left discussion group whose sessions I had attended as a guest from London. I knew that they were members of the communist party which called itself the CPI(ML) and was a self-proclaimed Maoist party, complete with the rhetoric of the Little Red Book and their bitter opposition to the two other communist parties in India. I said I knew about the torture they had suffered, but then, why had he ended the story there, I asked Anand.

He asked what I meant.

I had heard from reliable sources, including our mutual friend Darryl D'Monte, who had been part of that radical discussion group and was now the Bombay editor of the *Times of India*, that Dev Nathan and Vasanthi had gone on to join Indira Gandhi's party, the Congress, in a coalition against a rival communist party in the industrial constituencies of North Bombay. Was that turning the other cheek, or was it my enemy's enemy is my friend, or was it rank and naked opportunism?

Anand only said that this didn't negate their suffering.

Julie interrupted, turning to Anand and saying that my 'reaction' was typically that of upper-class Indians, and then turning to me, she said that I obviously didn't understand Indian politics.

'That may be true,' I said. 'Let's make a deal. You teach me Indian politics, and I'll teach you acting!'

The evening didn't end very well. I did screen one or two of Anand's documentaries, but not the disputed one.

The Drama department of Channel 4, whose series editor was my old friend Peter Ansorge, thought they were in trouble. They had commissioned a comedy drama series called *Annie's Bar* in 1996, set in a real drinking hole of the House of Commons and produced by a company called Ardent Productions. Several episodes of the series had been transmitted when Peter walked into my office.

'Have you watched *Annie's Bar*?' he asked.

'Only glimpsed a bit of last week's episode. Why?'

'Because it's in trouble,' he said.

'What sort? Copyright? Libel? Bad reviews?'

'Not the viewing figures we expected, and the further scripts by the writer are not, let's say, perfect.'

'Oh dear. Get him or her to redo them or get another writer?'

'Precisely,' said Peter. 'Which is why I'm speaking to you.'

'There must be hundreds of writers out there you can call.'

'We want you to write the next two episodes at least,' Peter said very calmly.

'Me? I can't write for Channel 4. I work here. That's what my contract says!'

'I've cleared it with the bosses. They said they can make an exception. You'll get paid the writing fee.'

'Why me?' I asked, genuinely puzzled and not fishing for compliments.

'Because I know how fast you can write, and we want you to inject a bit of humour and perhaps an Indian character into *Annie's Bar*.'

'Why is that urgent?' I asked.

'Come on, Farrukh. You know Ardent Productions is owned by Prince Edward!'

'Oh yeah. Didn't connect.'

'We can't have the series failing dismally. So, you start now?'

'I really don't know what *Annie's Bar* is all about. I mean the characters, the setting, the premise ...'

'I've given your secretary the tapes of all the transmitted episodes and the scripts of the others which we don't like. Just check them out.'

A real challenge. I said I would think about it.

'Don't think, just get on with it,' he said.

And then Peter pronounced the tall order—I had to produce the first script in forty-eight hours and the second in seventy-two.

That afternoon, I was driven to Prince Edward's production office and studios in Twickenham in Southwest London to meet the producers and cast before getting to the computer. The first thing Prince Edward asked me after polite introductions was what, in my opinion, would make the series a hit.

'Well, if you want instant success with your next episode, persuade your sisters-in-law, Princess Diana and Duchess Fergie, to make guest appearances, opening some event in the House of Commons or through some other bit of plausible plot that I can easily invent.'

Edward let out a deep breath, shaking his head and grinning.

'Very good idea, but it won't work. Fergie will want to dominate the show, and Diana is a loose cannon.'

Back home that evening, I had a deadline to meet for the weekly column 'Of Cabbages and Kings' which I had been writing for years for the *Asian Age* in India. The subject of the column was anything I chose—politics, anecdotes, opinions on anything in the world. It was a very tolerant commission. Time was short. I had to get down to viewing the tapes and meeting the deadline. What should the column be about? The easiest thing was to recount the above as an anecdote. I dashed it off and sent it and got down to scripting *Annie's Bar*.

The next day, the rest of my colleagues at Channel 4, except for Peter, had gone away for a few days and nights to a conference centre in the countryside to discuss the future programme mix of the channel. Peter and I were to follow once the *Annie's Bar* business was settled or at least under way.

I completed the first episode, submitted it, and a day later, Peter and I drove to the country to join the Channel 4 'away days'. As we entered the gates of the venue, we noticed several press and TV vans parked on the lawns. It was intriguing. Surely the media weren't interested in an internal Channel 4 conference? Our own press officer was anxiously waiting in the car park.

'Quick, Farrukh, get in the building. Run!'

'What's going on?' I asked.

'They're after you. You made some stupid remark about Princess Diana and the Duchess of York in an Indian newspaper, and the tabloid vultures are after a complete report and anything else you can tell them. Of course, the boss is furious'—he meant Michael Grade—'so keep your head down and mouth shut.'

I walked into the conference room to loud jeers and mocking applause from my colleagues.

Someone at the *Asian Age* must have read the column, realised that it would be of interest to the British press and leaked it. I escaped from the conference without being interviewed. Two tabloid newspapers carried the story in their gossip columns, using the words from my own column. My secretary warded off any further enquiries.

The only other occasion on which I interacted with British royalty was as a consequence of having written the film *Mangal Pandey*.

We were in pre-production of the film, and I was in Mumbai for it. Prince Charles was on a visit to India on some Commonwealth occasion. The British High Commission thought it would be a good idea for him to be seen inaugurating the 'shoot' of our film, especially as it had as its subject the historical events variously known as the Indian Mutiny and the First War of Independence.

Charles duly made an appearance at the ten-star hotel where a hall had been cleared for the contrived occasion. The cast and crew of the film were present, and the prince was led to the stage with the actor Aamir Khan and was filmed operating the first clapperboard. It was good publicity for the film too. Win-win.

After the clapperboard business, Charles was conducted down a row of the cast and crew of the film, accompanied by two smart-suited equerries who walked behind him. As the writer, I was somewhere down the line. The chief equerry had passed down the line and instructed us not to venture any questions to Charles but to speak only when spoken to.

When Charles came face to face with me, the producer of the film, Bobby Bedi, introduced me by name, and said I was the writer of the film and a British citizen.

'Ah, from whereabouts?' Charles asked and I told him.

'So, how long did it take you to write the screenplay?'

'Two weeks for the first draft, one year for the second,' I said.

He sort of got the joke.

'And "Farrukh" would be a Muslim?' Charles asked.

'No, I am a Parsi.'

'Oh, a Zoroastrian!' He knitted his brows. 'So, tell me, why are there so few of you?'

Instead of launching into a socio-historic reason, I said, 'Maybe something to do with our sexual inclinations?' whereupon the equerries behind the prince literally grabbed his shoulder and moved him on to the next person in the line—I think it was our composer A.R. Rahman.

But after that one project where I was offered credits and a fee, I found myself in situations where I had to come up with various ways to be a pseudonymed contributor and that was the birth of Kamal Kukuldash the Second.

One of the most popular genres spawned on television is the soap opera. When I was commissioning programmes for Channel 4, there were several jostling for attention on the British household screen, or perhaps they weren't. The fans of ITV's long-running

Coronation Street would probably pace their TV watching to accommodate the BBC's *East Enders*. These were long-running sagas of several families, the first who live in a street in Manchester and the second in the east of London. The soaps featured what masses of viewers would immediately identify with or at least empathise with. An Indian equivalent would be *Kyunki Saas Bhi Kabhi Bahu Thi*. There's such a thing as soap-addiction which has nothing to do with cleanliness.

There were issue-oriented episodes, ones which dramatised the imagined or much-vaunted current preoccupations of the populace, and there were family-oriented others, in which the eternal questions of the relations between spouses and lovers and siblings and parents and children would be enlivened through the entanglements of plot.

A few years into my job as commissioning editor, I determined to bid to the purse-string-wallas for funds to conceive and bring to the screen an Asian soap, and so was born *Family Pride*, a name chosen by the three writers on the project.

The writers, Barry Simner, Mahmood Jamal and one Kamal Kukuldash began work on the scripts. The mysterious Kukuldash remained unidentified and unphotographed in the publicity and announcements of the venture. He had to remain so—as the commissioning editor, while responsible for the production and quality of the product, I would be seen as indulging a conflict of interest if I appeared as co-writer. Of course, I was not paid a penny for the work, which could be passed off as editorial.

The pseudonym comes from history. Khusrau Kukuldash was one of the Turko-Afghan generals in the first Mughal emperor Zahir-ud-din Babur's invading army. Once Babur had established himself in the capital—the territories of Delhi and Agra—he distributed governorships and feudal suzerainty over provinces of the territory he had won to the generals who had enabled his victories. All except Kukuldash, who, because of his military prowess, was delegated over several years by Babur to subdue one rebellion after another on the borders of his newly established empire. Kukuldash was rewarded with blood, sweat and tears.

The production of *Family Pride*, with the veteran Pakistani actor Zia Mohyeddin leading the cast of mainly Asian actors, began in Birmingham, where the soap was set, and the three writers moved into a Birmingham hotel as the shoot began.

A few weeks into the shoot, it happened to be my birthday. When I returned to the hotel after the shoot, I walked down the corridor, quite exhausted, probably thinking about stepping out to an Indian restaurant in the Asian area of the city with my co-writers and a few of the crew for a celebratory dinner. As I entered the room, I found two young women sitting with their legs up on my bed and drinks in their hands.

'I'm sorry. Seem to have blundered into the wrong room,' I said, turning to leave.

'No, Farrukh, it is your room! Happy birthday!' they both said in unison.

I didn't know who they were. One was a white girl and the other an Indian, both probably in their twenties and attractive and dressed for a party.

'I'm sorry, I don't ...' I began.

'Don't be alarmed. We are your birthday present from Barry and Mahmood. We've started on your minibar. We're yours for the evening and can do whatever you want to.'

Call girls? A joke? I didn't know what to say.

'I don't ... I mean I've never ... I mean you should finish your drinks and ... just that. Then you're free.'

'Don't you find us attractive?' the Indian girl said. Both of them had strong Midland accents.

'You are very attractive, both of you, but ... I don't go professional.'

'Don't you want to know our names?' the English girl asked.

'Yeah, tell me and drink up. I'll call those bums!' I said and, picking up the phone, dialled Mahmood's room.

'Done already?' Mahmood asked, laughing into the phone.

'Bastards,' I said. 'Come and get your girls.'

They arrived in high spirits.

'So, no action?' Barry asked.

'He doesn't like us,' the Asian girl said.

'It's nothing to do with … These idiots know I don't, can't … you know …'

'C'mon girls, let's go to the bar. Farrukh, come down to the bar and we'll sing happy birthday for you.'

Writing *Family Pride* was fun. Apart from sneaking in my own written offerings and signing myself off with various pseudonyms as the episodes developed, Mahmood and I contrived some childish mischief. We named one of the white women characters Rosemary Marlow and the other, a putative Italian immigrant radio presenter, Rozanna Marwati—both of which Urdu speakers will recognise as risqué puns, the first meaning 'Fuck me every day' and the second 'She gets it all the time'. When the soap was on air, several viewers picked up the obscure facetiousness and complained to Channel 4 about the bad language.

The channel's controller called me in to enquire about these complaints. With a straight face I said there were no abusive terms or obscene dialogues in any episode.

'Some complainants say they mean different things in Urdu,' the controller said.

'Well, lots of English words form puns in different languages. My literary agent, for instance, is called Nicky Lund which in Punjabi means a tiny penis.'

'So, nothing we can be up for before the Broadcasting Standards Commission?'

'No,' I said. 'Much Urdu about nothing!'

THE SERIAL KILLER AND RED MERCURY

Eva, from her desk on the secretarial floor outside my glass cubicle, called me on our intercom.

'A feller called Charles Sobhraj wants to speak to you, Dolly. He's called quite a few times and won't say what he wants.' She began calling me Dolly Daydreams when she caught me sleeping under my Channel 4 office desk for the second time.

'Charles Sobhraj? Yeah, my god, put him through,' I said.

The French-accented voice came through.

'Monsieur Dhondy, my name is Charles Sobhraj. You might have heard of me.'

'Of course. You're the serial killer!'

'You could put it that way,' he said without the least hesitation.

'I thought you were in jail in Delhi.'

'That's all over. I am in Paris and want to come to London to see you.'

'See me? What for?' I was intrigued and taken aback. Had someone pinned a contract killing on my head?

'My cousin Raj Advani, he was in college with you in Pune, said you were the best man in Europe.'

'Raj Advani? Yes, I remember him. And I am, in many senses, the best man in Europe, but what does it mean?'

'You're a writer, yes? You see, I have written my jail memoirs, and I want to find a publisher in English. Raj tells me you would be the man.'

Charles Sobhraj's memoirs? Is he going to confess to and write about the perhaps forty murders he is said to have committed? Dynamite on the screen? Here I was, commissioning programmes for a national TV channel. Why wouldn't I want the confessions of a notorious serial killer?

'When can you come to London?' I asked.

'Tomorrow.'

'Give me an approximate time and take down the Channel 4 address. The nearest tube—metro—stations are St James' Park and Victoria.'

In my fourteen years at Channel 4, I had seen many strange characters—including a Rastafarian who wanted to do a conspiracy documentary showing the former Ethiopian emperor Haile Selassie, who had died in 1975, to still be alive—but a serial killer was still novel.

Sobhraj turned up the next morning, wearing a brown tweed jacket, cord trousers and a tweed peak cap. I couldn't see the reputed charisma of his face or figure. How could he have seduced the scores of women the books and stories about him say he had?

A Chinese girl had come with him. As they settled into my office, a relentless succession of secretarial and other staff of the channel passed outside. Eva had spread the word that I was seeing a notorious serial killer—I had told her who he was after his phone call—and everyone wanted a glimpse.

Charles had brought with him the printed manuscript of what he called his jail memoirs. He handed it to me asking what he should do to get it published. I asked him if it was exclusively about his years in jail, and he said that it was.

'What about the life and … er … experiences before going to jail?' I asked, hoping there would be something of the years during which he had committed the murders.

He said he didn't want to go into the years before. He obviously didn't want to confess to those.

'The best thing to do is to get an agent to take it on,' I said, even as I wondered who I should recommend. My own literary agent, Jacqueline Korn, was a dignified lady, a sort of queen mother of literary agents who would probably not appreciate this book and would even perhaps look askance at my acquaintance with an unsavoury character.

'I know the person who would be ideal to represent you!' I said. 'A friend of mine, Giles Gordon. He is Vikram Seth's agent.'

'Who is Vikram Seth?' Charles asked.

'Bestselling novelist,' I said and then presented Giles's credentials.

I told him how Giles had been to the Frankfurt Book Fair the previous year and walked into a bar where the editors of international publishers had gathered. He sat at the bar next to a young lady with a reputation for gossip.

'What have you got for us, Giles?' she asked, buying him a drink.

'Too big for your publishing house,' Giles is supposed to have said.

Nevertheless, as the evening wore on and the gin-and-tonics supposedly inspired confidences, Giles whispered to her that in his briefcase was the manuscript of Sean Connery's autobiography—affairs, politics, enmities, quarrels and all.

Late that night in his hotel room, he dialled the number he had researched for Connery in the US.

'Mr Connery, my name is Giles Gordon, and I am a literary agent. If you write your memoirs, I can get you perhaps six million dollars for them.'

'From your accent, Giles, you are a fellow Scotsman, and I haven't written my memoirs, but when I do, you shall be my agent,' said Connery.

Charles seemed convinced. 'He sounds like a good person.'

I picked up the phone and dialled Giles. When I mentioned the name and why I was calling, he said he was coming over right away. I introduced Charles to him, and they left together with the manuscript of the memoirs.

A week later, Giles called me to say the manuscript was a load of boasts in bad English without a hint of the criminality of the man. There was nothing worth publishing.

He said as much to Charles, whose resilience caused him to call me and ask if there was another agent I could approach. I said I would think about it, without telling him that Giles had told me that his 'book' was an unpublishable load of self-delusion.

I didn't want to sever contact with him as there was the vague possibility that he would volunteer, or be induced into revealing, the darker side of his story.

Some weeks later, late at night, my bedside phone rang.

Charles was at the Victoria Casino on Edgware Road, with his wife Chantal, who had returned to him from the USA after twenty-five years. He had lost his last penny playing blackjack in the casino and had no money to get his car out of the parking. Could I see my way to lending him enough money to get the car out, get some petrol and pay the fare of the ferry back to France? It was later that I learnt he was an inveterate gambler and perhaps the sequence of killings was a gamble with justice, a challenge to see if he could get away with murder.

Despite the lateness of the hour, I dressed and drove over to the seedy casino, having got enough money from a hole-in-the wall dispenser. The casino was the dregs, with fruit machines and crumply clothed old men sitting at gambling tables. Charles and Chantal were relieved to see me and took the money. They were going to sleep in the car in a park for a few hours and set out for the ferry at dawn.

In the months that followed, Chantal, in Paris and London, told me her story. She had run away from home with Charles when she was in her early twenties, and they had crossed over from Iran to Afghanistan. The driver of the taxi they had hired in Tehran to drive them to the border refused to cross it. They agreed or pretended to agree that he should drive them back to Tehran, and a few miles down the road, Charles 'disposed of' the driver. Chantal gave me no details about this disposal, but I drew my own conclusion. They drove to Kandahar, where they were arrested for being in possession of a stolen car. They were sent to separate, gender-segregated prisons.

Charles managed to escape or, more probably, bribed his way out of the prison and, leaving Chantal in her jail, made his way to India and Bombay. Chantal served her sentence, was thrown out penniless onto the streets of Kandahar, then rescued by an American backpacking traveller, went with him to India and eventually returned with him, who was now her husband, to the USA. She was at the time pregnant with Charles's child and gave birth to a daughter, whom the American husband generously adopted.

More than twenty-five years later, she watched Charles being interviewed on TV after being released from Tihar Jail in Delhi and on his way to being extradited to France. She decided she was still in love with him, abandoned her husband and two daughters, travelled to Paris, found Charles and proposed that they resume the relationship he had betrayed.

Charles turned up again in London one early morning and called me from the lodgings above a pub off the motorway leading into London from the South Coast. Some days or weeks earlier, Chantal had asked me if I would write a film script about Charles and that she would tell the story, as far as she knew it, and I could ask Charles about his supposed escape from Tihar Jail. When Charles said he wanted to talk to me, I assumed it was confession or, at least, anecdote time, especially as he said, 'Jus' come quickly, Farrukh. It will be helpful to you.'

In all the time I knew him, my friends, family and I joked about the possibility of him turning on me and perhaps murdering me to steal my wallet and credit cards. But it was always a joke. It never once crossed my mind that he would attempt another murder, but

I never invited him to my house and was very vigilant when we went to a restaurant to make sure that he wasn't poisoning my food or drink.

That early morning, wondering what the emergency was about, I drove over to the inn off the highway. Charles came down to the reception in the hotel section of the pub and asked me to step out into the inn's carpark with him. He got on his mobile phone and called his companions, two men in black leather jackets, and all four of us made our way to the carpark, where they had left their large truck. Charles didn't say what this was about. I didn't ask.

One of the men, who Charles said was Belgian and didn't speak any English, opened the loading door of the truck.

'Look,' Charles said.

The truck was full of furniture—ornate chests of drawers, mirrors, sets of chairs, perhaps a wardrobe and small tables.

'Antiques from Belgium and France,' he said.

'So?'

'We want to set up a business in London, selling them. London buys lots of antiques.'

I was intrigued. Why had he called me to show me his antiques?

'The thing is, Farrukh, we are all foreigners here and need a British citizen to get a lease on a shop, and for that, you have to have a British bank account and address and everything.'

'You'll need a shop in Portobello Road or Camden Town—places like that,' I said.

'It could be anywhere, near you, wherever is cheap for property. You just do this for us, and we give you proper money. Yeah?'

'And you'll run the business?' I asked.

'Just your name and passport and everything, and the money will go through your bank. Then you won't have to do anything.'

I nodded. This wasn't as straightforward as it seemed.

Charles took me aside as the two others climbed into the truck and began readjusting the furniture.

'We can give you even £100,000 for the whole year,' he said.

'For hiring a shop in my name?'

Charles looked serious and indicated I should go back to the hotel with him. He led me up the stairs to his room and said, 'I have to tell you. Look.'

He brought out from his leather suitcase a couple of what looked like catalogues and handed them to me. They were Russian. I opened one, flipping through the pages rapidly. There were photographs of tanks, armoured vehicles, anti-aircraft guns, automatic field guns, a section on small arms and what were probably specifications of each of them as the columns were dotted with numbers.

'London is the best place to do the business,' he said.

'These armaments? How will they get here?'

'Nothing comes or goes from here, just the paperwork. The stuff goes straight from the places to whoever is buying.'

The penny dropped. It was being sold by the governments or someone high-up in the military of the ex-Soviet countries, which still had, after the Soviet Union broke up, dumps of Russian arms. Belarus, Kazakhstan or the others would, through the antique dealers in London, supply the ticked-off shopping list to any and all—Al-Qaeda, Taliban, Jaish-e-Mohammed, Boko Haram, the Ku Klux Klan or whoever paid.

'I can't do this,' I said.

'What's the problem?' Charles asked.

The penny didn't just drop—it was slammed like a bullet into my head. After all, I had read and knew about him, but his question handed me the missing piece of the jigsaw. Charles Sobhraj couldn't, not wouldn't, understand why one would have qualms about being part of an operation selling arms or perhaps killing people. What was my problem? He had explained what the business was about and told me I would be paid an unbelievable sum for doing very little, so why would I not do it? Was he really some character out of Albert Camus or Dostoevsky? Some amoral being who had not relinquished morality but had never encountered or absorbed it?

My reply was, of course, disingenuous. 'I've already got a mortgage, and without a steady income, no one would allow me to take a lease on a property.'

'We can employ you and give you a salary, so you can show an income,' he said.

'My age,' I said. 'You have no idea of the restrictions of British banks. I won't be able to do what you want.'

His face fell. He had assured his partners in the enterprise that he had just the man in London to set the whole thing up.

I drove home, asking myself whether I had in some sense betrayed my own conscience. I was confident that Charles wouldn't find anyone else to set up their front for them. My refusal would kill the project. Was being asked to get a lease on a shop which may or may not be used for arms-dealing a crime? Even if I had agreed, this gang wouldn't be storing arms there. They would probably use it for some form of money-laundering.

My refusal did seem to have killed the London end of the project, but I found out later that they had set up the same deal in San Marino, a free port in Italy where fewer regulations applied and fewer questions were asked.

I realised something else about Charles. Betrayals, disappointments, even enmities could be put aside if any further material advantage was to be gained from an acquaintance or a relationship. As though there had never been the antique-shop-armaments episode, Charles rang me a few weeks later, this time from Paris, with a peculiar question: 'Farrukh, do you know anyone in the CIA?'

'How the fuck would I know anyone in the CIA?' I said, but then thought and added, 'Hang on, one of my former colleagues at Channel 4 wrote on the history of the CIA and will know people from the organisation.'

'Can I meet him?'

'I'll find out.'

I called John Ranelagh. He knew who Charles Sobhraj was and said he would meet him and, depending on what it was about, give him some CIA contacts.

Charles turned up from Paris, and I drove him to Grantchester, a village outside Cambridge where John lived.

He received us, and while I was shunted off to the stables belonging either to Mrs Ranelagh or a neighbour and was shown to the horses or they to me, Charles strolled around with John, getting, or being refused, contact with the American intelligence agency.

We drove back to London, and Charles seemed smug and pleased but wouldn't say what he had got from John.

Years later, I learnt that the reason he had wanted a CIA contact was to offer them a bargain. If the CIA could get the US administration to give him citizenship, a lifelong pension and change of identity so he and a partner of his choice could live happily ever after in some recess of the country, he would, in exchange, give them evidence about the terrorist and insurrectionary groups he had been acquainted with through the arms trade. Charles seemed happy at the time that the CIA would do this deal with him if he had the right sort of information they wanted.

In characteristic fashion, a few months later, Charles called me in the December of 1999 when there was a crisis in India. An Indian Airlines plane had been hijacked by members of the Pakistani terrorist outfit Jaish-e-Mohammed. The hijackers had forced the plane to land in Kandahar in Afghanistan and were threatening to kill all the Indian citizens on board unless the Indian government released, in exchange for the lives of these passengers, the Pakistani terrorists being held in Indian prisons.

Charles claimed to be a friend of Masood Azhar, the head of Jaish-e-Mohammed who had been in Tihar Jail with him, and that the terrorist was grateful to him. Charles had supposedly saved him from assault by other Indian jail inmates who, in patriotic fervour, had been against Pakistani terrorists. He boasted on the phone that he could intervene in this international crisis if I could put him in touch with the then Indian foreign minister, Jaswant Singh, who was dealing with the crisis and considering the hijackers' demands.

I told Charles that I was acquainted with several senior Indian civil servants and would immediately put his offer of negotiation to them, and they could probably convey it to the minister.

Hours after I had spoken to a friend, a high-up official in the Indian Administrative Service who might have a direct line to Jaswant Singh, the answer came back—they had noted the connections but didn't want to be known for having used a serial killer as an intermediary. They were, nevertheless, willing to accept the hijackers' terms. These were the terms Charles had told me the terrorists would probably set. Was he in touch with the hijackers or others in the terror group?

Jaswant Singh took charge of the operation, flew to Kathmandu and made an agreement with the hijackers to free the hostages. One of the hostages had been murdered in cold blood even before the negotiations had begun, but the rest were freed in exchange for the terrorist assassins.

Charles, to this day, claims that he was instrumental in the negotiation, having been the go-between. I know he wasn't.

I suppose I must have mentioned to Charles that I had a degree in physics because one day in 2001 he called from Paris with a peculiar question: 'Farrukh, what is red mercury?'

As far as I knew from having read about it in the popular science articles in newspapers, it was something Russian nuclear scientists claimed to have concocted from antimony, a small quantity of which could act as a powerful trigger for nuclear bombs. I told him this, adding that several other scientists were sceptical because such a substance would be unstable and couldn't exist, and asked why he wanted to know—he was not someone

I would characterise as a seeker of scientific knowledge. Charles wouldn't tell me why he was asking.

For the next two years, I forgot that he had, until George Bush and Tony Blair invaded Iraq in 2003 under the pretext of Saddam Hussein hoarding weapons of mass destruction—WMD, as they were called—chemical, biological and nuclear, with which Hussein apparently threatened Israel and even Britain and the USA. I joined the march of millions in London protesting the UK's involvement in this war. We demanded that Britain not join the USA and even discouraged Bush from waging war on Iraq.

It wasn't that I believed Hussein to be a benevolent democratic head of State—he was a dictator and tyrant, but such was the condition of the Middle East's religious and political cauldron that he was the sort of tyrant to keep the lid on it. Besides, the media of Britain had revealed that Blair and his publicity spokesperson had lied to parliament based on a 'dodgy dossier' about Hussein's possession of WMD. We anti-war demonstrators felt perfectly justified in this denunciation of Blair as a liar and a prime minister who was willing to sacrifice the lives of Iraqis—soldiers and thousands of civilians—and those of Britain's fighting forces in subservience to US policy and based on a manifest lie.

Then I remembered my chat with Charles. I called him. Why had he asked me what red mercury was?

This time he was forthcoming. He said he had been in negotiation with some clients who wanted to acquire red mercury and had approached his San Marino firm to get it from the ex-Soviet stockpiles.

'Did you get some? And sell it? To whom?'

'I went to Bahrain to negotiate with some Arab fellows about this. I have their messages, emails and some recordings which I secretly took of our meeting.'

'Bahrain? Could these clients have been Iraqis?'

'They could have been.'

'Can you come to London and bring the emails and all this with you. Like now?'

He didn't know why I was asking.

'You are probably sitting on a huge international story. If they were Iraqi clients trying to buy a nuclear trigger on behalf of Hussein's government, then these bastards Bush and Blair, much though I don't like it, could have been telling the truth about Hussein and WMD.'

Charles came over from Paris that night and lodged in a dingy hotel in Victoria.

I called Peter Oborne, a journalist acquaintance and columnist for the *Spectator*, a right-wing magazine which would certainly want to put the boot into the Labour prime minister. The editor of the *Spectator* at the time was Boris Johnson, who is now the Conservative prime minister of the UK. When I told Oborne about Charles's dealings, he said he and Johnson would meet Charles and me at his house in Highbury at half past seven the next morning for breakfast.

At Oborne's house, Charles boasted that he had coded messages from the Arab customers on email and that he had secretly recorded on his phone the negotiations with them about the price, date and place of delivery of the red mercury. Johnson was intrigued but said if this was true it was too big a story to break in the *Spectator*, which was a weekly without the front-page-news format the story required. He would call the *Daily Telegraph*, which would gladly run it.

He phoned a journalist called Mike from the *Daily Telegraph*, who came over within the hour. Having given Charles the contacts, I left them and went about my daily business. That evening, Mike called me and said that Charles was demanding a few hundred thousand pounds to even show them the emails and give them access to the recordings. Journalists were not legally supposed to pay for such stories, he said. It was between him, the newspaper and Charles was what I told him. I had nothing more to do with it.

Soon after that, Charles called. He said the *Daily Telegraph* was offering him peanuts as 'expenses', and he would, in time, sell the story to the USA. He was sure they would pay him a proper amount. Did I know anyone in the press there? I didn't, but there were certainly ways of getting to such a person. Charles said he would do it on his return from Kathmandu in Nepal, where he claimed to have some very important business.

What was he doing there? He said he couldn't tell me over the phone, but he did tell me later that evening, on his way from London to Paris.

He had fixed a meeting in Kathmandu with the Taliban, who wanted to buy a huge shipment of weapons from his San Marino firm. They didn't have the money in dollars to pay for them, but they had large quantities of heroin grown in Afghanistan. Being a localised religious order, they had no way of selling it on the international market and getting dollars in exchange. Charles had arranged for representatives of the Chinese triads from Paris to meet the Taliban in Kathmandu so they could acquire the heroin, sell it on the international market through their drug-dealing networks and hand the money to Charles's arms-dealing firm, which would in turn supply the Taliban with the ex-Soviet weaponry from neighbouring countries through overland routes.

Was this his fantasy? Was he really going to Kathmandu? All through the episodes of him trying to set up an antique-shop front, through the red mercury claim and now this, I was uncertain as to whether he actually had any access to arms he claimed he was selling. Was there really a business in San Marino? Who were the other criminals in his syndicate? Was he a prime mover in this enterprise as he claimed, or were some international arms dealers using him as a pliable idiot? I had no way of knowing.

A month or so later, I read in the papers that Charles had been arrested in Nepal for a murder he had committed in the 1970s and would face trial there. He had been using a false French name and passport and had spent twenty-eight days in the country instead of three as he had told me.

He was arrested in the basement of a casino, playing blackjack. A retired policeman, who claimed to have recognised him from having been on the murder case twenty-seven years ago, had spotted and arrested him in the casino. Charles was tried, convicted for murder, principally on the word of the ex-policeman who arrested him, and sentenced to life imprisonment.

To my great surprise, a few months after his arrest, Charles called me on a mobile from a Kathmandu prison and asked if I could research the availability of hot-air balloons in India. As he had done in Tihar Jail, he had acquired the use of a mobile by bribing the prison staff. I was in Bombay when I got this call, editing the script for a Vishal Bhardwaj film called *Maqbool*, a Hindi adaptation of Shakespeare's *Macbeth*, and asked one of my researchers to check it out, just to play along with the cartoonish absurdity of escaping from a walled prison in a hot-air balloon.

Siddharth, the researcher, came up with three Indian manufacturers. Charles asked me for the dimensions of the most compact one. The smallest balloon would be twenty by thirty metres and would have to have a metal gas-burner, which would be at least three-feet high. I conveyed this to him on a subsequent call, and he asked if the whole apparatus could fit into two suitcases. He obviously didn't understand the physics of hot-air balloons. I said no, and that was the end of it.

Years later, a speculative explanation for his trip to Kathmandu came my way through a chain of Chinese whispers. A friend of a friend, a Chinese individual, had perhaps picked up the story from the Chinese mother of another of Charles's children, whom he had abandoned for Chantal when she came to look for him in Paris.

Charles, the story goes, had set up the tripartite meeting in Kathmandu, as he had claimed, between the Taliban, the Chinese triads and himself as the arms dealer. He had intended to go through with the deal but would eventually betray all the parties involved to the CIA contact he had acquired through John Ranelagh, whom I had introduced him to. Someone in the Chinese community of Paris tipped off the triads, and they didn't turn up in Nepal. The CIA realised that Charles's cover as their agent had been blown and, through whatever means, persuaded the Nepalese government to arrest and jail him.

Charles, in jail for life in Kathmandu, constantly told his lawyer, according to her statements in the press, that if the Maoists came to power, they would release him as he was innocent of the two murders for which he was serving two life sentences and that he was framed. Does he mean that the Maoists, being viscerally opposed to all things American and the CIA, would be aware that he was a victim of American intrigue and free him?

Hot-air balloons, the triumph of Maoism in Nepal and then in March 2020, the worldwide outbreak of the corona virus, causing the Nepalese government to release prisoners over seventy-five years of age—hope yet, then, for Charles, who tells the media that he will go to Kolkata after being released and do charitable work with poor children.

In 2008, I published a book called *The Bikini Murders*, a work of fiction based on the life of Charles Sobhraj. I didn't use Sobhraj's name but called the main character, a serial murderer, Johnson Thaat.

The book was extensively reviewed in India as a biographical account of Sobhraj's crimes, and I was invited onto TV by the notorious anchor Arnab Goswami to talk about the book. A few minutes into the interview at the Times Now studio, Arnab said, 'I have a surprise for you.'

The screen cut to Charles in Kathmandu jail. Asked what he thought of my book, he said that it was outrageous and that he and his lawyers would sue me for millions for defamation.

He said, 'This Farrukh is just a middleman.' Presumably, his lawyers must have advised him not to use the word he intended.

Arnab was, I could see, enjoying the encounter he had set up. It was good television.

I wasn't in the least disconcerted and responded, 'I see, Charles, you are identifying with the character in my book. So, are you saying you committed the murders that the book says he did? And, of course, you are free to sue me for defamation of character, but being a person sentenced to life for murder, there's not much damage the book has done to your impeccable reputation.'

When he called me a 'middleman' again, I said, 'You obviously want to call me a "pimp". Please go right ahead. If Nelson Mandela called me anything of the sort, I'd be deeply hurt, but you can say what you fucking like!'

The cameras then turned, at Arnab's behest, to Paris, where a lady said she was a lawyer representing Charles Sobhraj and they were going to sue me for every euro I didn't have.

I recognised her. She was married to a killer called 'The Jackal', who was at the time imprisoned in France. I said so and that she had been the representative of genocidal murderers such as the Yugoslavian president Slobodan Milošević. She was welcome to sue me. If she had been alive in the seventeenth century, she would have certainly sued Milton for libelling Satan and bringing his impeccable character into heroic disrepute.

They didn't sue.

FILMS I DIDN'T WRITE

After successful ventures commissioning feature and documentary films came the opportunity to commission a radical story which would significantly advance the range and feasibility of Indian cinema.

Phoolan Devi had risen from being born into an oppressed caste of rural Hindu society to become one of the most notorious bandits in contemporary India. Her life and times, her character and crimes had been researched and written into a moving and compelling account by Mala Sen. She had spent years doing this, interviewing Phoolan Devi in jail, talking to her family and her bandit associates. The book was published to great acclaim by HarperCollins.

Twelve years before its publication, in 1979, when Mala and I were working together in *Race Today* and in the East End, we had decided to formalise our separation and get a divorce. It was Mala's idea. I didn't know whether she suggested it because she wanted to marry someone else or whether it was a question of gaining some symbolic freedom.

Her book was called *India's Bandit Queen*, and I felt that a film based on the book would not only hold a mirror up to the practices and injustices of contemporary India but also radicalise Indian cinema as it would ignore the conventions of Bollywood, such as the inclusion of imitatively choreographed song-and-dance sequences, and present real drama with a greater compulsion than the melodrama in which Indian films conventionally traded.

It would be a film that was neither Bollywood nor fall into the category of Indian 'art'—films which were either self-conscious and self-indulgent 'auteur' conceits or agitprop-ish films which could be called 'behalfist', made by concerned radicals on behalf of some oppressed section of society, profession or other category of 'sufferer'.

Mala had written a brilliant book, and ignoring the risk of being accused of nepotism, I paid a production company with vast experience in drama to support her in writing a script. The months passed, and Mala, while saying she needed a few more days or weeks to complete the draft, presented me, through the production company, with a tome the size of a telephone directory.

I began to read it. It wasn't a screenplay. It was a diatribe in which a multitude of characters stated their political and revolutionary points of view about Indian society's evils, land reform, the suffering of the peasantry and twenty other causes dear to the deeply socialistic and even revolutionary disposition and convictions of Mala Sen. All very real, very convincing but not anything one could turn into a film, with characters taking several pages to present a rhetorical point of view.

Disaster. I pointed this out to Mala, and she was adamant. That was what she wanted on screen. For seven hours? I asked. She said I was only considering the commerciality and not the truth of the presentation.

My boss Michael Grade called me to his office.

'This project you've got on, the feature film called *Bandit Queen*, is it on its way?'

'Getting there,' I lied.

'Can you tell me the names of the production company, the director, and can I see a script? Not to approve or disapprove, that's your job, but it sounds good—the way you describe it anyway. Pop the script onto my desk, I'll read it over the weekend.'

'Ah, still a bit of work to do on it,' I said.

'Will it get done soon? We've put a million in your budget, and if it can wait till next year, the other commissioning editors are clamouring for the cash ...'

'No, Michael. It's all set to go,' I persisted. 'I'll get the contracts for the director and producer and show you the script in a few days, and then we're off shooting.'

I don't think my body language or my brazenly straight face betrayed me, or perhaps he was distracted as he looked into the distance.

'Great,' he said.

I got back to my office and phoned Bobby Bedi, who had produced another film in India for me. When I asked if he would produce *Bandit Queen*, he said he had been waiting to be asked. It meant I had a producer. He was in London, and I asked him to come to the Wandsworth Studios that evening, where Shekhar Kapur, the Indian film director, two of whose films I hadn't commissioned but had acquired for broadcast, would be hosting one of my chat shows called *On the Other Hand*.

Bobby and I watched the recording of the show together and then invited Shekhar to the pub adjoining the studio. I bought drinks and told Shekhar there was a serious subject I needed to raise: Would he direct *Bandit Queen*, the story of Phoolan Devi?

He said he couldn't say yes without seeing a script.

I understood that, I said, but this was an emergency. There wasn't a script, but there would be one in a few days. Had he read the book?

He said he hadn't but had read all about it. 'Who's writing the script?' he asked.

That was the precise moment I decided that I was. There was no one else I could compel or rely on to deliver it within the timeframe to avoid Grade's threat of taking the money out of my budget.

'I am,' I said.

I'll never know what Shekhar thought of that then.

'I need a director to commit, or I'll lose the project,' I pressed. 'Look, by the time I drain this beer, Shekhar, please say yes or no, so I can start phoning other directors in India. But, of course, you are my first choice.'

He bit his lip and stayed silent till my pint of beer was down to its last inch.

'OK, I'll do it.'

We shook hands, Bobby, Shekhar and I.

I had a director and producer and could name them, but no script and a commitment to write one.

It was risky. I couldn't commission myself officially and couldn't under any circumstances pay myself or take credit on the screen. I was sanguinely conscious of all that. But, time! Working at my job wouldn't leave me any.

The next day, Caroline Thomas, the deputy commissioning editor for Music and a dear friend who sat a few cabins down from mine, on hearing my dilemma, offered me the key to her parents' cottage outside Bordeaux in France.

'Take a few days off—say you're working on the project away from the office.'

Which is what I did. Or we did.

Over eight days in Bordeaux, writing six to eight hours a day, by and large sticking to the information in Mala's book but weaving it into a film plot; taking time off each evening to visit the chateaus of the famous wine-producing region to taste and bring back bottles of wine; riding and dismantling Caroline's brother's racing bicycle without being able to put it back; having barbecues in the summer evenings and listening in the main to Nusrat Fateh Ali Khan and Bob Dylan tapes, the first draft of the screenplay was done.

It was variously discussed, modified and then filmed in the badlands of central India, where I visited for ten days, living with Bobby and Shekhar in the borrowed hunting lodge of the local maharaja. We drove to the set in hired jeeps with an armed ex-bandit in each for security against newer contemporary bandits who would stay away if they knew—and their intelligence networks were infallible—that the legendary Man Singh was riding shotgun.

The film tells the story of the oppressed-caste girl who, raped and humiliated, rises above the persecution and takes revenge.

In one scene of the screenplay, Phoolan Devi is stripped naked in the village square by the dominant-caste Thakurs who have captured and raped her. She is then made to walk across the village square to the well to fetch water for her tormentors—an extreme form of humiliation. I included this in the screenplay because Phoolan Devi herself had given a vivid description of the horror she had been subjected to, and I wrote the scene following her account precisely.

The actor Seema Biswas, who played Phoolan Devi, despite having read the script and signed a contract without raising an objection, refused to do this nude scene. Shekhar and Bobby understood her reluctance, and we collectively had the option of changing the scene, omitting it or modifying it. Shekhar insisted on keeping it as it was written and suggested recruiting a 'body double' who would agree to do it.

Without proclaiming his directorial strategy, which he explained in detail to the actor who played the body double, Shekhar had a flimsy fence constructed all round the square. The scene's action commenced within it, and the actor, stripped of her ragged clothes, began her walk to the well. As the camera rolled, Shekhar directed the stage-hands to demolish the fence, revealing the shivering actress to the hundreds of villagers gathered behind it. Some had climbed to the roofs of the adjoining houses to get a better view of the 'sooting'.

The camera captured their genuinely astounded reactions.

The scene as Shekhar had it shot was, for all the horror of the reality, filmed with a subtlety that made it shocking but far from pornographic.

I had asked Darcus to come along from London with the British film crew to India, which he had never visited. As we drove from the Delhi airport to the guest houses where the crew was booked to stay, we passed through the impressive imperial centre of New Delhi. Darcus looked out at the domineering buildings and the avenues of the city.

'Dhondy, who built all this?' he asked.

'The Brits,' I said.

'They intended to stay, boy,' he said casually.

When in the next few days, as the pre-production progressed in Delhi, Bobby arranged a sightseeing trip for the London crew, I drove down in the hired coach with them to Agra to see the Taj Mahal and then on to the historic pavilions of Fatehpur Sikri.

This latter red sandstone enclosure was built by the Mughal emperor Akbar in gratitude for the birth of his first son, which he attributed to the blessing of Sheikh Salim Chishti, a Sufi saint who had predicted the birth and had a shrine just outside the walls of Akbar's construction.

This was a grand collection of pavilions, and Akbar's ambition, it is said, was to have habitations and his empire's capital built round it. It never happened. Historians say the river nearby changed course, and being without water, the plan for a city had to be abandoned.

As we reached the tourist spot and alighted from the coach, we were besieged by the touts and 'guides' who hang around historic sites, offering genuine guidance or selling souvenirs.

'No bar flies, no bar flies,' Darcus said. 'Dhondy here knows more history than you all!'

We went into the complex, and Darcus asked me the obvious questions.

I told him that Akbar was reputed to be the greatest of the dynasty as he attempted to reconcile all the differences of religion amongst his nobles and subjects.

'So, no tragedy then?' Darcus asked.

'Actually, there is a very legendary story which is tragic, associated with Akbar,' I said and proceeded to tell him the famous, perhaps apocryphal, story of Akbar's son Prince Salim falling in love with a courtesan of the Mughal court called Anarkali, whose name means the bud of the pomegranate. Salim declared his love and announced that he was going to marry her. Akbar, dismayed, said that was not possible. Salim would succeed him as emperor of India, and he couldn't make an empress of a mere courtesan. He was free to use her services, as that was her profession, but making her a wife was out of the question.

As I told the story, the crew, mostly women, gathered round to listen.

Salim was defiant, I continued, and his father sent him off to the wars, hoping he would be killed instead of bringing disgrace on the Mughal dynasty. But Salim returned triumphant. Akbar asked him to relent and give up his demand of marrying Anarkali, but his son stubbornly insisted that no power on earth could command him to surrender his love. Akbar said he had already made arrangements with the royal family of Persia, one of whose daughters would be engaged to Salim, and eventually accede to the Mughal throne. Salim refused such an arrangement, and for his defiance, was thrown into prison by his father.

Akbar then summoned Anarkali and offered her a large sum of money and pension for life if she would leave India and go to Afghanistan, where she could live out her days in comfort. Anarkali refused. She would marry the man she loved and who loved her. Akbar doubled the sum on offer, but it made no difference. Anarkali refused.

Akbar was furious and ordered the execution of Anarkali—who was, it was said, pregnant at the time—by the cruellest means: of being suffocated to death by being entombed in the hollow of one of the pillars being built in a new palace in the western capital of Lahore.

'So it was ordered and so it was done,' I concluded.

Not a dry eye under that Fatehpur sky, at least so I thought from the reactions of my female colleagues. Darcus said nothing.

In the early hours as our coach made its way back to Delhi, a voice, talking to itself, broke our intermittent slumbers.

'But wait! The boy brings a whore into de house and say I want to marry she. I say no! He say he's in love. I say these are not matters of love, these are matters of social and political arrangement. The boy still say no. So I get him outta de way, and I call de woman and say take de money and go. She say no. I say I'll double de cash. She still say no. You know what I say? I say, wall the bitch!'

From that night on, if there was any hitch in the filming or on set, people would shout, 'Wall the bitch!'

In these months, as the film was in preparation, Mala engaged the voluntary service of Kamini Jaiswal, an eminent lawyer, who pleaded for Phoolan Devi's release through the courts. The politics of the state of Uttar Pradesh played its part. The then chief minister Mulayam Singh Yadav, who was entitled to interpret the terms on which she had surrendered, calculated that releasing Phoolan Devi would win the votes of several million who belonged to her caste and sympathised with her. It was the way of India's democracy. After her release, the film, released in 1996, assisted in propelling her into India's parliament, but more of that later.

Bandit Queen was the most famous film I didn't write.

There were other films before this, to which too I couldn't put my name. Similar circumstances had brought one of these about. Laurens Postma, an innovative director, came to me with a story about a black DJ and musician who commits suicide on live TV. It was a fascinating plot, but he hadn't managed to turn it into a viable screenplay and realised this himself after it was commissioned. Laurens had called it *Midnight Breaks*, and its conceit was that it would be shot entirely at night and only break into a daylight scene at the very end.

So, putting shoulder to the wheel, when he appealed to me knowing that I had written TV and films before, I wrote it, again without acknowledgement or money, but with the satisfaction of knowing that an original film was being broadcast in 1986 under the aegis of my department and that I had made a good friend of the director who would go on to work with me on several projects.

And the same happened with Jamil Dehlavi's *Immaculate Conception*, a story of primitive subcontinental beliefs set in and around a Sufi shrine in Pakistan. Again, I worked with the director and supplied the script because he said he couldn't trust anyone else to know the background, supply observed and accurate dialogue and make a proper story of it. Jamil induced some big stars to work with him, and the movie, released in 1992, went on to win prizes at international festivals.

The next film I didn't write came about in a similar way. Pamela Rooks, a young Indian director, came to me in 1996 through Bobby—by then a very respectable and renowned producer—proposing that she turn Khushwant Singh's famous novel *Train to Pakistan* into a film. The novel, set in the days and horrors of Partition, is regarded as a classic and certainly as the prolific Khushwant's most celebrated work.

After I commissioned the project, Pamela began writing the script, having moved with Bobby to a hotel in Goa, perhaps inspired by the producer's stint of isolated, concentrated writing of *Bandit Queen* in Bordeaux.

In a few weeks, he sent me the screenplay Pamela had produced, with a severe note saying that both he and Pamela thought it didn't work and that he had a deadline. He had already lined up the cast and crew. They were in the process of pre-production, booking locations, recruiting extras, etc., and a significant part of the budget had been either spent or legally committed. There was no question of aborting the project.

I read the script, and it wasn't going to work. I asked Bobby on the phone what he intended to do. He should get another writer, pronto. He said there was no one he could think of who would work to the deadline the production had to stick to, if the whole project were not to go into massive overspend, except me.

I must say here that none of these producers and directors, who extended the flattery of saying they could think of no other writer, ever said it was for the quality of the drama. I hope they meant it, but they always attributed their faith in me to speed up, to meeting deadlines and to acceptability. Oh well.

I went to Goa, borrowing my cousin's flat, which happened to be in the same village as Bobby and Pamela's hotel. I got down to writing on my portable typewriter and, on the second day, suffered from painful stomach cramps. I went to a local doctor in the high street, and he, after some tests, prescribed a medicine, which the pharmacist supplied without specifying what the dosage should be. I couldn't be bothered to go back to either him or the doctor and took what I arrogantly thought would sort me out.

I was very, very sick, having taken four doses, one every three hours, instead of, as I found out when I was forced to go back to the doctor, just one a day.

Nevertheless, starting from scratch and devising my own story from the novel, which I read on the plane from London to Mumbai, the screenplay was done in time. Bobby told me that at the private screening to launch the film, Khushwant himself ultra-modestly told Pamela that he thought it was better than the novel.

The last film I didn't write remained unacknowledged for a reason very different from the others which were Channel 4 commissions. It was soon after I resigned from the network to resume my writing career, which had been, at least publicly, interrupted by the prohibitions of my employment—not being allowed to write for Channel 4 or for any other station, and not having the time to write a book, though I did manage to write three during my fourteen years of commissioning.

I was approached by Jamil Dehlavi and Akbar Ahmed. Akbar, whom I knew as a fellow undergraduate at Cambridge, had, in the years after we graduated, built a reputation as something of an Islamic academic, albeit of liberal inclinations.

On an afternoon in 1997, the two of them took me to lunch and asked if I would write a screenplay about Muhammad Ali Jinnah, the founder and father of Pakistan. As Pakistanis, Akbar elaborated, they wanted a grand film to rival or equal Richard Attenborough's *Gandhi*.

I immediately said I was out of sympathy with Jinnah, his leadership and his demand to partition the subcontinent, which had led to millions of deaths and a historical tragedy.

They had anticipated my answer and my objections but asked me to consider the undoubted truth that I was viewing Jinnah's actions and ideas through the prism of Indian nationalism.

My father and family had been ardent Indian nationalists and supporters of Nehru and Gandhi, and I had been brought up hearing arguments against Jinnah, of whom one British official of the Raj had purportedly said, 'Ah, Mr Jinnah, the man who has a problem for every solution!'

'Yes, I suppose I am viewing Jinnah through lifelong convictions and a feeling that Indians and Pakistanis are one people and should never have been divided into separate nations,' I retorted.

'We may even agree with you,' Jamil said. 'But Partition was not all Jinnah's doing. Nehru and the Congress played an instrumental part in stimulating or causing it.'

I had heard these arguments before, but now Jamil said they dearly wanted me to come up with a story and write the screenplay and would I keep an open mind and read Stanley Wolpert's historically objective biography of the man?

Could I refuse without displaying bigotry? I said I would read it, along with other biographies. Akbar asked me to come back to them and tell them that there was a balanced story to be told, even though he actually wanted Jinnah to be portrayed as mythically heroic—he repeatedly alluded to Attenborough's film, saying Jinnah deserved equal treatment.

I read the books, and yes, some historical opinion overruled my innate nationalism, even though I couldn't and won't believe that Jinnah didn't foresee the slaughter that would ensue from Partition, and it was, still is, unforgivably short-sighted, if not selfish. Even after reading the sympathetic biographies by Wolpert and a few Pakistani writers, it left me in no doubt that Jinnah was a lawyer who had won an argument and got lumbered with a country. He had had no idea what to do with it or where it would go. He had fought all through the Independence struggle for a Muslim-majority country, but in one of the first speeches he gave after having achieved this, he claimed that Pakistan would be secular. He couldn't see that Pakistan would inevitably declare itself an Islamic nation.

I told Jamil and Akbar that I had a story to tell, but it may not be the one they wanted told. I outlined my plot, which wasn't unsympathetic to Jinnah and began with his death and ascent to heaven, where he is questioned by the angel Gabriel.

They approved of my story, and Akbar offered me a £12,000 fee. I agreed.

'There's only one thing,' Akbar said. 'You can't have onscreen credit for the screenplay or proclaim in any media that you wrote the film.'

I didn't quite get it, which he must have seen from my expression, so he went on to explain. 'The potential financiers of the film are all ardent nationalistic Pakistani businessmen. You are an Indian by birth, a non-Muslim Parsi and have a reputation for being a Marxist. If you are known to have written the film, they won't finance it.'

I understood and had decided it would be interesting to write. I would settle for the money and giggle all the way to the bank.

I gave Jamil and Akbar the final screenplay. Throughout the process of casting, Jamil consulted me. He cast Christopher Lee, the actor famous for playing Dracula, as the elderly Jinnah. It was a brilliantly appropriate piece of casting, and Lee enthusiastically embraced the role.

I didn't go near the shoot. On Christmas, Akbar sent me some more money saying he wanted to give me a bonus beyond the agreement.

Once the film was complete, Akbar negotiated a showing at London's National Film Theatre. I was invited by Jamil and went with Piki to the screening. I enjoyed it and was reassured that it was close to what I had written, except for some sentences of Islamic rhetoric that Akbar had written into Lee's speeches. The credits at the end attributed the screenplay to Akbar and Jamil.

After the show, Akbar was with the Pakistani high commissioner and other grandees, and when I encountered him, he looked apprehensive, unsure of what I would say.

'Congratulations, Akbar,' was what I said, offering my hand. 'Great script!'

He took my hand, smiling nervously, and said, 'Thank you, thank you!'

That was the end of that, till I met Jamil some weeks later. He and Akbar were in bitter dispute. It was over the credits for the film and the budget papers, which Jamil had got a copy of and was dismayed to see that very many of Akbar's relatives had been credited with having done things they had no part in and been paid extravagant fees. There were relatives who were 'script consultants' and had been paid ten times what I had, legitimately and uncomplainingly, received as the payment for the entire screenplay.

Jamil then told me that Akbar had shown the film to General Musharraf, who had recently taken over the government of Pakistan through a military coup. Mush had loved the film and, as a reward, had appointed Akbar as Pakistani high commissioner to the UK. Jamil was least pleased.

In the following weeks, as their dispute progressed and was even about to be taken to court, I received a phone call from one

Seumas Milne, who said he was a journalist with the *Guardian* and was investigating the origins of the film. He asked me straightforwardly if I had written the screenplay.

I said I didn't know what he was talking about.

'So, it's a no comment? You refuse to say one way or the other?' he asked.

'Nothing to say,' I said.

The conversation ended, but a few hours later, he called back. 'Farrukh, I have here a slip of paper which declares that you have sold the screenplay of *Jinnah* to Akbar Ahmed for the sum of one pound. It's signed by you.'

I did not recall signing such a piece of paper, but in the process of handing over the screenplay, I must have. Akbar must have wanted to protect himself against all contingencies is what I vaguely remember thinking.

'I don't recollect such a document,' I said.

'There are no two ways about it,' he said. 'Either this is your signature, and you did write *Jinnah* and signed the script over to Mr Ahmed, who is now the high commissioner of Pakistan, or you are accusing him of forgery!'

'I am not accusing anyone of anything.'

'Then you did write *Jinnah*,' he said very coolly.

He had me there. I don't know where he had got hold of that chit, which I subsequently saw and then confirmed my signature.

The fact of the authorship was out. Apart from the *Guardian*, several newspapers picked it up, and the story spread to Pakistan.

A prominent Pakistani newspaper called me. 'Mr Dhondy, you did write the film *Jinnah*?'

There was no way I could now deny it. 'Yes, I did.' I said. 'And if General Musharraf is handing out diplomatic posts for doing it, I would gladly be Pakistan's ambassador to Tahiti and promise to look after Pakistan's interests after I have seen to a few of my own.'

The idiots published the quote verbatim. I have always suspected that most subcontinentals lack a sense of irony.

Jinnah was released for a brief spell in Pakistan. It had, certainly with Christopher Lee playing what is probably his most creative role, the potential for international popularity. Jamil insisted that the legal disputes between various parties had stymied the distribution. I don't suppose that world audiences, apart from some bigots in Pakistan, would have given a flying fox's fuck that the film was written by an Indian Parsi with a leftish reputation.

Films are, as a form, perhaps 19 per cent art and 81 per cent commerce—not exact figures, but bear with me! Distribution is all. In most cases, there is bargaining about the cost and extent of distribution, and for some films, as with *Jinnah*, there are battles over it.

And so it was with *Bandit Queen*.

When the film was finally ready, Bobby invited guests to a private viewing in the Alliance Française in Delhi. The audience, he reported, was perhaps disconcerted but positive and admiring. Among the invitees were the writer Arundhati Roy and her husband Pradip Krishen.

Before *Bandit Queen*, I had commissioned a film called *Electric Moon* for Channel 4, which Roy had written, I had script-edited, Pradip had directed and Bobby had produced. We were, I thought, all friends.

It came, then, as a bit of a shock when Bobby received a court notice forbidding the distribution of the film, followed by articles in the press by Roy, accusing the producer, director and writer of traducing Phoolan Devi's rights by depicting the violent rapes she had described to Mala.

Later, we came to know that Roy had encouraged Phoolan Devi to launch a case against the film, protesting the depictions of rape and to prevent its distribution.

The case was heard in the Delhi High Court. A group of supporters for the case accompanied Phoolan Devi to court for each hearing. Bobby, who was being sued as producer, and Mala, as writer, had hired the services of prominent lawyers. The one who represented Mala, Arun Jaitley, would go on to be India's finance minister. The ongoing case meant the distribution of the film anywhere in the world was legally blocked.

The case lumbered on for months, when one day, Colin Leventhal, Channel 4's head of Finance, walked into my office and complained that it was costing him millions: the insurers of the network's other films had heard of the case and raised premiums or refused cover. He pulled out a chequebook and some forms which he asked me to sign.

'What for?' I asked

'To authorise you to sign cheques on Channel 4's account,' Colin said.

I was puzzled.

'Go to Delhi and fix it,' he said. 'Your secretary has your plane ticket. Your clothes are in a bag in a taxi waiting to take you to the airport. Now!'

He walked out before I had a chance to protest. I landed up that night in Delhi. Regardless of the lateness of the hour, Bobby called Phoolan Devi's husband.

'Farrukh Dhondy *saheb* London *sey ayenh hain abhi, saath* chequebook *layeh hein*.' I was here from London and with a chequebook. The husband got it. Bobby asked if that would solve the problem.

Of course, it would, the husband Umed Singh replied. '*Mein palang mey samjha deyta* Phoolan *ko*'—I will convince her in bed—is what he said. If the financial negotiations were successful, Phoolan Devi would, of course, drop the case and support the film.

At seven the next morning, Bobby met Singh at the Delhi race course, with our car and Singh's driving into the central ground inside the race track. It was like a scene out of a mafia movie. Bobby got out and went to Singh. My cheque for £40,000 changed hands with a promise of a further amount from the film's distribution company, owned by Amitabh Bachchan.

Before midday, accompanied by a jobbing lawyer she had picked up, Phoolan Devi walked past the supporters of the case gathered on the steps of the court, went in and asked the judge to drop the case. It was dropped there and then.

Bobby had, even while the case was being heard, approached the Film Federation of India to consider nominating *Bandit Queen* as India's entry for an international Oscar. It was duly entered, and the news that it was the country's official entry was reported. A friend, supposedly on the inside of the Californian Oscars institution, called me to say we stood a very strong chance as the votes came in. But the Film Federation of India received instructions from the court to withdraw the film from the Oscars. So it was written, so it was ignominiously done. Shekhar Kapur was deprived of a potential Oscar.

Phoolan Devi repeatedly told the press that she enthusiastically supported the film. In the political campaign that she fought to get into parliament, she and her husband would tell their electoral audiences to watch the film to see how she had been brutally treated and who the victim was and who the perpetrators.

Having had the case withdrawn, I returned to my office in London. But it wasn't the end of the story.

I received a phone call from a person saying he worked at Robert Laffont, a French publisher. He asked me to delay the release of Channel 4's film for six years and that they would make it 'worth my while'. I pretended I didn't know whom he represented and why he was making this absurd and corrupt demand, though if he was who he claimed to be, I could guess why.

Laffont had, some years previously, sold the film rights of their publication of Dominique Lapierre's novel *City of Joy*, set in Calcutta, to Hollywood. The film was a success, and Laffont was looking for another book set in India to sell to the US producers. Inspired by the success of *City of Joy*, Laffont had commissioned an English writer and sent her to India to research and write a biography of Phoolan Devi, which they might have wanted to turn into their second Hollywood film. The release of Channel 4's *Bandit Queen* would have killed that enterprise.

I assumed, when this person said he would make it worth my while, that he was offering me a bribe to suspend a film that belonged to Channel 4. I said I was sorry his French firm had faced this disappointment but that was a twist of historical fate.

'Agincourt, Waterloo and now *Bandit Queen*,' I said, invoking the famous battles between the two nations, before putting the phone down.

There then followed another nasty episode. Those who had supported the court case sent a letter signed by eight or ten individuals to Michael Grade asking him to sack me as I had done a disservice to India. Michael had seen the film and thought the letter absurd. He made a rude remark about what he would like to do with the letter and gave it to me to frame a reply. My reply basically said they would be disappointed to hear that I wouldn't be sacked, and I added two succinct words.

Three of these signatories were people I knew. Two of them had had Channel 4 commissions through me—Roy for her feature film and Pankaj Butalia, whom I had commissioned to make a documentary he had pitched called *Shakespeare in Mizoram*.

A third signatory, Praful Bidwai, was a friend of Mala's, who had contracted through a traffic accident, perhaps a year before all this, an infection which the doctors said could prove fatal. There was, Mala had said, no cure. Except that there was! Through a fateful coincidence, Firdous Ali, a friend, happened to be in my office when Mala gave me the news. Firdous, alert to our conversation, said his relatives, both doctors in the Midlands, were working on a cure for precisely that disease—something to do with bone marrow. He called and persuaded them to send some of the medicine to India.

It was sent, and for all I know, may have saved Bidwai's life. And here was his signature asking for me to be sacked from my job.

The only retaliation open to me was through the force of imperfect rhyme, which I employed in my weekly column for the *Asian Age*. The limerick began, 'There was a man called Butalia …', but perhaps revenge should only bite once.

Though Channel 4 kept me busy and stopped me from writing for TV, I managed to write three books in my time there. One was called *Janaky and the Giant and Other Stories*, for younger children and in the genre of fairy-tale fables. The other, *Bombay Duck*, is a novel which attempts in part to represent the growing clash between an international consciousness of equality and the religious prejudices of India. It was inspired by the idea of inauthenticity: of Bombay Duck not being a duck, spaghetti bolognese not being known in Bologna and chop suey not being a Chinese dish. The novel was shortlisted as one of two finalists for the Whitbread Prize and, like Napoleon at Waterloo, came second. The third was *Black Swan*, a young adult novel about the Shakespeare plays actually being written by playwright Christopher Marlowe and his slave boyfriend.

My romances and partnerships too changed with time. As the years passed, I had met and befriended Loretta Jennings at Archbishop's, where she had joined as a teacher. She was in a partnership at the time we met, as was I with Piki, and living with her boyfriend. Loretta and her partner eventually decided, independently of any friendship I had with her, to end their relationship.

I was still committed to Piki, and both of them knew of the existence of the other and my relationship with each. They intellectually, if not emotionally, adjusted to the unfairness of it and didn't label it as such. Something in the ideas popular with those who considered themselves the revolutionary conscience of our generation in the late 1960s urged an accommodation to even such a triangle.

But eras change, and I suppose the zeitgeist, the animating ideas, the dominating determinations—social, political and personal—can alter even in one lifetime. Perhaps that's what happened in my parallel relationships with Piki and Loretta. The years passed, the children I had with each grew, and they both eventually tired of the duality. In their reticence to engage with me and this triangular arrangement, they drifted into what I perceived as a personal and sexual estrangement. I had gotten busy with the Channel 4 job, which occupied me sometimes late into the night and certainly took me all over the world. These may have been intolerable periods for both Piki and Loretta. The estrangement and distance I felt led me into a relationship with a colleague at Channel 4.

Part of the time, I began living in Oxford with Bernadette O'Farrell, who was the deputy commissioning editor in the Documentary department. We had one daughter, whom I named Tir, taking the name of the star Sirius in the Avestan language from a calendar of holy Zoroastrian names. Born to Loretta, the name of my eldest daughter, Tamineh, is a modern Persian version of my grandmother's name, Tehmina. Her brother Danyal was named after a Mughal prince, Emperor Akbar's son. The twins, Piki and my daughters, were called Shireen, after my mother, and Jahan, after the princesses of India who used the Persian word, meaning 'universe', in their titles.

As Tir grew, Bernadette too drifted away. I used to spend days and nights with Piki and my children, even when attending to Tir in their Oxfordshire home, and Bernadette possibly resented this, even though we had, in discussion, agreed to such an arrangement. But arrangements and agreements don't govern the heart or even the mind. Bernadette and I ceased to have anything one could call a relationship, and we agreed I should leave.

I returned to Piki, to London and the house we used to share, and resumed my life with her and my children. Of course, relationships change and the definition of the very word evolves. Maybe one can never forget the past, and 'forgive' is too patronising a word as none of us dare cast the first stone. But my return didn't feel like the healing of an estrangement. After all those years of being together, an ease and naturalness grows and relationships change but endure.

FILMS I DID WRITE

By 1997, I had been the longest-serving commissioning editor at Channel 4. The possibilities of new programmes, formats, adventures and experiments with the small screen continued to be attractive. It seemed one of the best jobs one could have. But the hectic demands of the job and the fact that I couldn't openly write TV or films for Channel 4 or indeed any rival channel was frustrating.

It was the fiftieth anniversary of Indian Independence, and as I thought of programmes I could commission to commemorate it, it felt like a good time to move on and find the freedom again to write. I had written, staying up late into the night and grabbing hours here and there, three books in the fourteen years I had worked at the channel, but yes, I had decided it was time to move on and maybe even give the network the opportunity to explore multicultural programming through a fresh perspective.

In August of that year, I handed in my resignation, was given a great farewell and left Channel 4, with a mixture of sadness and anticipation of the future.

Several possibilities and projects suggested themselves.

My friend Dev Benegal and his beautiful wife Anuradha Parikh approached me to write a film. It was to be an expose of the sexual underbelly of Mumbai's upper-class life. It was called *Split Wide Open* and had some pretty strong material about a gay threesome, a rich paedophile and an exploited child who accepted her situation in return for the comfort and riches she received.

The film was completed and submitted to the Indian Board of Film Censors. They came back with more cuts than Julius Caesar had suffered. Anuradha, who produced the film, went to argue with them.

The chairperson of the board apparently told Anuradha, 'Why are you complaining, Miss Parikh. We have given you two "fucks"!'

In 2003, my friend Mohan Chopra introduced me to Meenu Bachan and her husband Phil Blackburn, who together had just floated a film company called Inspired Movies. They asked me to write a film with songs throughout. They wanted to make a film for Western audiences which had a sort of Bollywood form.

I wrote the film, which came to be called *Take Three Girls*, and asked my friend and ex-colleague at Channel 4 Peter Ansorge to join the firm and produce it. Peter and I got the team together. I asked Kabir Bedi to play the main male role. Even though it was not a big-budget movie, a genre through which he had built a stupendous international reputation, Kabir agreed. We would go on to become good friends.

Having started this as a name-dropping incident, I should recall the circumstances under which my name was dropped, from proceedings in which it should have been extolled, thanks to Kabir.

In 2004, I was invited to Italy on a lecture tour, speaking to university students of literature and English about my writing. After a successful round of talks and readings in Bologna, I was transported to the mosaicked city of Ravenna to address a large student audience with the assistance of a bilingual chairperson. In introducing me and my writing, the chair mentioned that apart from the books they had been compelled by their course to read, I had also written films for the Indian industry.

Before I could get into the short story I had bookmarked, a hand went up from the audience.

'Do you mean you write for Bollywood?'

'Yes,' replied the chair. 'Now we are delighted that Mr ...'

A few more hands went up before she finished her sentence.

'So, do you know Kabir Bedi?' a bold young lady asked.

'Yes, he's a friend of mine. He recently acted in one of my films.'

There were 'oohs' and 'aahs' all round the hall, and several more hands shot up, but their owners didn't wait for their questions to be called.

'What's he like?'

'Is he married?'

'Does he have a girlfriend?'

'Don't be silly. Of course, he has a girlfriend!'

'Have you seen *Sandokan*?'

The questioner was referring to the hugely popular role that Kabir played in the Italian series about an oriental pirate.

'What aftershave does he use?'

'Is his voice dubbed?'

Before I could frame even one answer, the chairperson held up her hand to bring order to the house.

'Mr Dhondy is here to read his stories. Questions about his writing or literature now, please!

I began reading, aware of a certain restlessness in the hall. Rather than finish reading my story, I stopped at a nodal point and ingeniously asked the students to write a possible ending to it for homework.

'Now, let's get on with your questions. Even Kabir.' I knew that's what they wanted. Who wants literature homework when you can have Sandokan.

Smiles all round, and again a dozen hands shot up. Their teachers lining the wall frowned. I talked about *Take Three Girls* and about Kabir's role in it as the emperor who built the Taj Mahal. I had to be content with writing myself out of the morning's script.

Years later, I narrated this to Kabir and his wife Parveen Dusanj, and they both laughed, unconcerned at my humiliation.

Now, back to the making of *Take Three Girls*. As we worked on the film, I realised that Inspired Movies was financed by a British Indian businessman who was taking advantage of a government scheme, floated by the then British prime minister Gordon Brown, which gave tax concessions for investing in the revival and revitalisation of the British film industry.

According to the deal, an investor could put 40 per cent of the tax they owed the Inland Revenue into the production of films. It was a good deal for any business.

When *Take Three Girls* was complete, Inspired Movies asked me to write another film. I did. It was called *Exitz* and was set in Goa. The Hollywood actor Malcolm McDowell was to play the male lead and Perizaad Zorabian, a beautiful Parsi actor from Mumbai, the 'heroine'.

I came with the foreign crew, Meenu, Phil, Malcolm and the director—my mate Laurens Postma—to Mumbai.

I was living in my own flat rented by Bobby in Mira Bagh and the crew and Malcolm checked into the Taj in the south of the city.

One afternoon when I went to see them and as we sat by the luxurious swimming pool with cocktails, Malcolm seemed extremely restless. I asked him what the matter was.

'I am in India, dammit! I don't want to sit by the pool with other Americans, drinking cocktails. I want to see India—not with tourist guides—but the real India, the way Indians live. Where are you now, you're not in the hotel?'

I said I had my own flat up in North Bombay.

'Can I go with you? Can I see it?' he asked.

'I've got a spare bedroom. You can come and stay if you want.'

He was excited and suddenly animated. He got up, asked me to hang about, went to his room, packed his stuff, brought his bag down and checked out. He was taking me up on my invitation for three days, before the crew moved to Goa.

We took a taxi to my place. I walked him round the neighbourhood, and we ate what Ganesh, my Nepalese cook and Man Friday, had prepared for dinner.

'What did you intend to do in the morning?' Malcolm asked.

'I was going to go for a haircut but we can ...'

'No, we can't anything. I want to come with you for the haircut.'

In the morning, we walked to Bandra railway station, a mile away. Along the metal railings of the station, there were several barbers' stalls—nothing more than wooden packing cases on which the customers sat while the itinerant barbers cut their hair, with their machines, razors, cisterns of water, soap and scissors laid out on cloth mats on the pavement.

I sat down on one of the crates and had my haircut.

'I want one too,' Malcolm said. He was accommodated on an adjoining crate, draped with a cloth cape and given a cut. A huge crowd gathered to watch a white 'sahib' availing of the street-barber facility. They stood round and stared through the entire procedure. The barber was bristling with pride. He said he would waive the charge, but Malcolm and I insisted, and instead of the regular thirty rupees per cut, we paid fifty for each.

I then said we would visit the fish and meat market next to the station to buy some crabs and take them home for Ganesh to make a South Indian crab curry for the night.

Malcolm was fascinated. The fish and meat bazaar was, he remarked, 'so clean'.

We went on that day or the next, I forget which, to a textile shop, where Malcolm bought several handloom shirts.

The crew went off to Goa for the shoot. *Exitz* was edited in London, and Phil, Meenu and her sister Vibha Bhatnagar asked me to think of the next film. They seemed extremely enthusiastic about my work, and I had become their regular writer in residence. They said I could choose the theme and the crew.

I wrote *Red Mercury*, which was about three young Islamist fundamentalists on the run and forced to take hostages in a restaurant. It was reminiscent of the actual Spaghetti House Siege, about which I had written the young adult novel *The Siege of Babylon*. The film may have had some echo of the book but was entirely different. Charles Sobhraj asking me about red mercury was obviously on my mind, even though the narrative of the film had nothing to do with him.

I got in touch with Roy Battersby, who had directed the four-part drama *King of the Ghetto*, to ask if he would direct *Red Mercury*. Michael Wearing, a former head of Drama at the BBC who had commissioned *King of the Ghetto*, now a freelancer, would produce it with Peter Ansorge, now the resident producer at Inspired Movies.

They assembled a fabulous and famous cast including Stockard Channing, Pete Postlethwaite, Juliet Stevenson, and three young Asian actors, Navin Chowdhry, San Shella and Alex Caan.

The film was invited to the Montreal Film Festival, and we took it proudly to Canada.

After the screening of the film to a packed and appreciative audience, Meenu and I were invited onto the stage for the question-and-answer session.

I answered questions about the intentions of the film, the parallels to real occurrences and so on, then someone asked what the film had cost. Both Michael Wearing and Roy Battersby had vociferously complained about the skimpy budget of one million pounds which had been allocated for the production. I was about to answer the question, quoting this figure, when Meenu grabbed my wrist. As she was the producer, I naturally deferred to her. She told the audience it cost five million pounds. I was astounded.

That night back at the hotel, I asked Peter about the five-million figure. He too didn't know what Meenu had been talking about. Back in London, where Peter had a desk in the Inspired Movies basement office near Great Portland Street, we discovered the truth through a document he got hold of.

The accountant of Inspired Movies had produced a budget sheet for the tax authorities which inflated every cost to five times the amount actually spent. So, for instance, while I was paid something like £10,000 for the script, the 'budget' on paper said I had been paid around £60,000, and there were a few named 'script consultants' attached, whom I had never met or worked with, and each of them had been paid some incredible sum.

The purpose of the false accounting was clear. The financier of Inspired Movies inflated the budgets to cover the full 40 per cent of his tax liability, while actually deploying, on the evidence of *Red Mercury*'s actual budget, perhaps 8 per cent of the sum. That way, he got to keep 32 per cent of his tax liability 'legally'.

The realisation that my screenplay commissions were not the result of my talent but part of a tax dodge was a bit of a blow. Inspired Movies, having falsified the budgets and made their money, had no interest in deploying more cash on distribution and advertising. The films, regrettably, remained in the can and made their way at best to DVD.

Despite the downer of working with Inspired Movies, my movie-writing career continued and expanded to Bollywood. I happened to be working on an edit of a film in Mumbai in 2005 when Bobby said he had just received a call from the famous director Subhash Ghai asking if I was in town and whether he could see me as he wanted me to write his next film. I was curious. Apart from having worked with the very talented Shekhar Kapur, who isn't really a Bollywood myth-maker, I hadn't worked with or written for a classical Bollywoodian director. I said I would certainly meet him.

Bobby fixed the meeting and said I should be in Subhash's Bandra office by ten next morning.

I was. Subhash wasn't. A receptionist told me he would be in any minute. He wasn't. I left the building in the meantime and found myself some street food. Slightly indignant, I went back to Subhash's office just before twelve. Still no sign of the maestro. Just as I said I was leaving, he walked in with a retinue of eight, mostly young, men.

He greeted me heartily, saying he was glad I had come and that he wanted to discuss a film he wanted me to write. We went into what must have been a reception room. It was quite bare, with a circle of chairs for the whole company. Subhash introduced the group of young men as his assistant directors, or ADs as they are known in the film circle. I was used to having two or three ADs in a film. Subhash appeared to have seven. The eighth gentleman, perhaps in his seventies, was introduced as a distinguished film writer.

'He has written hundred and ten films,' Subhash said by way of a modest introduction.

'Hundred and seventeen!' the old gentleman said.

'Yes, seventy of those were superhits,' Subhash added, perhaps compensating for the statistical error.

'Eighty-one,' the old gentleman corrected him in a gruff, matter-of-fact tone.

'So, when can we discuss this film you want me to write?' I asked.

'Right now,' Subhash said.

'Is it based on a book? You'd told Bobby it was historical.'

'No, no, this is a sitting,' Subhash said.

I didn't understand.

'And how do I know what you want me to write?'

Subhash seemed puzzled at my puzzlement.

'In the sitting, I will give narration,' he said.

I hadn't encountered this procedure but noticed that everyone else took it as routine.

Subhash introduced me as 'our writer', and just as he did, a secretary walked in with a clipboard and piece of paper and gestured as though to hand it to me.

'What's this?' I asked.

'Your contract,' Subhash said. 'You see, you have to sign a non-disclosure clause in it. And the payments and everything, all there.'

The secretary held out an envelope.

I took it, again not knowing what was going on.

'Your advance, two lakhs,' Subhash said.

'But I haven't heard or said or written a word.'

'Farrukh, Farrukh, this is how we do it in India. I have agreed on all payments with Bobby. He should have told you.'

Bobby hadn't.

I glanced over the contract. It said I would be paid a very tidy sum. And I now had in my hand more than the equivalent of £2,000 as just advance. I signed.

The 'sitting' began. Subhash gave us the outline of a story. I interrupted him several times with doubts, but no one else said a word. Eventually, the old gentleman—who was wearing an Indian suit of thick printed material, which I thought much too hot for the Mumbai climate—spoke up.

'Subhash, Subhash,' he said, raising his hand to silence the room. 'In the 1950s, there was this film with Errol Flynn ...'

I can't recall the details now, but he continued to say something about a gun confrontation between two people. I didn't gather why we were being regaled with this story and thought it rude to ask.

A couple of hours on, the 'sitting' ended. I told Subhash I had got the outline of the period, characters and theme, so should I go and invent a proper story and plot, write out an outline and show it to him before proceeding to pen the screenplay?

He said I should come again the next day at the same time, and there would be another sitting. I didn't go at ten the next day but a little after twelve. That was a smart thing to do as the deputies were just gathering. The sitting proceeded as before, and very little was added to it. After the sitting, I went up to Subhash privately and said, since he didn't want to see an outline, should I proceed with a full first draft of a screenplay? Of course, I should, was the response.

I may have taken a week or so to write *Kisna*, as it was finally called. I handed the screenplay over to Subhash and said I was on my way to London. I would await his views anxiously and then would attempt to address any concerns in the second draft. He seemed happy.

A month went by. I was back in London and there was no news on the screenplay from Subhash. When I emailed a few times, one of the ADs wrote back saying it was fine and the sittings were continuing. Nobody said anything about my draft screenplay.

A few weeks later, I returned to Bombay and called Subhash. Yes, yes, yes, they were all happy with the screenplay, and if I attended the next day's sitting, they would give me their additions and modifications.

At the sitting, I was given additions—at least in parts legitimate, if melodramatic—to the way I had told the story. The only contribution I couldn't place was from the veteran writer of eighty-eight or whatever super-hits—about the Hollywood film with the guns and the stand-off. I worked at the second draft for a few days and handed it to Subhash, who said it was great. He said the script required, as was in the original story he narrated in the sittings, three principal British characters. He would come to London to recruit them. On his request, I suggested the names of casting firms I had come across in my time at Channel 4.

Subhash and a couple of his ADs, by now nine in number, turned up in London and booked a suite at the Taj in St James' Court. The casting agent had been commissioned, and I was asked to attend the auditions.

The casting took a few days. The film was set in the era just before India gained its independence from British colonial rule. The main female role was that of a late teenage British girl, saved from ruthless Indian nationalists by her Indian serving boy from childhood, Kisna, to be played by Vivek Oberoi.

Perhaps twenty or so young British female actors were presented to Subhash and auditioned over three days. Then came decision time with the casting director, Subhash and me.

'Tell me finally, Farrukh. Who would you choose for acting as your heroine Catherine?'

'I liked three of them, but my final choice would be Antonia Bernath. She brought an inner understanding of the role. I could feel her having lived with the history of the period.'

Subhash looked grim. He turned to the casting director Sarah.

'Who would you choose?'

'I think Farrukh is right,' Sarah said. 'Antonia would be my first choice. She was so emotionally engaging.'

Subhash paced about the room holding his chin.

'Well, you know, Antonio'—that's how he pronounced her name—'she is … you know, for a film in India, the heroines, well … It's no … she won't be what audiences … you know.'

'No. Please explain, Mr Ghai. What are you saying, I don't understand. She seems absolutely to fit the role,' Sarah said.

'You don't understand. In Indian films … Antonio is … not for our audience …'

A look of complete impatience shot across Sarah's features.

'Farrukh, what is Mr Ghai trying to say?'

'He is saying that Indian films expect heroines with big lalas and no morals,' I replied.

'I don't believe it!' Sarah said.

I defused the situation, looking at my watch. 'The actors for the male role should be at the reception.'

'Antonio' got the role.

A month or so later, I happened to be in Delhi, again working with Bobby, when Subhash rang me cheerily.

'I will pick you up at six in the morning tomorrow, and we will then fly together to Ranikhet.'

I hadn't expected a call from him and didn't understand what he was talking about.

'What? Fly where?'

'For the shoot we start tomorrow,' he said.

'But I am not on the shoot. My job's done. Screenplay delivered, cast in place …'

'You're not reading the contract, Farrukh. It says two weeks on the shoot.'

He was right. I hadn't read the contract.

'But I have to earn my money here working on Bobby's projects, Subhash!'

'Don't worry about money. Bobby said he will pay your salary for the two weeks with our shoot.'

Bobby was now at my elbow.

'You are turning down two weeks' holiday in the Himalayas with plane transport paid for?' he said. That is Bobby's style.

I was on the plane. We drove the last lap from the airport to the Himalayan hill station of Ranikhet in a Landrover. We went along winding roads and came to the grounds of a beautiful colonial house on a hilltop. There must have been more than twenty trucks, vans and Landrovers parked in the grounds. There were what seemed like hundreds of people milling about.

Under an awning to the side, cooks were busy at large pots on imported gas fires. As we stepped out of the car, the ADs greeted Subhash as courtiers greet royalty. We were led into the old, Victorian house and shown the different rooms.

'This is for Vivek,' said the AD who was guiding us round, and then another room was for someone else, and finally we were shown to Subhash's large first-floor suite.

'Your room, Subhash sir,' the flunkey said. Subhash looked happy.

'And where's my room?' I asked.

'Oh, you are not here,' Subhash said. 'You are very special, so we've booked a room for you in the Ranikhet Club.'

'There is a car assigned to you, Farrukh sir, with a driver who is waiting. Your luggage has been transferred to the car.'

It was getting dark by the time the car drove me to the Ranikhet Club. I felt a bit indignant. It seemed as though the important people had been housed in the central residence, and I was being fobbed off alone to some club.

The club was on a promontory overlooking a deep forested valley. The residential rooms were set in a straight line with a narrow veranda overlooking the precipice. They may have, it seemed to me, at one time been army barracks but had now been converted to luxury rooms with en-suite bathrooms.

A receptionist or caretaker awaited my arrival and greeted me as I stepped out of the car. The club was deserted. There was no one apart from me in residence that night. The receptionist accompanied me to my room and said I would only be on my own for a night as the three English people, the two ladies and the gentleman actor, arrived the next morning.

'That would be Antonia, Caroline and Michael?' I asked.

'That's right, they are all in your film,' he said.

I got it. I had been hauled up to Ranikhet to be host to or even nursemaid to the British actors. Subhash's little strategy. It made sense. I was to perhaps be a cultural interpreter if needed.

They arrived the next morning, all seemingly dazzled by their first time in India, by the sights, sounds and landscape. Below our rooms, on a terrace perhaps thirty feet down the cliff, were tennis courts with nets to stop the balls careering over into the deep valley.

I had, of course, made the acquaintance of all three of them during the casting in London. Michael Maloney and Caroline Langrishe were distinguished and famous actors, and Antonia was a young actress with a sparkling stage career.

We had breakfast together before setting out for the main residence. They were full of questions. Were there any Buddhist temples nearby? Could they observe a Hindu ceremony? Would there be any time for trekking in the valleys? Could I identify the species of beautiful birds they spotted? I said I would find out about the first three questions and the only answer I had to the last one was that the white-and-purple birds were Himalayan magpies, larger than the similarly patterned black-and-white ones in Europe and just as badly behaved.

The filming progressed. I would go every day to the locations and watch the shoot. Characters I hadn't written cropped up on the set. I asked Subhash what they were doing there, and he said he put them in to add colour.

Both Michael and Caroline were not used to the Indian style of directing, or perhaps it was Subhash's unique style, in which he would replace the actor on set and contrive to act the scene out as he would like it. Antonia seemed to adapt to every circumstance.

On one occasion, Caroline was supposed to be playing the piano, and after several takes, Subhash asked her to vacate the stool and sat at the instrument himself. Caroline stormed off the set, saying, 'Do it yourself, then!'

I was called in to pacify her. I did my best, and both Michael and Caroline confessed that they didn't particularly enjoy Subhash's style of directing, but they loved being in Ranikhet.

One evening before taking the car to the main residence for the evening, I wandered into the club bar. Several young men were playing snooker and sitting round chatting. It was the first time I had seen anyone apart from our crew in the club.

As I got to the bar, one of them approached me.

'Are you Farrukh Dhondy?'

I said I was. He offered me a drink and said a mutual journalist friend had told him I would be at the Ranikhet Club for a film shoot. He and his friends had come up from Delhi to play polo, he said, and invited me to a party nearby that evening.

'Are you a journalist too?' I asked him.

'I'm a baker,' he said.

'You have bakeries here or in Delhi?' I asked out of politeness.

Another young man who had joined us said, 'He is the owner of Britannia biscuits, yaar!'

We drove in a caravan of fancy cars to the party. It wasn't nearby. We must have driven thirty miles through winding Himalayan roads to a beautiful large house on a hillside. There were barbecues and rotisseries set up in the compound, and whole goats were being roasted by a battalion of hired workers on open fires. There were all manner of young men and women who had come up from Delhi for this grand party. I ate and danced and drank into the small hours and then asked my host how I would get back. He said a car would set out at seven in the morning. It seemed rude to demand an earlier ride.

I got back to the club and my room mid-morning, exhausted and hungover. I slept, and when I woke up, it was early evening. I wandered out and found my car waiting for me. I was driven to the main house, where the trucks were still parked and the extras were having dinner on the trestle tables on the lawn.

As I walked into the house, Rajat Kapoor, one of the actors in the film, was sitting on the stairs with his head in his hands.

'How are things?' I asked. 'Where are my people?'

'They were not required for the scenes today, so they went off to see some temples or something,' he said. 'And the one day I needed you, you weren't bloody there!' He frowned and shook his head. 'He changed your lines and made me say some stupid thing,' he said.

'Like what?' I asked.

He described the scene I knew. 'Then he insisted I had to say, "There is a rising wind from the howling wolves against your fouling and your governance!"'

'It doesn't make sense,' I said.

'That's what I told Subhash, and he said if I didn't want to say the lines as instructed, I could take the next train back to Bombay.'

'So, you said those lines?'

'Did I have a choice?'

'Don't worry, I'll try and get them cut out in the edit. I'll make a big fuss,' I said.

I don't think he was convinced. I left Rajat and went up to Subhash's suite. The director was sitting in an armchair, and a man was massaging his shoulders.

'Ah, Farrukh,' he said cheerily, then turning to the attendants, said in Hindi, 'Can't you see Farrukh sir has arrived, fetch him that orange wine from the fridge.'

Subhash had very kindly noticed that I had been drinking rosé in Delhi and had brought a crate of it up for me particularly.

The cold wine was fetched.

'It's pink, not orange, and called rosé,' I said.

'What do I know, I only drink whisky.'

After some small talk, I came to the point.

'You gave Rajat some lines. He spoke to me and recited them. Subhash, please, they don't make sense.'

'Farrukh, Farrukh, Farrukh,' he said and then in Hindi, 'You think you're the only one who knows English? I have done some checking.' He repeated the English word 'checking'.

I understood. I finished my drink, went downstairs, dismissed my driver and drove the car to the club. I walked down the row of rooms and knocked at Michael's door.

Michael opened it. Caroline and Antonia were in the room, all of them with drink. As soon as they saw me at the door, they all stood up and in chorus theatrically recited, 'There is a rising wind from the howling wolves against your fouling and your governance!' and burst into laughter.

'Your petty revenge,' I said. 'Poor Rajat. You wait, I'm going to modify each of your speeches into embarrassing nonsense and hand them to Subhash, saying they are Shakespearean in style and intent.'

They couldn't stop laughing.

A FRIENDSHIP AND THREE-MINUTE EGGS

I first encountered V.S. Naipaul—or, at any rate, his way of thinking—in his first book about India, *An Area of Darkness.* I wasn't to encounter the man himself till years later.

In London, through my friend and painter Tarun Bedi, I met Naipaul's younger brother Shiva Naipaul. On occasional evenings, over drinks in a pub, the persistent political argument or difference between me and Shiva would be the inevitable topic—he had not a distrust but a deep contempt for any left-wing sentiment or idea. His mockery of socialists didn't seem to derive from any firm commitment to capitalistic or feudalistic principles or espousal of conservatism but seemed a visceral reaction. It was as though he had inherited the conviction as people of faith or ultra-nationalists do.

It was much later that it occurred to me that his seemingly instinctive stances were reflections or imitations of those his elder brother held. I eventually met Vidia when we shared a platform at Warwick University for a forum on some literary topic. We made our contributory speeches, were asked questions and then audience and speakers were invited for a drink. I didn't quite interact with him outside of this, but he told a friend of mine, 'That fellow Dhondy doesn't believe in anything, does he?'

Having strongly rejected from the platform that assessments of works of literature could be or should be subjective, I was disconcerted and puzzled by Vidia's comment. From reading

English in my final year at Cambridge, I had certainly picked up the critical idea that there were standards and criteria for the assessment of a literary work. F.R. Leavis of the university had written several elegant and convincing books, championing particular novelists and poets, denigrating others and backing up his pronouncements. It seemed to me, and to probably all the undergraduates reading English in that era, to be the critical doctrine to follow. Elsewhere, there was a cult of subjective judgement which decried and denied the existence of any code of criteria, reducing every work to an equality without allowing for one to be more equal than another.

I had diligently bought and continued to avidly read everything that Vidia published—his novels set in Trinidad, his second book of discovery of India unrelentingly titled *India: A Wounded Civilisation* and the books of travel in southern USA, Africa, South America and countries which were converts to Islam.

In 1990, a few months after we shared the stage, his third book of exploration on the country, *India: A Million Mutinies Now*, was about to be published. The producer of *The Book Programme* on BBC radio called and asked if I would interview, in the style of a review, Vidia about his new book. He sent me the book, and I read it without putting it down, through a day and night, and then skimmed it again for notes on what I would ask Vidia.

At seven in the morning on the day the recording and broadcast of the show was scheduled, my phone rang. I was asleep but awoken by the ringing, took the call.

'Mr Dhondy, this is Naipaul, Vidia Naipaul,' he said, not intending, I am sure, to echo James Bond's idiosyncratic style of introduction.

'Er ... yes,' I said.

'We are to speak on the television this afternoon. What shall we speak about?' he asked in a matter-of-fact tone, although the timing of the call, coupled with this question, made me think he may have betrayed some anxiety. Had the possibilities of the interview kept him awake?

'Well, the BBC has asked me to review your latest book on India, which I've very much enjoyed, and to possibly range in general over the rest of your work and perhaps ask you about your reaction to the criticism some of your books have received.'

'Ah. Which books were you thinking of?'

'Not the novels, but perhaps the ones featuring your travels in Africa and the Muslim world?'

'I see,' he said and paused.

'I look forward to it.'

'Yes, yes, goodbye,' he said and put the phone down.

As soon as I got to my office at Channel 4 that morning, *The Book Programme* producer rang.

'Hi, Farrukh. I just got a call from Naipaul's agent, Gillon Aitken. I believe you spoke to Naipaul this morning.'

'Yes, he called me at bloody seven in the morning.'

'Well, Gillon says Naipaul doesn't want to be interviewed by you?'

'What? Why?'

'He said you told him, "Negroes don't like your books."'

'What? I said nothing of the sort. It's not the kind of language I use, and why would I have said any such thing? Oh shit, so it's off?'

'No, no. It's not off. You're on, and we're sending the cab to pick you up. I told Gillon that if Naipaul won't be interviewed, we're giving Mr Dhondy half an hour to say whatever he likes about Naipaul's work.'

I was a bit taken aback, but he continued, 'Can you think of what you'll say? I'm sure you can do half an hour of your views on any and all of his work? You have carte blanche.'

'OK. There's plenty to say. I love his work.'

'Fine. See you at the recording.'

An hour or so later, he called again.

'Naipaul has changed his mind. You will be talking to him.'

The recording was scheduled in a room of a 'boutique' hotel in South Kensington so that Vidia could walk to it from his flat. He always wore a hat when he was outside, and he arrived, took it off and took his place. I had brought three first editions of his books with me and placed them on the coffee table in front of us.

I asked him about this latest book on India and said that it seemed to me a change of heart or a progression from his previous books.

'Oh dear, you're already giving me marks,' he said.

He seemed determined to treat the interview as a hostile encounter, though the questions I asked were, if not flatteringly put, devoid of any snide critical intent—which is what I think he expected.

The interview was meaty enough, and when our time was up, before he rose to go, I asked if he would sign my copies. He said he would sign just one and did so. He took his hat, nodded to the producer and left. The producer and crew looked as though they were breathing sighs of relief. I was assured it had gone well, was brilliant and all the usual guff producers feel obliged to tell their interviewers.

It was perhaps a year later that Gillon rang me and invited me to lunch with Vidia.

'Is this a joke, Gillon? Vidia hates my guts!'

'All that's changed,' Gillon said. 'You know the new Lady Naipaul …'

'I read that he got married to a Pakistani lady.'

'Yes, Nadira, who reads your columns and books, loves them and wants to meet you, so Vidia's called you to lunch. Is Bibendum good?'

Bibendum was a fancy oyster joint in South Kensington, and yes, I said, it was good.

Vidia was sullen as he took his place at the lunch table, while Nadira was effusive as Gillon introduced us. As we ordered the wine, she asked what I had been doing. I said I had returned from

Jamaica where a crew I had commissioned for Channel 4 was making a series of observational documentaries in the accident and emergency department of a hospital situated in the notorious Trench Town of Kingston. We had decided to follow two dedicated doctors at work and away from it and construct stories from the observed footage. There was a wealth of narrative to work with as the crew gathered material.

'I only went for a few days to supervise the end of the project,' I said.

Nadira was curious. 'Jamaica? What's it like there?'

'I didn't do much holidaying, just went for the shoot. It was very interesting.'

'In what way?'

'Let me tell you. The first day I was there, the crew and I were walking through the grounds to the entrance where a tall security guard was seated on a high stool.

'"You de television crew?" he asked, still seated.

'We said we had permission to enter, and he said he knew that, but we had to hear him out first.

'"I am de Nat King Cole of Jamaica," he said. "You have feh flim me firss! Check dis!"

'And he burst into passionate song: "Mona Lisa, Mona Lisa ..."

'I thought he did sound like Nat King Cole.

'And as he hit the third line of the lyric, gunshots rang out from beyond the compound wall. One shot, and then three or four more. They sounded pretty close.

'We didn't know whether to duck for cover or start running in the open towards the entrance.

'Nat interrupted his singing with, "Don't mind dem boys, don't mind dem ..." and coolly resumed the song. "Mona Lisa, Mona Lisa, you're the lady with the ..."

'We were inside the building by this time, and three men, one bleeding copiously through his shirt and trousers, hanging on to the other two, came rushing past us into the emergency ward.

'The camera had been running and had captured Nat's words and a topsy-turvy sequence of our flight. I told the crew, "Fantastic. I hope you got the gunshots. We start the series with that sequence."'

Vidia, opposite me at the table, was rocking with laughter.

I was no longer persona non grata. Before we left the restaurant I was invited to dinner and to any weekend I chose in the Naipauls' Dairy Cottage in Wiltshire in Southwest England.

Straight after dinner, I was on a flight to New York to be with my sister Zareen. My brother-in-law Ramesh Bhasin was in a hospital with very little or no chance of recovery from the cancer that had started, without warning, from the back of his brain and spread rapidly through every organ of his body. I went straight to the hospital from the airport. My two nephews and my niece, Sanjay, Arjun and Niharika, and friends who happened to be in New York were all in a small room adjoining the one in which Ramesh, unconscious, was strapped to several life-sustaining machines.

Zareen, tearful, told me I should whisper in his ear and hold his hand, 'and if he is at all conscious, he will squeeze it'. Following her instructions, I said he did, though it may have been my wilful imagination that sensed the faint squeeze.

After two days and nights, the consultant in charge called Zareen and me aside and said it was not possible to try any further. They had to have permission to disconnect the life-support machines. Zareen began to cry and said she couldn't do any such thing. The doctor looked at me. I would have to sign the papers to put an end to Ramesh's life.

He was one of the best human beings I have known, generous to a fault and could make anyone he was speaking to feel that they were unique and important—and laughed at the silliest of my jokes.

I spoke to the kids and signed the form. The nurses disconnected the machines. Though someone said there was a life-like stirring of his body after the machines were disconnected, Ramesh passed away. The funeral was presided over by a Hindu priest in Jackson Heights, a neighbourhood occupied predominantly by immigrants from the subcontinent. We made speeches and sang the songs he loved. I kept my composure throughout, and a day later, boarded a flight back to London.

The cabin was nearly empty, and as the flight crossed the ocean, the finality of the last few days struck me. I began to cry. The air hostess leaned over.

'Come on, sir, the food's not that bad!' she said.

She made me smile and spoke to me. I told her about Ramesh, and she was very kind.

Vidia became a good friend, and on one of his birthdays, I was invited with perhaps eight others to dinner at a South Kensington restaurant called Lucio's. Jeffrey Archer happened to be at the same restaurant a few tables away. I had met Jeffrey a few times through Channel 4.

As he and his party left the restaurant, Jeffrey came up to where I was sitting next to Vidia and said, 'Farrukh, introduce me to the great man. I'd like to shake his hand.'

I turned to see who it was at my shoulder and, of course, introduced them. Jeffrey seemed gratified and left.

Vidia hadn't caught his name as I was introducing them. Everyone else round the table had recognised Jeffrey.

'Who was that?' Vidia asked

His guests laughed. One or two said who it was. I don't know if Vidia recognised the name.

'So, how do you know him, Farrukh?' someone asked.

'They probably met in jail,' Gillon Aitken said, making a joke about Jeffrey's jail time a decade ago.

Being a part of Vidia's birthday celebrations became something of a routine. On one of his sixty-something birthdays, Nadira proposed that I bring him a kitten as a present. We visited an animal shelter together, where a fluffy little white-and-brown fellow was my choice, but Nadira said we should take the black-and-white stray with the sly eyes. On the day of Vidia's birthday, I drove to the shelter and picked up our acquisition in a cat cage. Nancy Sladek, the editor of the *London Review* and a dear friend of Naipaul's, was with me as we drove in the warm August sunshine in my open-top Saab to Wiltshire with the cat cage on the back seat.

Vidia seemed at first circumspect about this unexpected gift, but soon began to stroke the little fellow. He announced later that it was christened, or rather named, Augustus—presumably after Julius Caesar's son Octavian. No modesty there! But yes, Vidia, outspoken in his views, was modest about himself.

Years later in 2001, I was in Bangalore working in an animation studio when my mobile phone rang.

'Is that Mr Dhondy? This is the BBC's *The World at One*. We would like to speak to you about your friend V.S. Naipaul.'

'Oh my god … he hasn't … he …'

'No, no, Mr Dhondy, he has been awarded the Nobel Prize for Literature,' said the voice. 'Can we call you on a landline at 1 p.m. GMT, which will be 6.15 p.m. in India?'

Vidia and Nadira had always said the Nobel committee would never consider him—much too controversial. And now he had it.

I called Dairy Cottage, and Nadira answered.

'It's gone crazy here,' she said. 'TV crews and reporters from all over the world.'

'OK, if he's busy, just say I called to say how happy, etc.,' I said.

'Don't be crazy, if he knows you're on the phone, he'll want to speak to you. He's doing some interviews.'

'Then don't disturb him.'

'He'll be furious if I don't and finds you called from India. Hang on.'

Half a minute later, Vidia came on the line.

'Farrukh, Farrukh, you've heard of my little spot of good luck,' he said.

'What to say, boss? I knew it had to happen. Congratulations, Vidia, and please go back to the interviews. Thanks for taking the call.'

When I returned to Britain a few weeks later and turned up at the Naipauls', I found that Augustus had made a home for himself in the Wiltshire countryside and ruled Dairy Cottage with the sceptre of indulgence afforded to him. Augustus was, to me at least, disdainful, and I noticed that he was partial to expensive fresh fish and barely tolerant of the standard canned cat food I was on occasion deputed to offer him.

Vidia loved him dearly. Years later, after Augustus was past the normal feline lifespan and had to be injected to his euthanistic death, Vidia held him in his lap as he passed away.

In an interview I did with him on stage at Mumbai's Literature Live Festival in 2012, where he was given a lifetime achievement award, I talked about Augustus to bring in a personal note. Vidia did respond, but he choked and his eyes were filled with tears. I moved the interview on.

The next day, while Vidia and Nadira left for Goa, I stayed on at the festival for other speaking engagements. I attended a few sessions as a member of the audience, and one of them was with the famous Indian playwright and friend Girish Karnad. I was looking forward to his session and got myself a seat in the front. From the stage, Girish announced to the anticipating audience that he was not going to talk about his career as a dramatist in this session as billed but was going to express his dismay at being invited to a literary festival which could stoop to giving V.S. Naipaul an award for his lifetime achievement.

He was not content to just register a protest against this, he said, but would also explain why this award should never have been given to Naipaul. The organiser of the festival, Anil Dharker, who was in the audience, stood up and challenged Girish saying that this was not what he had agreed to when he was offered this platform.

The packed audience began to voice their displeasure at the turn of events and at Girish's determination to deny them what they had come to hear. Girish, rather disingenuously, said OK, he would talk about his career, which included his appointment as the director of the Nehru Centre, the cultural venue of the Indian High Commission to the UK, where he had to diplomatically maintain his silence about his disagreements with Naipaul, who was, he said, in his anti-Muslim stance attacking the very fabric of secular India.

Despite several heckles from the audience, Girish went on to make his case against Vidia, calling him a bigot and a racist, whose views on India ought not to be countenanced. He quoted from statements Vidia had been reported to have made and from his books and articles.

I didn't want to heckle, but waited till the end of what was, by any account, a diatribe rather than a reasoned argument with facts and accurate quotations in context. Towards the end of the session, when Girish said he would take questions, I raised my hand and stood up, ready to make my contrary contribution.

The festival stewards, who took the microphone to would-be-questioners in the audience, were approaching me when Girish shouted, 'Not Farrukh, anyone but Farrukh!'

'So, case for the prosecution done and no case for the defence allowed?' I asked.

Girish, standing at the edge of the platform now, began gesturing for the microphone to be taken from me.

'Don't be silly, Girish. Every TV channel and newspaper will be waiting at the door to get reactions to what you've said—not least from me,' I said.

I was right. After the organisers intervened to end the session and I walked out with my friends, I was mobbed by television crews and newspaper representatives.

I said what I had to. Vidia's writings on the countries which were converted to Islam, such as Iran and Pakistan, were stories gleaned from interviews with people in power and those without it. They gave the reader a rounded picture of the social and political practices and prejudices of those countries. This was a unique and necessary exploration. He had nothing to say about Islam or the Prophet. Besides, he was married to a believing Muslim and had adopted her two children, who were free to follow the faith into which they were born. What he had said in his books on India was that the several Muslim conquests of India were, in very many senses, genocidal. Vidia attempted to defy the Gandhi-Nehruvian historian's edict by arguing that this systematic assault, both physical and cultural, must be historically acknowledged and not swept under the carpet in the interest of a secular front against British colonialism. This stance may have been instrumental and positive in the phase of the Independence movement, but that phase was over, and history must tell the truth.

The *Times of India* asked me for a column saying just that to be submitted in a few hours, and it was published the next day.

Vidia enjoyed controversy, but I am in no doubt he wanted to be the winner of it.

A decade earlier, I happened to be in Delhi at the same time as Vidia and Nadira. I went to see them at the Maurya Sheraton where a suite had been named after him and made available to them. I was due to fly out to Mumbai the next day.

'Can you stay a day more?' Vidia asked.

'For what?'

'I've been invited to meet the cultural wing of the Bharatiya Janata Party tomorrow, and I'd like a neutral witness to be there, as there's sure to be some nonsense about it.'

'The cultural wing of the BJP? That's an oxymoron!'

'Now, now.'

This was 2003, and the BJP was in power at the centre.

The next day, we drove to the venue in the British-designed part of New Delhi. The police were out in force at the gate, keeping the TV camera crews and reporters at bay as we drove through the gates of the BJP's office compound. As we alighted from the car and were met by a delegation, they told Vidia that they had kept the media out. He nodded.

The hall was full, and I took my place somewhere in the middle of it. Vidia began by saying he hadn't come to say anything to them but to listen to what they had to say. He had some questions. He wanted to know about their policies and, as he put forth his questions, various people in the audience identified themselves and spoke about how they were changing history books, about their disagreements with the previous policies of the Congress Party, and so on.

Then, some stalwart stood up and demanded to ask Vidia what he thought of the Babri Masjid incident in which thousands of followers of the BJP had invaded the locked-up, disputed premises of a mosque in Ayodhya built by the first Mughal emperor Babur in the sixteenth century.

Vidia said he didn't want to get into the rights and wrongs and the contemporary politics of the issue, but he would say that Babur's construction of the mosque on that site was an act of hubris. I wondered whether anyone in that audience knew the word hubris or appreciated what Vidia was saying.

As the meeting ended and we stepped out into the grounds, we were surrounded by reporters and cameras. They had found their way through the gates and were waiting in a seemingly belligerent throng.

'Sir Vidia, do you support the murder of Muslims in Gujarat?' someone shouted.

'How dare you!' Nadira shouted back. 'I am a Muslim, and he has never supported killing anyone.'

I had hold of Vidia's arm now to steer him through the crowd which was unrestrainedly pressing against us.

'So you support the attack on the Babri Masjid ... you want to build a temple ...'

The questions came hard and fast now.

Vidia was about to answer when, dragging him through the crowd, I said, 'Say nothing! They are trying to set you up.'

'But Farrukh, I want to be set up,' he said.

I wasn't having it. I dragged him towards the waiting car, and we got in and drove away with the media crowd banging on the windows in frustration.

'Thank god you were there. See what Vidia meant when he said he wanted you to be a witness?' Nadira said.

In the next edition of the popular weekly news magazine *Outlook*, there appeared an article by the historian and writer William Dalrymple giving an account of the meeting at which he hadn't been. It was a wilfully distorted account, claiming that Vidia had supported the assault by BJP-led mobs on the Babri Masjid building and that his historical contentions were biased and wrong. Dalrymple went on to say that the great contribution that Muslims had made to India were kurtas and kebabs.

I felt I had to reply, and I did, in the rival publication *Tehelka*. I pointed out that Willy was not at the gathering and I was. That his account of the exchanges was inaccurate and, among other things I wrote, that the most revolutionary contribution of Islam to India was the absence of the caste system—a religion that vigorously asserted that human beings were equal before god.

I was intentionally rude in that rejoinder: 'Come on, Willy, grow some balls and say what you really mean.' It might have given offence at the time, but Willy took it all in his stride or was generously above my pettiness as he has since invited me and Vidia to the platform at the Jaipur Literature Festival, of which he is a prime mover and leading light. We remain friends. The first invitation to speak at the event was extended to me in 2012, soon after the publication of my first book of translations of the thirteenth-century Persian poet Rumi.

Two years later, Sanjoy Roy, one of the other organisers of the festival, visited Vidia and Nadira in their South Kensington flat. It was the fiftieth anniversary of the publication of *A House for*

Mr Biswas, and Sanjoy asked if Vidia would speak at the festival. Nadira said he would attend and be interviewed but wouldn't give a speech.

Sanjoy said that was perfect and suggested that Shashi Tharoor, a member of parliament and writer, would conduct the interview.

'No, no, not Tharoor,' Vidia said. He probably had in mind the fact that Tharoor's wife had died under suspicious circumstances, and Tharoor had been accused in the press of having a hand in her death. Vidia perhaps didn't want the shadow of scandal being a distraction.

'How about Tarun Tejpal?' Sanjoy asked.

'Er ... no, no, not Tarun,' was Vidia's immediate response. Tarun, a good friend of Vidia and mine, had also gained notoriety through an accusation brought by his female employee of sexual misconduct in a lift.

'Then who would you like to do the interview?' Sanjoy asked.

'How about Farrukh?' Vidia suggested.

'Dhondy? He's not an intellectual,' Sanjoy said.

Nadira was astounded. 'If he's not an intellectual, then I'm the proud empress of China,' she said.

'No, no,' Sanjoy said. 'He is a fantastic choice. We were going to invite him anyway. I know him well. I will get in touch today and ask him to do it.'

When he had gone, Nadira picked up the phone.

'Sanjoy Roy says you are not an intellectual,' she told me mischievously.

She didn't immediately tell me anything about when or why he had said this, but it posed no distress.

'He's absolutely right,' I said. 'Only Frenchmen and Bengalis are "intellectuals". As Auden said, the common man thinks an intellectual is someone who beats his wife.'

Thousands turned up to listen to Vidia in Jaipur in 2015 and the interview went well. The festival had got the fiftieth anniversary of *Biswas* wrong. They were two years late. I didn't point that out.

In 2008, Patrick French published Vidia's authorised biography titled *The World Is What It Is*, the first sentence of Vidia's novel *A Bend in the River*. Patrick was assigned the authorisation as Vidia and Nadira had read French's biography of a British officer of the Raj called *Younghusband* and been impressed by it.

Patrick was often at Dairy Cottage when I visited and would interview Vidia in private. On one of these occasions, I overheard Vidia telling Patrick about his regrets at having availed of the services of sex workers. When Patrick left that evening, I asked Vidia why he had thought it necessary to tell him all that. Did he want it in the book? Vidia said the truth must be told or the biography would be worthless.

Perhaps a year or so later, I was in Brisbane, Australia, on a film-writing assignment and was asleep in a hotel room. In the early hours of one morning, the phone rang. It was Nadira.

'Where are you?'

'You know where I am because you phoned this room in the hotel in Brisbane.'

'Don't act clever, the boss wants to speak to you,' she said.

Vidia came on the phone.

'Farrukh, Farrukh, I was told where you were, and I'm sorry, it's late, but I had to speak to you.'

'Tell me,' I said. 'I hope everything's OK.'

'No, it's not. We've just received the proofs of Patrick's book and read it. Patrick has betrayed us.'

'How?'

'Well, he says I beat women and that I buggered Margaret. That's what the book says. It's a lie. I don't beat women, and I never buggered anybody. It's a lie, a lie.'

'I thought Patrick was a friend. Why has he done this?' I asked.

There was a long pause. Then Vidia said, 'Farrukh, you don't realise how deep socialism has gone!'

To this day I haven't a clue as to what he meant.

The book was published, and it did contain the bits which Vidia said were untrue as, having authorised Patrick to write the biography, he couldn't legally challenge its content or veracity.

My interviewing Vidia seemed to have become a part of life's duties.

Nancy Sladek, editor of the British magazine *Literary Review*, asked me to interview him while I was staying for a few days at Dairy Cottage. She wanted his views on his own reading and generally on writers. Vidia said he would appreciate it if I didn't use the miniature tape recorder I had brought with me but would follow the method he used in his travels of research for his books. This meant asking questions and keeping a notebook open and paraphrasing the answers in jotted notes without interrupting the flow of the conversation. I complied.

There were two such interviews for Nancy and the *Literary Review*, some years apart, and each of them, when published, prompted national headlines because of the opinions Vidia expressed:

E.M. Forster? 'Went to India to screw young men!'

Henry James? 'Unreadable!'

James Joyce? 'I never read blind writers!'

Dickens? 'The first two books—Boz and Pickwick!'

William Faulkner? 'A muddle—sentences that unnecessarily go on forever!'

The most provocative thing he said which caused huge controversy in the national press and undoubtedly in the universities and among the British and Indian chatterati was in the second interview: 'Women can't write, you know. Reading the first paragraph of a novel, I can tell if it's by a man or a woman.'

On hearing this outrageous opinion, I pushed him a bit further.

'So, Jane Austen?'

'Pure gossip. She's only renowned because she was writing at the height of the British Empire. If she had been Croatian, nobody would have taken any notice!'

'And George Eliot?'

Vidia was thoughtful and hesitant. 'Tell me about her, Farrukh.'

Not wanting to interrupt my questioning just then, I resumed the interview.

He wasn't going to retract the mischievous bombshell pronouncement, but in a later conversation, when I said I thought *Middlemarch* and *Daniel Deronda* were masterpieces, he said he thought *Silas Marner* a great work and George Eliot's best.

The statement about women writers caused the storm and the controversy that I am certain Vidia intended. Why? It wasn't merely attention-seeking. Somewhere, I suspect, there was a streak of Trinidadian mischief, the instinct to create controversy, in these provocations.

Vidia's remarks didn't get me to revise my opinions about writers. I still think E.M. Foster a remarkable writer, if not perfect, and while not ranking Jane Austen with Dickens, I told him I didn't agree with his views on women writers.

Neither did other writers of ten national publications. In any case, as the storm over the statement raged, I asked Vidia if he would subject himself to the test of knowing from the first paragraph whether a book was by a man or a woman. He said he would.

I went to the shelves upstairs and chose six books, by men and woman, trying to avoid the obvious Jane Austens and Dickens. The game was on.

Vidia won. He got the four women and the two men by reading the first paragraph, with the cover and the rest made inaccessible by me as he read. He may have read these books at some time, but his memory for first paragraphs of obscure novels must have been phenomenal if he could recall them from a selection of roomfuls of books in his house.

He once asked me, 'Farrukh, why do these people go on about my prose style? What is this prose style?' He wasn't being disingenuous or asking for a compliment. It seemed a sincere question.

'What do you think it is?' I countered.

'I try to use the simplest words if I have a choice,' he said.

My answer would have been that Vidia's works are in window-pane prose. You are invited to see through it to the object or emotion beyond. The contrast is with writers who use stained-glass prose, where the picture in the glass is the proffered object of attention rather than what one can see through it.

In one of his innovative books, part novel, part history, part disguised autobiography, called *A Way in the World*, Vidia created a character named Lebrun, a fellow Trinidadian, a sage, a Marxist and a man who through ideology transcends nationalism and race. Vidia based this intimate portrait and his interaction with the fictional Lebrun on the figure, character and career of C.L.R. James.

Vidia presents Lebrun with sympathy and insight, but in the end, the character he creates, with very many parallels to C.L.R.'s life and person, remains Lebrun.

In the late 1970s, C.L.R., living with his wife Selma in Willesden in London, faced some sort of a household crisis. His nephew Darcus approached me and said C.L.R. wanted to move out of his house, forced by Selma through their disagreements which were political and personal. Darcus said he had nowhere to go and would I, since I had a spare room in my flat, accommodate him for a few days till he could think of a more permanent place for his grand-uncle?

I agreed, of course. I knew C.L.R. from the days when he addressed the BPM and induced me to write the pieces which then led to a publisher asking me to write my first book.

C.L.R. stayed in my flat with me for several months. I still held a job as a teacher at the time, and before I went to school each day, I would give him his breakfast of a three-and-half-minute boiled egg with toast. He would wake up an hour before I did and begin to demand the precisely timed egg with coffee. Apart from being an acute and unique interpreter of Marx's work, he was a connoisseur of the texture of boiled eggs and could tell a three-minute-and-fifteen-second one from a three-minute-and-fifty-second overdone one. It was a remarkable ability.

In his early years, C.L.R. was an aspirant writer in Trinidad. He earned his living there as a teacher in the prestigious Queen's Royal College, the school which both Vidia and Darcus in later years attended. He wrote short stories and a novel while trying to establish himself as a writer from the colonies. It was when he came to Britain, following his friend the cricketer Learie Constantine, that he began, through reading and his contact with the radical British left, to move towards an understanding and advocacy of Marxist doctrines and goals. He soon called himself a Trotskyist and actually interviewed Trotsky in Mexico a few months before he was assassinated.

Trotsky asked him what the black Americans could do for the revolution, and C.L.R. asked him what the revolution could do for the blacks.

After a few years, C.L.R. was deported from the USA and returned to Trinidad and Britain.

My intimacy with C.L.R. began when he lived in my flat.

He had written about all the things he talked to me about—the factionalism of the left in the USA and why he had, on a proper study of Marx and an assessment of the historical currents of the contemporary world, come to the conclusion that Trotsky was noble and high-minded but wrong. C.L.R. was a revolutionary who had evolved into an interpreter of Marx as applied to the actual world.

His political writings and activity, in the USA and in the Caribbean—where he edited a newspaper in the era of imminent independence for the West Indian colonies and advocated a federation of all the islands—predated the rise of the Civil Rights and then the Black Power movements in the USA. His vision of a single nation of the British Caribbean islands, which could then 'provoke Martinique, Guadeloupe and even Cuba to find their way into it', never materialised. The selfish ambitions of Jamaican,

Trinidadian, Guyanese and other politicians prevailed. The islands became separate 'nations', and James referred to them as 'pathetic pieces of dirt in the Caribbean'.

When Darcus and the Race Today Collective refurbished a second-floor flat above the magazine's offices, they made a home for C.L.R. there, and he moved from my home to his own. I would visit him there on most days. He would be sitting up in bed, watching cricket on the TV or listening to Mozart or the Beethoven quartets or reading, for the umpteenth time, Thackeray's *Vanity Fair*. He would ask me to fetch him bottles of claret. He could, to my dismay, tell the cheap wines from the more expensive ones. He only left his bed to go to the bathroom. The rest of the day he would sit leaning on pillows and reading or watching cricket on TV.

Ironically, one of the most creative Marxist minds I have read or encountered was more widely known for his cricket writings. His autobiography of sorts was shaped round the world of cricket in the West Indies and was called *Beyond a Boundary*. In Britain, he assisted Neville Cardus, a famous cricket columnist for the *Manchester Guardian*, the precursor to the *Guardian*, writing columns on games that Cardus or the newspaper sent him to report on.

He said cricket was to the West Indians what the Athenian games were to the Greeks. The ethics of cricket, its code of team spirit and fair play were moral influences on the ex-slave societies of the islands.

Another of his assertions was that all creation, black or white, in the USA and the West Indies was now, through the cruelties and passage of history, part of the Western intellectual tradition. The influence of the African heritage had been wiped out through the years of slavery and struggle in the New World. Any inclination towards reviving some tribal or other African traditions was, in his view, pantomime.

On one occasion, the revolutionaries of the island of Grenada—its prime minister Maurice Bishop, political leader Jacqueline Creft and another member of the government, which had come to power through a coup and declared a socialist regime in the island—came to ask his advice on how to advance the 'revolution'.

I was with him when they arrived, and he sent me to fetch some red wine, specifically claret, preferably from one of the chateaus from the Saint-Émilion region. I told C.L.R. that there would be no such wine in the shops of Brixton, and I would have to go some distance, and I had to.

When I returned to the flat, the Grenadians were listening diligently to C.L.R. 'Forget about preaching to the population about Marxism and Leninism, or even about socialism. You can't have nutmeg socialism!' he was saying, alluding to the island's main export. 'Give them good governance. That's what you are called upon to do.'

He said they should provide refrigeration plants for the island's fishermen so that they could freeze and export the vast percentage of their catch, which at present went to waste. He then talked about nutmeg farms and crops.

As they were leaving, he shouted after them: 'And don't kill no nuns!'

He was devastated when Bishop, Creft and eight others were arrested in 1983 by Bishop's deputy Bernard Coard—part of the New Jewel Movement which had carried out another coup—and were summarily executed as 'counter-revolutionaries'. The executions led to chaos on the island and an invasion by the US troops, who landed from the air and installed a puppet government in Grenada. Coard and his murdering cronies were thrown in jail.

At Channel 4 at the time, the Grenadian coup, its revolutionary pretensions, its break-up into factions and the murder and mayhem that followed seemed the ideal subject to research and record as history through a documentary or feature film.

Darcus, who knew the territory, Bobby Bedi as the producer and I set out to explore the possibilities.

I went to the island's jail and asked to see Coard, who before the coup had been a primary school teacher in London and whose acquaintance, as a schoolteacher myself at the time, I had then made.

He was happy, he said, to see me and tell me his side of the story. We were allowed two sessions, and he tried to tell me in some detail how Bishop, a friend and comrade of his, had become dictatorial and a tyrant within the party as well as corrupt and self-aggrandising. Coard's persuasive, to his mind, justification for murdering Bishop made me think of Brutus who in all nobility stabbed Caesar alleging that he was ambitious and it being a grievous fault he had to answer it grievously.

On the third visit to the jail, the superintendent said that Coard had refused to see me anymore. He had spoken to his wife Phyllis, a Jamaican from a rich family which owned the Tia Maria liqueur franchise, and she had apparently said, 'Farrukh Dhondy? No, we can't talk to him.'

We gathered stories from several others on the island before returning to London. A documentary about the coup and the sad story of the socialist revolution couldn't be made. There weren't enough of the key participants alive, and those that were, weren't willing to talk to us. The story was still compelling, and I took the time to write it as a screenplay, but it was never made into a film.

C.L.R. died the same year of the coup, in 1983. It was not an unexpected passing. If I were to assume the avatar of an Indian disciple, I would say he was one of my gurus, and his political stances, profoundly expounded in his books and very simply in his conversations, had a lasting effect on my own perceptions and opinions.

Darcus took his body to be buried in Trinidad. A few years later, the editor from Random House who had published my novel *Bombay Duck* asked me if I would write a biography of C.L.R. using my acquaintance with him as a thread. I did, and it was published in Britain and then republished in the USA, where there was a new wave of curiosity about this black thinker and writer.

I think back on three of the people who had determining effects on my later life, Darcus, Vidia and C.L.R.—all Trinidadians by origin. A coincidence, as I didn't encounter them through each other, though all of them were more than acquainted, Darcus through a blood relationship with C.L.R. and through being his ideological disciple, Vidia owing to the fact that C.L.R. followed his writing career, and Vidia created a version of C.L.R. in his fiction.

As someone wise said, 'For we know in part and prophesy in part ...' and that perhaps points to the shortcomings of the recollections one shores against one's ruin, whatever that means.

I have had the good fortune of knowing many people who have made a difference to the world. There is no pride in being acquainted with those who did so by eliminating people, but there is in the humble friendships with people such as Vidia and C.L.R. who dented the world's civilisation with their thoughts and writing.

Vidia's contribution, at least and best in his non-fiction, can be assessed as the penetrating vision of a mind which looks at the world without any nationalistic or ideological bias. Of course, that assessment will be challenged and disregarded by those, perhaps even including me, who do look at the world through some ideological lens. But his writing will continue to speak with the voice of universal values of judgement, undoubtedly critical of some acts, thoughts and even cultures.

C.L.R. contributed through his evolution an approach to Marxism which best fits the contemporary world and uses but leaves behind the works of Lenin, the rants of Mao and the irrelevant dogmas and rhetoric of the 'communist' and Trotskyist parties and factions of the world.

And then there were others like Darcus, whose life, determinations and contributions to the shaping of an emerging, postcolonial, multi-ethnic Britain are, even in a small way, the stuff of history. Darcus didn't write many books, but he did put down in articles and compilations the political advancement of black and Asian Britain.

In extolling the achievements of these three, I have deliberately chosen the friends who are dead, their contribution a closed book, though it has an inevitable impact on the future.

'For now we see through a glass darkly,' but I hope I have seen—even through the darkened glass of memory, people and palpability—'face to face'.

AFTERWORD
A TARGET AUDIENCE

Autobiographies of writers don't normally include, or are not obliged to include, accounts of the birth and growth of their children—unless one is A.A. Milne, who wrote all his books for his son Christopher Robin and cast him as a character in them. Or, of course, Rudyard Kipling, who wrote the *Just So Stories* for his children and, we are told, read it to them as he wrote.

I wrote my first four books before my children were born—of the young Asians and West Indians of Britain in the 1960s and 1970s, and then my vaguely fictionalised, partly autobiographical *Poona Company*.

The first book I wrote with one of my children in mind, my son Danyal, as a possible reader was *Janaky and the Giant and Other Stories*, with a wishful deviance from reality which young people's literature traditionally indulges.

My children, Tamineh and Danyal, daughter and son of Loretta; the twins, Shireen and Jahan, daughters of Piki; and then Tir, precisely and to the day twelve years younger than the twins and the daughter of Bernadette, have all travelled to India—at first with me and then in their teens, twenties and later, with their friends and partners. They visit their cousins, their aunt Zareen and tour the resorts, check out the historical monuments and do whatever else travellers and tourists do on the beaches of Goa.

All of them, growing up and schooled in Britain, had no formal approach to Indian history and, though not being in any form a historian, I set out to write an opinionated guide for them. I tackled Indian history, from the prehistorical archaeological finds of the Indus Valley Civilisation to the election of the BJP government of Narendra Modi, and directed my children and anyone who wanted to buy the book, say at airport stalls, to places connected to the historical chapters. I wanted to call it *India for Idiots*, but the publishers thought it would put readers off, and so it was, in imitation of D.H. Lawrence, I suppose, published as *India, My India: A Stab at Its History* in one volume and at the same time in three slim ones, dividing the work into historical periods.

All my children grew up as close siblings and included my cousin's daughter Lyla Patel, their 'cousin-sister', as Indians would say, a few months younger than Tamineh and a few months older than Shireen and Jahan. I hoped my children as well as Lyla would read *India, My India* and have some inkling of what they were looking at when they visited Humayun's Tomb.

I call it an opinionated history for the reason that I disagreed in some ways with the ten history books I read and twenty others to which I referred before I started writing.

The books on the Indus Valley Civilisation, for instance, don't come to any idiosyncratic conclusion about where that civilisation originated, who its inhabitants were and where they went. My deductions or speculations based on the evidence that the same books presented was that they were ancestors of the Dravidian civilisations, who were driven south by the invasion of the nomadic and militant Aryans from Central Asia and with whom the Dravidians amalgamated their religion to produce what is today Hinduism.

In writing about Hinduism, the book contends that the Ramayana essentially portrays the antagonism between the Aryan kingdoms of the north, personified in Rama of Ayodhya, and the Dravidian kingdoms of the south, personified in Ravana of Lanka.

The Aryans are aided in their triumph by the armies of the third ethnic group of India, the Adivasis, who are represented by the 'vaanara' or forest-dweller Hanuman.

At the other end of the historical spectrum, the evaluation of Nehru as a 'socialist' struck me as ignorant. It's certain that Nehru had the sensibility which embraced the ideal of social equality and the upliftment of the masses. In his ambition to rapidly develop India, he was faced with the problem of the lumpiness of capital—a lot of money gathered in one lump to be put to use. The taxable economy of the India he inherited wouldn't pay for the steel works, energy-generating projects such as hydro-electric power, roads, educational institutions and other infrastructural elements of growth. He had to borrow money, and the Soviet Union was, in exchange for international political partiality—disguised in this case as 'non-alignment'—the only bloc willing to lend it.

Nehru, inevitably, through calling his developmental schemes 'Five Year Plans' in imitation of the Soviet Union's seven-year ones (Nehru was in a hurry?), was labelled a socialist, if not a crypto-communist. Taking a step back from the labelling and assessing the intent and progress of his schemes clearly leads to the conclusion that Nehru was no such thing. He laid the foundations for development and built the structure which enabled India in the following decades to take a great capitalist leap forward. Perhaps that's not quite what he intended, but that's what he did.

As for the rest of my work, I dedicated a collection of short stories to my children, including LP—Lyla Patel. It slipped my notice that the book, taking its name from the longest story in it, was called *Adultery and Other Stories*. My daughter Tamineh pointed out that only I could ironically dedicate a book with that risqué title to all of them. I tried to tell her that the story 'Adultery' was not about the violation of the seventh commandment but about the interpretation given to it by a teacher in my school, who said it was an injunction against diluting milk with water. That didn't convince her.

Even as I write this, and not simply because I am writing it, the memory of those I have mentioned in these pages and have recently died comes vividly to mind. C.L.R. James died long ago, but in recent years, I have suffered the loss of first Dara Cama, then Mala Sen, then Darcus Howe, Firdous Ali, Vidia Naipaul, Ratnakar Kini and Darryl D'Monte. I guess we are all on the runway, and such a flight holds no terror for me. I can confront it without hope, belief in god or a promise of eternal anything—how boring that would be! The prospect of hell is not terrifying either; think of the interesting people one could argue against.

And as I write, I also ask myself again, why does one write? I began one chapter of this attempting to answer that question and answered it in devious ways. Perhaps the real reason one writes is the reason spiders spin webs. It's what comes naturally—a spider can't help it and can't stop, and it's a trap for sustenance.